Weekend Millionaire Mindset

MIKE SUMMEY
ROGER DAWSON

McGraw-Hill

New York Chicago San Francisco Lisbon London
Madrid Mexico City Milan New Delhi San Juan
Seoul Singapore Sydney Toronto

McGraw-Hill books are available at special discounts to use as premiums and sales promotions, or for use in corporate training programs. For more information, please write to the Director of Special Sales, Professional Publishing, McGraw-Hill, Two Penn Plaza, New York, NY 10121-2298. Or contact your local bookstore.

 This book is printed on recycled, acid-free paper containing a minimum of 50% recycled de-inked paper.

Dedications

- To my mother, Jacqueline Kiser, who more than any other person instilled in me the drive and determination to succeed in whatever endeavor I attempted.
- To the many people from whom I have learned valuable lessons that cumulatively make up the heart of my Weekend Millionaire Mindset. Without you this book would not be possible. I sincerely thank each one of you, but I won't try to name you here, because I have done so throughout the text that follows.

Mike Summey

- To my darling wife Gisela, who has taught me so much about love, life, and happiness.
- To my three amazing children Julia, Dwight, and John.
- To my two beautiful grandchildren Astrid and Thomas

Roger Dawson

# Contents

Foreword by Carleton H. Sheets   vii

Preface: Why Read This Book?   ix

Part I. The Weekend Millionaire Mindset   1

1. What Is the Weekend Millionaire Mindset?   4
2. The Lifestyle of Success   11
3. The Lifestyle of Failure   19
4. The Lifestyle of Ordinary   27
5. What Constitutes Wealth   36
6. Debt: Constructive or Destructive?   45
7. Beginning the Journey to Financial Independence   55

Part II. The Formative Years   65

8. Going to War   68
9. Everyone Is Not Equal, but Opportunities Are   73
10. It Takes Planning to Be Successful   78
11. Ideas Must Be Implemented to Be Valuable   82
12. People Help Those Willing to Help Themselves   89
13. Patience and Persistence Are Unstoppable   94

Part III. The Learning Years   101

14. Growing Requires Stretching, Getting Out of Your Comfort Zone   104
15. The Grass Isn't Always Greener   120

Contents

16. You're Rewarded for Performance, Not Promises   127

17. The Ability to Do and the Skill to Manage Are Different   135

18. Learning Is an Everyday Task   141

19. Seek Positive Advice When Setting Life's Goals   150

20. Believe in Yourself, Cancel the Pity Party   156

21. People Continue to Help Those Willing to Help Themselves   160

Part IV. The Earning Years   165

22. Accepting Personal Responsibility   168

23. Knowing Where Your Money Goes   176

24. Developing a Pattern of Investing   180

25. Developing a Personal Budget, Tracking Your Money   188

26. Repel Negative Influences, Focus on the Positive   201

27. The Application of Audio Learning   208

28. Don't Let Frustrations Deter You   214

29. Practice, the Key to Power Performance   222

Part V. The Skills You'll Need   229

30. How to Stay Motivated   231

31. Goal Setting   235

32. Integrity   244

33. Consistency   249

34. Changing Your World by Changing the Way You Think   255

35. Smart Decision Making   262

36. Time Management   268

37. Think Like an Investor, Not Like a Consumer   279

Part VI. A Kick in the Pants That Will Improve Your Life   283

38. Creating Desire   285

39. Eliminating Excuses   291

40. Getting Started   296

Foreword

The present book should probably have preceded Summey and Dawson's highly successful first book, *The Weekend Millionaire's Secrets to Investing in Real Estate*. All the techniques and strategies in the world, designed to help you make money, overcome fear, gain self-confidence, have courage, or achieve financial independence, will only work if you have control over yourself. This book deals with the self-awareness and mindset it takes to adapt to change and bring success to whatever you undertake.

Many people who read this book will start with negative thoughts and beliefs about themselves. They may think that they're not smart enough or educated enough. Or they may feel that because they're part of a minority or are female, or speak with an accent, or they just don't have the time, and one or all of these doubts, may have limited their ability to achieve success— to accomplish what other successful people have accomplished. This book will remove those negative thoughts and eliminate the doubts.

To further compound their problems, most people are surrounded by parents and friends and spouses who constantly remind them of what they "can't do." This is why over 90 percent of the people in this country, if they lose their job, are only one paycheck away from disaster.

In my How to Buy Your First Home or Investment Property program, I advise people to be careful whom they talk with about their ambitions. Many people are so jealous of others who become successful or try to become successful that they simply can't find it in themselves to be supportive. They are reminded of their own failures in life.

Change is the order of the day. If you aren't successful and you want to be, you have to change. The problem is that change is frightening and continues to be for many people until we stop and realize that we are constantly changing from the day we are born. We only stop changing when we die. The key is learning to control change and turn it into a positive. In my opinion, that's what this book accomplishes: It shows you how to change your mindset and shift your paradigm. It helps you see the world, in a very practical and positive way.

What's the difference between a person who labors to make $15,000 a year and one who makes $150,000 or even $1,500,000? What traits identify these people as being different from others? Read this book and you'll find out!

Armed with the ammunition this book contains, becoming successful investing in real estate or any other business endeavor becomes significantly easier. This is a book that reads like a fun and exciting novel. It is not only an excellent guide to becoming financially successful; it will help you in just about every other aspect of life as well.

Congratulations to Summey and Dawson for a book that should be required reading for every high school student in America and most of the adults too.

Carleton H. Sheets

Author of *How to Buy Your First Home or Investment Property with No Down Payment*

Preface

When we wrote *The Weekend Millionaire's Secrets to Investing in Real Estate*, between us we had over 70 years of experience investing in real estate. Both of us started out without capital and without any formal training. Apart from a few self-help books and audio courses, it was all a matter of street smarts. We just got out there, started making some offers, and figured out how it worked.

What surprised us was what we learned about real estate investing after we wrote the book. We set up a chat room on our Web site (www.weekendmillionaire.com) and started having regular Monday night chats with readers of the book and listeners to our audio program *The Weekend Millionaire's Real Estate Investing Program*. We heard from thousands of participants about how they were doing with their investment programs. The comments we got were diverse.

Some people took a pragmatic attitude. One person told us that he realized he'd have to make at least 30 offers to get one accepted. Another told us she made an offer that was rudely rejected and that was enough to convince her that the program wouldn't work.

Some people were impatient. One reader told us that his goal was to have a net income of $30,000 a month by the end of the year. We told him that the goal was very doable, but it was not likely that he could attain it by the end of the year. A $30,000 a month income would require owning something like 15 to 30 rental houses free and clear. We explained that this would take some time to accomplish.

Others clearly understood that real estate investing is not a get-rich-quick proposition. Their objective was to buy one rental house a year for the next 15 years, which is realistic.

Preface

Some readers were optimistic and enthusiastic about building wealth quickly. They were like youngsters at a beach who plunge headlong into the waves. Others were more cautious and wanted to put their toes in the water first.

All of this left us wondering why we had been so successful. It certainly wasn't because of any breaks we'd gotten. Both of our parents were poor. Neither of us got much past high school. We were both flat broke when we started out. We came to the conclusion that just one thing separated self-made millionaires from people who were not so successful financially—their mindset. It was how they viewed the world. It was the lessons they learned during childhood and early adulthood that caused them to see the world differently. It was the mindset they had toward solving problems and handling setbacks. They were risk-takers who leaped at opportunities with confidence, knowing they could adjust and learn if necessary. They weren't paralyzed with fear and too cautious to act.

That's what this book is all about. We'll teach you how to develop the mindset you will need to become financially independent ... and we're not just talking about real estate investing either. You will be able to apply what you'll learn to all your endeavors. You'll read about Mike's journey from the poverty-stricken coalfields of West Virginia and Roger's journey from England to America with only a few dollars in his pocket. You'll learn how they used their tough upbringing to learn lessons that made them financially successful. You'll learn how they used setbacks and failings to teach themselves how to handle disappointment and to improve their mindsets.

We know that by the time you finish this book, you'll have a whole different mindset about wealth, what it is, and how to accumulate it. You may learn that some of your beliefs about money have been completely wrong. But most important, you'll have a fresh new opinion about financial independence, as well as an innovative approach to turn your financial situation around and get it heading toward the wealth you may have thought was out of reach for ordinary people. So get comfortable, turn the page, and get ready for a fascinating experience!

Mike Summey
Asheville, North Carolina
Mike@weekendmillionaire.com

Roger Dawson
La Habra Heights, California
Roger@weekendmillionaire.com

PART I

The Weekend Millionaire Mindset

Y ou are about to embark on a journey that will challenge your thinking, upset the status quo, and change your life. Many self-help books
are based on research and theory and read much like textbooks. This book
also includes research and theory, but what sets it apart from so many of the
others is that Mike Summey and Roger Dawson open their hearts and minds
to share personal stories, some very emotional, some painful, and some
downright funny, that have helped them develop their Weekend Millionaire
Mindsets.

In Part I we define the Weekend Millionaire Mindset; what it is, what it
isn't, and the positive effects it can have on your life when you understand
how to use it. It's not magical, it doesn't require a college degree to understand, and it proves that you don't have to be born with money to enjoy
financial independence. The Weekend Millionaire Mindset shows you *how
ordinary people can achieve extraordinary success.*

We start by defining the difference between the Lifestyle of Success, the
Lifestyle of Failure, and the Lifestyle of Ordinary. As you read about the

similarities and differences between these lifestyles, it will allow you to identify the traits and characteristics you possess and help you determine which lifestyle you are living. Until you establish where you are, you can't set a course to get you where you want to be. If you're in Pittsburgh and you want to go to Dallas, it doesn't make much sense to map out a route to get there from Orlando. Likewise, if your goal is financial independence and you're currently in debt, have poor credit, and no job, it doesn't do you much good to study how someone with great credit, cash in the bank, and a good job would do it.

As you journey through this book, you will be able to pinpoint your position in life and determine the course of action you need to take. As Mike and Roger share their journeys from very modest backgrounds to financial independence, you will see how they encountered many of the same obstacles you encounter and what they did to overcome them. You'll learn that they relied on patience and persistence, rather than luck; that setting aside time to learn each day had more to do with their success than specific events. You'll also learn that they haven't done anything you can't do if you really want to.

Developing a Weekend Millionaire Mindset and becoming a Weekend Millionaire is not an event, it's a course of action. What you'll find in this text is how to learn from day-to-day events and use common sense to build your future. Whether it's earning your first bicycle, building a business, learning to fly airplanes, or becoming a millionaire, you can't arrive unless you're willing to take the journey.

Yes, life is a journey. It consists of a changing, shifting series of events that ultimately leads us all to the same place … death. While that's a sobering thought, the amount of joy and excitement, accomplishment and reward, and the peace of mind we get from the journey, depend on our willingness to keep learning new skills and seeking additional knowledge. Since we all know what our final outcome here on Earth will be, shouldn't we focus on doing or not doing things between birth and death that make our life more enjoyable rather than miserable? And the beauty of it all is that we get to decide how much or how little of the trip we enjoy. It all starts with our mindset; how we approach problems, how we react to outside influences, how well we control our emotions, and what we decide we want from life. We get to choose whether we face the future filled with excitement and anticipation or whether we view it with fear and despair.

The Weekend Millionaire Mindset will help you establish a road map to wealth and financial independence. How well you follow the map determines how well you enjoy the trip and how soon you arrive at the destination. Now turn the page and let's begin by defining the Weekend Millionaire Mindset.

1

What Is the Weekend Millionaire Mindset?

O ne of the things that constantly astounds us about life in this great country is not so much the great contrast between the rich and poor but the astonishing contrast between the successful and the unsuccessful. Some people seem to achieve great wealth with seemingly little effort, and all too many are unable to survive without the help of others. And this in the wealthiest country the world has ever known!

All people are created equal, we are told. Look through the maternity ward window at your local hospital and at the newborn babies. Can you tell which of them will be successful? I doubt it. They all look physically much the same and they all have many more brain cells than they will ever use. Which one will be building an empire of wealth and influence, and which one will be standing on a street corner saying, "I'm homeless, can you spare some change?" It's really hard to tell, isn't it?

Why do some people zoom down the highway of financial success, while others end up as road kill on life's economic highway? That's what happens to so many well-meaning, hardworking individuals. Sometimes it's short-sightedness. They spend more money on casino gambling or lottery tickets than it would take to build a safe and secure financial future. Others are so cautious they are afraid to take any risks at all; they want a sure thing. Although their styles are vastly different, the results are often the same—they are rarely able to build wealth and achieve financial security.

Is the willingness to take risks a key to financial success? That sounds right. Most wealthy people will tell stories of the giant risk they took on the way to success. But beware of coming to that conclusion. It's deceptive because we always hear about the people who successfully take risks, we don't hear about the thousands who take similar risks and lose. We hear about the $10 million lottery winner, but we don't hear about the more than 10 million people who lost a dollar trying to win. What we will teach you is that the willingness to take informed risks is a key to the Weekend Millionaire's Mindset.

In this book, we are going to explore that mindset. We're going to teach you how changing the way you think can change your life and especially your financial future. In fact, if you're ever going to change your life and your financial future, you're going to have to change the way you think—and change it a great deal.

Look at it this way: Instead of thinking, "What do I have to do to become rich?" start thinking, "What am I doing wrong that's keeping me from already being rich?" If you're not doing well financially in this country, you're doing something substantially wrong. The economy in the United States today gives you opportunities that people have only dreamed about in past centuries. Not since Venice was the most powerful merchant state in Europe during the Middle Ages has this kind of opportunity existed. And the incredible thing about America is that the opportunity to build wealth exists for everyone, not just a privileged few. If you're not financially successful in this country, you're doing something wrong, and the first step to changing your future is changing the way you think.

You read a book by starting at the beginning and reading through to the end. You build a life by starting at the end—what you want to become—and figuring out what it will take to get you where you want to go.

The Hare, the Tortoise, and the Eagle

If you're destined to become road kill on the financial highway, you probably fall into one of two categories. Take a look at the menu down at the Financial Road Kill Café and you'll see that it's filled with tortoises and hares.

Hares get run over because they are always in too much of a hurry to build financial success. They buy into get-rich-quick schemes. They don't want the hassle of working to be successful. They want big success, and they want it now. They buy lottery tickets, play slot machines, and bet on horses. Even though they've lost a small fortune over the years, they are convinced their big hit is just around the corner. After all, they reason, they have a friend named Joe who has an uncle whose son-in-law lives in another state and he once won a million dollars in the lottery. It is so easy to get seduced by the siren song of instant riches. We confess to feeling a little giddy when we see that the Powerball Lottery prize has reached $200 million. Somebody has to win it. Why not us? Wouldn't it be great to have all that money! Soon the right side of our brain is off on a delicious fantasy that drowns out the logical thinking left side of our brain, which is screaming, "Don't you realize that for the prize to be $200 million there has to be more than 200 million losing tickets?" The odds are absurdly against us.

Hares don't seem to realize that by running in a dozen different directions and always looking for that "lucky break," they are asking to get run over. Because they are failing to take advantage of the genuine opportunities that exist in this country to achieve true financial independence.

The tortoises, on the other hand, religiously get up and go to work five, sometimes six, days a week, receive a regular paycheck, pay their house payments, car payments, and credit card bills on time, and choose to save a portion of their salary each month rather than waste money gambling. They are much more conservative than the hares, and they don't take a lot of chances. They plan for the future, make regular deposits to company-sponsored retirement plans or IRA accounts, invest in mutual funds, buy a few shares of stock, and keep a respectable amount of money in the bank. They are convinced that by continuing to invest a portion of their earned income, it will assure them of a safe and secure retirement income.

Twenty, 30, and 40 years ago that wasn't such a bad plan. You could get a good education, go to work for a large company, religiously contribute to their profit-sharing and retirement plans, and retire with enough income to live well. But not today. Depending on corporate pension plans to see you through is Pollyanna thinking these days. Look at what happened with companies like Enron, Kmart, WorldCom, and others. Tens of thousands of good, hardworking people saw their futures eradicated by corporate greed or incompetence.

The Weekend Millionaire Mindset is different! Unlike the tortoises and hares that make up the vast majority of the financial road kill, Weekend Millionaires are more like eagles. Eagles soar above it all, and their perspective gives them wisdom. They see tortoises and hares scurrying about in their own little worlds unable to see the big picture. The Financial Road Kill Café is full of tortoises and hares for two very different reasons. The hares tend to bolt into the roadway without looking, often right under the wheels of oncoming traffic. Tortoises, on the other hand, ease onto the road, not realizing that the semitruck two miles down the road will run over them because they are moving so slowly. Some will even venture halfway across the road, pull their head in their shell and just sit there. Maybe they're trying to decide whether to go ahead and cross to the other side or come back to the side where they started.

People who are failing financially are either like hares or like tortoises. Hares, because they are always rushing into get rich schemes and never developing a long-term financial strategy. Or tortoises, who will agonize for days or weeks before making a decision and then, after making it, change their minds and not see it through: just like the tortoise frozen in the path of a speeding semitruck, not knowing whether to advance or retreat.

Have you ever seen an eagle hit by a truck? It just doesn't happen! There are no eagles on the menu at the Financial Road Kill Café! The soaring eagle doesn't dive into oncoming traffic, because he can see the cars coming from a greater distance. He moves at a faster pace, but does so with a different perspective; one that comes from knowing the surroundings and acting with the wisdom that comes with being able to see the big picture. Successful people are like this. They develop the ability to anticipate pitfalls and avoid them, but also plan a strategy to deal with them in case they do arise.

The tortoises and hares of the world share thoughts such as, "Those people were luckier than me. They were in the right place at the right time. If

I'd had the same opportunities they had, I'd be more successful too." They would rather make excuses than put forth the effort that success requires. They have yet to learn that nearly all luck is nothing more than the intersection of preparation and opportunity. The tortoises and hares spend more time looking for excuses than it would take to solve most problems. They have discovered that making excuses is a lot less work than developing a financial strategy and making it work. That would require realizing that what they were doing in the past was wrong and they need to take responsibility for it. Fear of taking responsibility for their financial shortcomings causes them to continue trying to cross the same highway. Of course, the results never change and they ultimately become economic road kill.

Developing the Right Mindset

We first introduced the concept of becoming a Weekend Millionaire in our book *The Weekend Millionaire's Secrets to Investing in Real Estate* (McGraw-Hill, 2003). In it, we taught you how to get rich investing in rental real estate in your spare time. What we didn't cover was defining what it takes to develop the mindset needed to become a Weekend Millionaire. While the Weekend Millionaire Mindset concept is simple, it does require you to look at life from a different perspective. If you have the ability to anticipate problems and are prepared to deal with them when they arise, you will always enjoy more success than those who are surprised by problems and don't have a clue what to do when they come up.

In this book we will explore what it takes to develop a Weekend Millionaire Mindset and show you how it can guide the life decisions you make in ways that will lead you to achieve financial independence. We all have bad things happen to us at times, but if we would just realize that there are valuable lessons to be learned from each negative experience, we could turn them into good learning experiences. In fact, a big part of developing a Weekend Millionaire Mindset is learning to distill positive lessons from what appear to be bad experiences.

Throughout life we face the age-old question, "Is the glass half full or half empty?" Those with positive outlooks see the glass as half full, while negative thinkers see it as half empty. (As our college educated children pointed out to us, this assumes that you want the glass to be full. If it were half full of hard-to-dispose-of toxic waste, you might want it to be empty!) Step one in developing a Weekend Millionaire Mindset is to look for the good in life, not the bad. Nurture the good things, learn from the bad things, and above all, take personal responsibility for the mistakes that you make. When we start taking personal responsibility for the decisions we make and accept what happens as a result, we are on our way.

Becoming a Weekend Millionaire isn't difficult, but it does require the right mindset. It requires making a commitment to the three Ds of success: Discipline, Dedication, and Desire. Discipline is developed by making the small decisions, like getting out of bed when the alarm goes off rather than hitting the snooze button. Dedication comes from making decisions to persevere with a course of action until it is brought to a successful conclusion; in other words, by deciding not to be a quitter. Desire is increased by constantly measuring the results of the decisions we make. In this case, are we better off today than we were yesterday? Weekend Millionaires don't measure themselves against others, they measure themselves against the way they were last week, last month, or last year. They have a tremendous desire to be better with each passing day.

Throughout this book, we will be exploring thoughts, actions, and experiences from our lives that have enabled us to develop Weekend Millionaire Mindsets. Both from humble beginnings, we have been able to apply this mindset and rise out of poor surroundings to achieve wealth and influence. We have proven that it's not having formal education or being born with a silver spoon in your mouth that leads to financial independence; it's having the right mindset that brings success.

From his humble start as an emigrant shipboard photographer, Roger has worked for a retail department store and been president of one of the largest real estate firms in California on his voyage to becoming one of the nation's most in demand corporate speakers and a leading expert on the art of negotiating. Mike's journey from the poverty stricken coalfields of southern West Virginia to becoming a financially independent real estate investor, author, and public speaker took him from door-to-door encyclopedia sales, to construction work, plant work, and through years in the politically charged billboard business. Although very different in styles, mannerisms, personalities, and personal goals, our experiences in life have proven to us that ordinary people can achieve extraordinary success. Now let's move on to the next chapter so we can start sharing some of these experiences.

Key Points from This Chapter

- Don't be so shortsighted that you take unreasonable risks and waste your life chasing get-rich-quick schemes.
- Don't be so cautious that you're unwilling to take any risks.
- Learn how to take informed risks.
- Don't think, "What must I do to become rich?" Instead think, "What am I doing wrong that's keeping me from already being rich in this, the wealthiest country the world has ever known?"
- You read a book from beginning to end, but you build a life from the end to the beginning. You decide what you want from life and then develop a plan to get it.
- To avoid becoming road kill on life's financial highway, don't race into things with little thought, like the hare, or move too slowly and indecisively, like the tortoise.
- Develop the perspective of an eagle; look at the big picture and then swoop in to take advantage of opportunities when they arise.
- Learn to distill positive lessons from otherwise bad experiences.
- Nurture the good things and learn from the bad things.
- Take personal responsibility for both your successes and your failures.
- Commit to the three Ds of success: Discipline, Dedication, and Desire.

2

The Lifestyle
of Success

L et us begin by saying that throughout this book when we refer to success, we are talking mainly about financial success.

We realize that success means many things to many people. If you ask a monk if he is successful he might reply, "Yes, because I feel closer to God than ever before." If you ask a baseball player if he is successful, he would tell you how many home runs he has hit or how many no hitters he's pitched. He wouldn't tell you about how much money he's making from his auto dealership. Ask a mother if she's successful and she will tell you how well her children are doing in college. Ask an alcoholic if he is successful and he might tell you, "Yes, I've been sober now for 92 days."

Yes, success comes in many forms, but in this book we want to teach you how to develop the mindset required to achieve financial independence. We're going to stay focused on teaching you how ordinary people can achieve extraordinary wealth. So you puritans out there who are successfully broke, we're not talking about you. If you're happy working 40 hours a week, 50 weeks a year, for 40 years and then ending up with nothing more to show for it than a worn-out body and a Social Security check, God bless you. However, if you want to get off this 40-50-40 plan of life and become financially independent while you're still young enough to enjoy it, then you are holding in your hands the book that will give you a road map to success.

What is this Lifestyle of Success? Is there something magical about it? Are some people just luckier than others? Isn't it amazing that you can drive down streets in America and find neighbors, living side by side, both earning the same income, yet one has a lovely well-maintained home, nice clothing, new cars, and all the trappings of success, while the other lives in a house that needs painting, wears hand-me-down clothing, drives an old clunker, and is always broke? Why? What does one do that the other doesn't?

Over the next few chapters we will define the differences between the Lifestyle of Success, the Lifestyle of Failure, and the Lifestyle of Ordinary, and do so in a way that will let you determine which lifestyle you are currently living. We'll begin with the Lifestyle of Success.

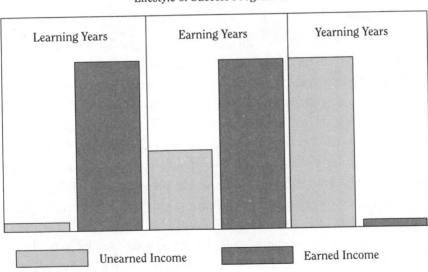

Lifestyle of Success Progression

Figure 1

The graph in Figure 1 shows the growth process that occurs when we live this Lifestyle of Success. The left or vertical axis of the graph represents income, while the bottom horizontal axis represents time. For simplicity, we have divided time into three phases. The first phase corresponds to youth, the middle phase stands for middle age, and the final phase signifies retirement years. You could also say these phases represent the Learning Years, the Earning Years, and the Yearning Years. We'll talk more about the first two of these phases later.

The columns in the graph represent income. The column on the left in each phase is unearned or investment income; money you don't have to trade your time or labor to earn. The column on the right in each phase is earned income, or what you work for.

Let's first look at the youth phase. Notice that during this period, nearly all income is earned income and there is very little if any unearned income. That's the way most people begin life as adults. They have to get a job and work for money to pay the bills and provide sustenance. Their Standard of Living is determined by what they can earn.

For those people living the Lifestyle of Success, the middle portion of the graph shows what happens as we move into our peak Earning Years. As you can see, earned income is still high, but we are beginning to show a rise in unearned income. This indicates that we are still working full-time, but we have begun making investments that are starting to kick off money that we don't have to work for.

Finally, as you can see from the graph, we are able to move into the retirement years and achieve the same Standard of Living from our unearned income without having to work. That's a nice thought isn't it? Not only is it a nice thought, it's what happens when we live the Lifestyle of Success. But, once again, what is this Lifestyle of Success? Let's use another graph to illustrate what we have to do in order to achieve this lifestyle.

As in Figure 1, here in Figure 2, the left or vertical axis represents money, and the bottom or horizontal axis represents time. We do not show specific numbers on either axis, because this graph is designed to illustrate a concept, not specific amounts of money or periods of time.

The line identified as Earned Income represents the earnings from your job. Whether it's a little or a lot, it's the amount you earn working. The Standard of Living line represents the amount of money you spend to main-

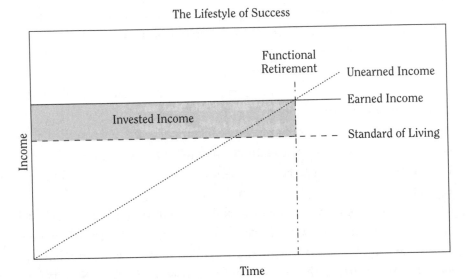

Figure 2

tain the lifestyle in which you are living. If you are living the Lifestyle of Success, this line is below the Earned Income line.

The shaded area between the Earned Income and Standard of Living lines represents the amount of money you have to invest after paying your bills. When this money is invested, it creates the third line on the graph: Unearned Income. This is the amount of money your investments earn. It is money for which you don't have to trade time or labor.

This may be an oversimplification of how to achieve financial success, but let's take a closer look at the concept. You will notice that in the beginning the Unearned Income line is at zero. Unless you are fortunate enough to have a trust fund or inheritance bestowed upon you, you will start just as we both did, with no investments and lucky to have a job.

What's important at this stage of life is not so much what you make, but what you spend. If you discipline yourself to live on less than what you make and invest the difference, no matter how small it is, you will begin having some Unearned Income. If you continue this practice and leave the Unearned Income alone and allow it to compound, what starts out as a tiny trickle gradually becomes a flowing stream of income, and the Unearned Income line on the graph continues to grow.

As we saw in Figure 1, by the time you get into your true Earning Years, your Unearned Income begins to become a significant part of your overall income. By allowing this Unearned Income to stay invested and to continue to compound, it creates a snowball effect. The money from your Earned Income that you are continuing to invest, together with the Unearned Income that is accruing, makes the time it takes for your investments to double grow shorter and shorter. What may take 10 years to double the first time may double again in six years and again in four years, etc.

Invest for Success

For those of you who are thinking that this is the tortoise way to financial success, you're right. It's a slow and methodical way to wealth, and it works. What we are discussing here is the concept of wealth building, not the speed. We'll get into ways to speed up the process later, but for now we want to be sure you understand that the one absolute rule for wealth building is: "You can't spend everything you make, you have to invest for success." This rule forms the basis of the Weekend Millionaire Mindset.

By establishing a lifelong commitment to investing, the Unearned Income line continues to grow until eventually it equals or exceeds your Earned Income. This crossing point, as shown on the graph, is called Functional Retirement. This is when you reach the point at which you can continue to live the lifestyle you are accustomed to living without ever having to work for money again. There is no age associated with Functional Retirement. It can come at age 25 or 35 or 45 or 55, and it does not have anything to do with whether you quit your job or not. It is merely the point in life where you could quit your job if that's what you wanted to do.

Mike set a goal at age 20 to become a millionaire by age 30 and retire at 50, both of which he reached. (We'll talk more about the importance of goals later.) What he didn't understand when he set this goal was the difference between quitting work and Functional Retirement. Today he is as busy as ever, but he is doing what he wants to do, not doing things he has to do to earn a living. Big difference!

Today, there seems to be a common thread that runs through all the get-rich-quick schemes being advertised. That thread is being able to quit your job. Developing a Weekend Millionaire Mindset is not about quitting your job; it's about having a more productive and rewarding life. Many people love their jobs; what they hate is the fact that they have to work to survive. Life is so much more rewarding when you do things because you want to, not because you have to.

Even if you aren't an economist, you can see from Figure 2 that if you discipline yourself to live on less than what you make and invest the difference, gradually over time the unearned income from your investments will grow until it matches or exceeds what you earn on your job. When this happens, you have all kinds of options. You can choose to continue working and increase your standard of living. You can choose to stop working and maintain the same standard of living for the rest of your life. You can choose to work part-time and still increase your standard of living, but at a slower rate. You can choose to quit working, increase your standard of living by a portion of what you've been investing and continue to invest the difference so your unearned income also continues to grow. You can choose to keep the same standard of living, continue to work and invest for several more years, and then both quit your job and substantially increase your standard of living. The options are numerous.

"But," you say, "how can we invest when we can barely pay our bills now?" Answer: It's simple! You reduce your standard of living for a period of time just as you would if your income were suddenly cut by 10, 15, or 20 percent and you couldn't find another job to replace your loss. Is it easy? NO! Is it possible? ABSOLUTELY! Are you willing to do it voluntarily? MAYBE … MAYBE NOT!

We know that it's hard when you're first getting started. When Roger came to the United States from England, he had saved up enough money for a one-way air ticket and $200 in capital. That's not much to start a life in a strange country 8,000 miles away. He accepted the first job he could get, as a management trainee at Bank of America in Menlo Park, California. It paid $65 a week—before deductions! "Strangely enough," he'll tell you, "it seemed like a lot of money. I had only been making $20 a week in England, so I thought I'd died and gone to heaven." But soon his lifestyle started catching up to his income. He bought a $200 car instead of riding a bike to work, and began treating himself to an occasional 19 cent hamburger at McDonald's.

The Lifestyle of Success

It wasn't long before $65 a week wasn't enough to live on. After nine months he left Bank of America and went to work for Montgomery Ward, the now defunct department store chain, for $93 a week. Then he could afford an apartment instead of a room in someone's home, and a $900 car instead of a $200 car. Also, he started a very important habit: He began saving money. Each week he would buy a $25 U.S. savings bond. It cost only $18.75 to purchase, but would be worth $25 when it matured. When you're grossing $93 a week, it takes a great deal of discipline, extreme dedication, and a strong desire for a better life to keep you from succumbing to the temptation to dip into your savings. Those meager savings enabled him to buy his first house the following year, and his second one the year after that.

That's the three Ds of success that we discussed in the first chapter. Unless you develop the Discipline to take the steps necessary to achieve success, the Dedication to stick with it until you succeed, and a strong Desire for a better life, you probably won't enjoy the Lifestyle of Success.

"But," you say, "money isn't everything, we want to be happy too." To which we respond: "Is one mutually exclusive of the other, or have we just been brainwashed into thinking so?" Are the only two choices we have to be rich and miserable or poor and happy? Couldn't we be well off but moody? Seriously, we're amazed at the number of people who equate riches with misery. Look at your own personal experiences: Have you encountered more miserable poor people or more miserable rich people? Could it be that the sacrifices made in the beginning by people who achieve financial success are viewed as misery by those who are not willing to sacrifice? How many times have you heard someone say, "I'm going to enjoy all I can today, because there is no guarantee I'll even be here tomorrow, let alone 10 or 20 years from now?" Before you say this, consider whether this is a valid statement or an excuse born out of jealousy by people who didn't have the Discipline, Dedication, or Desire required to achieve financial success.

"But," you say, "if it's so easy, why isn't everyone doing it?" Well, that's a good question, but in order to answer it, we need to look at other lifestyles that people follow and try to determine their similarities and differences from the Lifestyle of Success. Let's start by moving to the next chapter, where we will analyze the most destructive of these, the Lifestyle of Failure.

Key Points from This Chapter

- Success means many things to many people. In this book we're primarily talking about financial success.
- Don't rely on the 40-50-40 plan of life where you work 40 hours a week, 50 weeks a year, for 40 years, and end up with only Social Security on which to retire.
- The lifestyle of success requires limiting your spending during your earning years so you can build investments that will produce money for which you don't have to work.
- Functional retirement doesn't mean that you quit working. You may, in fact, work with more passion and vigor than ever before. It means you can do what you want to do, rather than what someone else wants you to do.
- Even if you are struggling financially, you can still save a little for investments by adjusting your lifestyle.
- The amount you save is not as important as developing the habit of saving.
- Develop the three Ds of success: the Discipline to take the steps necessary to achieve success, the Dedication to stick with it until you succeed, and a Desire for a better life that is strong enough to keep you inspired.
- Don't think of wealth and happiness as being mutually exclusive.

3

The Lifestyle of Failure

It goes without saying that no one sets out in life to be a failure. Think back to all those dreams you had as a child about growing up and one day becoming a prosperous adult. Sure, back in elementary school we all had thoughts like that, even those of us who grew up dirt poor. We knew that when we grew up and got out on our own we would get a good job, find our niche in life, and be successful. Then about the time we entered middle school, we started looking around and saw that many adults weren't living that dream. Maybe it was even our own parents who were struggling. Roger remembers a seminal moment in his upbringing: "Both of my parents worked very hard, but never became wealthy. My father drove a London taxicab and my mother was a bookkeeper. I remember when I was about six years old, watching them read the menu posted outside a café and wondering if we could afford to eat there. Even that young, I remember thinking, 'I never want to live like that.'"

By the time we got to high school and knew it wouldn't be long before we had to face the world, many of us started collecting excuses; companies were downsizing rather than hiring, jobs were going overseas, prices were going up faster than wages, the only good jobs required a college degree, and college was just too expensive.

This dose of reality brought many reactions. Some young people with bleak outlooks on the future turned to drugs and alcohol to mask their fears and cover up perceived inadequacies. Others quit school and got menial jobs so they could buy cars or chase the latest fads. Even those who finished high school and went on to college were bombarded with credit card offers and the lure of easy money. The sad part is that all of these things unknowingly start many young people down a road destined to lead to a Lifestyle of Failure.

In the last chapter, we graphed the Lifestyle of Success and explained how it worked. Now let's do the same with the Lifestyle of Failure.

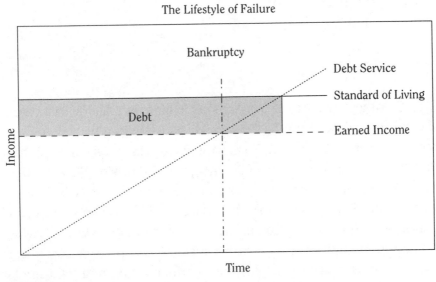

The Lifestyle of Failure

Figure 3

If you go back and review the graph in Figure 2 and compare it with the one above, you will notice that they look nearly the same. There is a spread between Earned Income and Standard of Living, and the difference between the two creates a diagonal line just as there was in the Lifestyle of Success graph.

Although the graphs look the same, the difference is huge. Instead of the gap between Earned Income and Standard of Living being income to invest, in Figure 3 it represents debt. Instead of the diagonal line representing a growing stream of unearned income, here it represents the increasing burden of debt service. And most important, instead of the point where the diagonal line intersects the Earned Income line representing functional retirement, here it represents bankruptcy or the point at which you can no longer service the debt.

Credit Card Debt

As we said in the beginning, no one sets out to become a failure in life; so how do they get themselves into a pattern of overspending that leads to a Lifestyle of Failure? Well, it's easy, and credit cards are one of the major contributors. Do you realize that each time you charge more to a credit card than you can pay off at the end of the month, you lower your standard of living for the next month and each month thereafter until it is paid? Let's look at an example.

Assume that you earn $3,000 per month and are living a lifestyle that takes it all. If one month you spend an extra $1,000 and put it on your credit card, not only do you not have the money to pay it off at the end of the month, but in order to make the minimum payment, you have to give up something you have been accustomed to having or start charging it. Let's assume that the minimum payment is 2 percent of the outstanding balance, which would be only $20. If you're like most people, whatever you were buying with this $20, you don't do without it; you just charge it on the credit card. No big deal, right? Well, let's see.

At this point, you think, "No big deal! I paid off $20 and put back $20 so I'm even." Wrong! If the interest rate on the card is 18 percent, $15 of the payment went to the bank in the form of interest for the use of their money. That means you only paid the balance down by $5, but you charged $20. You're not even, because now your outstanding balance has grown to $1,015.

Next month you again pay the minimum payment and continue enjoying your same standard of living by once again charging an amount equal to the minimum payment back to the credit card. This time the payment is $20.30 with $15.22 going to interest, and only $5.08 being applied to the outstanding debt. After making this payment, your balance has now risen to $1,030.22, and in just two months you have paid out $30.22 for which you have received absolutely nothing.

If you continue this same scenario for just one year—making the minimum payments and charging back the same amount so you can maintain the same standard of living—you will pay payments of more than $260 and your balance will go up to nearly $1,200. Do this for another year and you'll pay out an additional $312 and end up owing $1,430. The sad part is, you will have paid out over $570 and your debt will have increased by $430, all because you overspent by $1,000 one month and weren't willing to reduce your standard of living until you could pay it back. Not only will you have gotten nothing for the $570 you've paid out, your minimum payment will have grown from the original $20 to over $28.

The reason we say credit card debt lowers your standard of living is because it's not until you decide to do without some of the things you're accustomed to having and stop charging them back to the card that the balance begins to go down. What's really scary is the fact that if you never add another charge after the initial $1,000 and continue to pay $20 per month, you will have to do without whatever you were buying with this $20 for nearly eight years before the debt will be paid off.

In the above example, we are only talking about $1,000 in credit card charges. We know people with $10,000, $20,000, $30,000 and more outstanding on their credit cards and they still can't understand why they are struggling to keep their heads above water. Unfortunately, these are the same people who continue to make the minimum payment each month and keep charging more. Imagine how depressing it must be to work hard all month and then have to pay $400, $500, or $600 or more in credit card payments for which you get nothing?

Many people continue to charge until they're unable to keep making the payments and have to file for bankruptcy. And the really sad part is, they often get right back in the same dilemma within years of filing the bankruptcy.

The Lifestyle of Failure

Others think they are solving the problem by getting a debt consolidation loan. As our friend Jim Rohn says, "A debt consolidation loan is when you take several very hard-to-make payments and convert them into one impossible-to-make payment."

The problem of debt service eating into lifestyle is not restricted to poor people. During the recent real estate boom, millions of people refinanced their homes to get cash. Roger recalls having dinner at a fancy restaurant in Beverly Hills with a friend of his who is the former head of Bank of America's international banking system. The restaurant was packed with people and there was a long line trying to get in. The prices for food and wine were outrageous, and they were still fighting to get in. This was 2003 at the height of a deep recession.

Roger said, "I thought that we were in the middle of a big recession. Where did all these rich people come from?"

"They're not rich," his friend told him, "they just feel rich because real estate prices are booming and they have refinanced their homes to get cash out. They feel rich but they're actually just getting deeper into debt." Refinancing real estate to get capital to invest in additional income properties is fine, just don't do it to raise spending money. Pulling cash out of your investments to pay for consumable items would be comparable to a farmer eating his seed corn.

The problem is not confined to young people who are just getting started either. Mike received an e-mail from a gentleman in his 40s asking for some advice on purchasing a real estate investment. In his e-mail he remarked that his income was approximately $100,000 annually, his credit scores were good, but that he had over $50,000 in credit card debt. Mike's response to him was the suggestion that he get rid of the credit card debt before doing anything else. There are few investments that will give a better return and solidify your credit rating more than paying off credit card debt.

We use this credit card example to illustrate the destructive effects of consumer debt. Many people, especially young people in college, become ensnared in the trap laid by credit card companies while they're still in school. They are bombarded with credit card solicitations that offer the lure of easy money.

To many college freshmen, probably away from home for the first time, these credit card offers are their first experience with credit. Suddenly, they are in college, dreaming of the high-paying jobs they will have when they graduate, and these dreams are solidified by the fact that they're now being offered credit; not by one bank, but by several. Wow! It can't get much better than that.

When he was a young man just getting started in life, Mike mistakenly thought that the more credit cards you had, the better your credit rating would be. Although he was smart enough not to run up big balances on them, at one point he had more than 60 cards. They were everything from bank cards to department store cards, oil company cards, and others. He thought it was cool to pull out his wallet and have a long string of credit cards drop out in plastic sleeves. He soon learned that the availability of all that unsecured credit hurt rather than helped his ability to obtain credit for important things like real estate investments. Today he uses two bank cards exclusively—one for business-related purchases and one for personal items—and he pays them in full each month.

As we researched this problem, we were continually amazed at the number of college students and other young people who, like Mike in his early years, have six, eight, 10, or more credit cards. One young man who was 23 years old proudly showed us his 53 cards. We were also amazed at how quickly they learn to borrow from one card to make the payment on another when money is a little tight, which is most of the time for students.

When we talked with students, few of them expressed much concern about running up their credit card balances. The standard response was: "Yeah, we know it's bad, but as soon as we finish school and get a job, the first thing we're going to do is pay off the credit cards." The intention is good, but the problem is, just when they think they'll be ready to start paying off these debts, they are hit with the reality of life. Suddenly they have rent to pay; groceries, clothes, furniture, cars, insurance, and other things to buy; and the regular monthly expenses of electricity, telephone, water, TV cable, and more kick in. In addition to all of these, many also have student loans to repay. The fact is, paying off debts accrued while still in school isn't as easy as they thought it would be. They often find that what they assumed

The Lifestyle of Failure

were a few minor credit card bills have ensnared them in a trap of revolving consumer debt that takes years to pay off.

Our friend Michael LeBeouf, Ph.D., author of *The Millionaire in You*, made an interesting point about this phenomenon. He said, "Times have really changed since my college days. I remember that first day when I was registering for school; it seemed that everywhere I turned, there were attractive young ladies with sandwich board signs hanging across their shoulders advertising the brand of cigarettes, of which they were passing out samples. If the tobacco companies were to try that today, they would be hit with lawsuits and tossed off campus. What I can't understand is why no one seems to equate the way credit card companies are hooking young people on debt with the way the tobacco companies tried to hook them on cigarettes 40 years ago. Just go to any college campus on orientation day and look at the banks trying to solicit kids to apply for their credit cards."

But it's not just college students who get strapped with consumer debt—even kids still in high school fall victim. For them, the culprit is most often car loans. Sure, it's every young person's dream to get his or her first car and have the freedom that comes with mobility. But once again, their wants are often greater than their ability to pay. Often, high school students actually drop out of school in order to get a job making enough to pay the car payments. In fact, if you discuss this with high school principals, they will tell you that buying a car is one of the biggest reasons that kids drop out of school. (Mike's son Jason is the author of *Be Cool, Stay in School*. He founded the "Be School, Stay in School" program and received a citation in the Oval Office from President Clinton for his work in encouraging high school students to stay in school and graduate.)

If they are able to keep up the car payments, these youngsters also become targets of the credit card companies. The fact that they're responsibly handling the loan on the vehicle makes them a prime target for more credit. This causes them to get sucked into the same vicious spiral in which many college students find themselves.

Remember in the 1970s when we lowered the age for legal responsibility from 21 to 18? Young people hailed it as a great victory for their generation. "If we're old enough to die in Vietnam for our country, we should be treated as adults," they would cry. Guess who was behind that change? The big banks! Before we lowered the age that young people could be held legally responsible for their debts, people in that age bracket could default on huge debts and the banks had no legal recourse against them. It wasn't the triumph young people thought it was; it was a windfall for the banks.

No one starts out to be a financial failure, just as no one sets out to become a drug addict. It just grows on them little by little, bit by bit, until the hold becomes so tight it takes professional help and a strong will to break the addiction. Why do we as a society allow this to happen? Could it be that credit has become so universally accepted that we have lost touch with how destructive it can be?

Granted, not everyone gets caught so deeply in the financial quagmire we have just discussed that it leads them to bankruptcy; in reality, only a few do. We believe that less than 10 percent of the people in America actually enjoy a Lifestyle of Success, and only a similar percentage suffer the disgrace of the Lifestyle of Failure. If that's the case, what happens to the other 80-plus percent? That's a good question, and to answer it let's move on to the next chapter and discuss the lifestyle we believe most people follow: the Lifestyle of Ordinary.

Key Points from This Chapter

- When we're young, we all dream of becoming wealthy, but those dreams can be easily hijacked by growing consumer debt as we mature.
- Using a credit card instead of paying cash is so easy to do, but it can cost you dearly if you use it to make purchases you can't repay when the next statement comes due.
- Don't refinance your property to get spending money. Only do it to raise more investment capital.
- Paying down credit card debt is one of the best investments you can make. Paying off balances on which you're being charged 18 percent interest or more is the same as making an investment that earns an 18 percent return.
- Students should be cautioned about the dangers of easy credit before being sent off to college.
- Credit cards can get students hooked on debt the way that tobacco companies used to get them hooked on cigarettes.

4

The Lifestyle
of Ordinary

A h, the Lifestyle of Ordinary: How should we describe it? Safe, secure, dependable, steady, stable, reliable, responsible, conscientious, trustworthy, sensible, and mature, or should we just sum it all up and call it ORDINARY. This is the lifestyle most people live. "So, what's wrong with that?" you ask. Nothing, if you're content to be ordinary. But if you want to achieve financial independence, you have to understand the differences between the Lifestyle of Success and the Lifestyle of Ordinary. The vast majority of people living the Lifestyle of Ordinary actually think they are living the Lifestyle of Success. They pay their bills on time, their credit is good, and they can show you investment accounts to support their claim. So what's the difference?

Remember back in Chapter 2 when we talked about the 40-50-40 plan of life? These are people who work 40 hours a week, 50 weeks a year for 40 years and end up with nothing more to show for it than a worn-out body and a Social Security check. These are the people living the Lifestyle of Ordinary. All those adjectives we used in the first sentence of this chapter describe this plan pretty well. The people living this lifestyle are the solid working citizens who work hard, handle their affairs impeccably, but just can't seem to get a break. They are convinced they're doing everything right, but for some reason their ship never seems to come in. Although they live within their means, have investment accounts, IRAs, 401(k)s, and all the trappings of the Lifestyle of Success, they just can't seem to make it to the good life that comes with financial independence. Why? What do they do that keeps them from reaching this goal? That's what this chapter is about.

Just as we did in the previous two chapters, we can graph the Lifestyle of Ordinary. Figure 4 below graphs the overall behavior of people living this lifestyle. We will explain this in detail and then later in the chapter show you how those who enjoy the Lifestyle of Success avoid the missteps made by ordinary people.

The Lifestyle of Ordinary

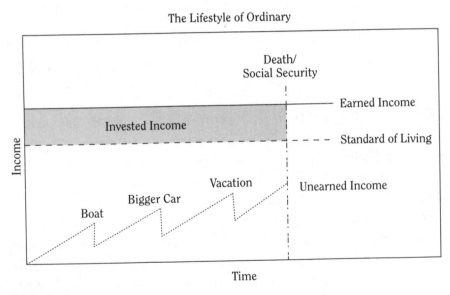

Figure 4

Once again the vertical axis represents income and the horizontal axis represents time. In this example, you can see that people living the Lifestyle of Ordinary live a Standard of Living below their Earned Income and invest the difference. Just as with the Lifestyle of Success, this creates a diagonal line representing Unearned Income. So far so good!

The Lifestyle of Ordinary

The Unearned Income line is growing, just as it should, but then it takes a dip labeled "Boat." This happens when Mr. Ordinary discovers that he can pay his bills on time and has money in the bank, so he decides he can afford to buy a new boat. Problem is, he dips into the funds he's investing for financial independence to pay for the boat. This reduces his investments and causes his Unearned Income to take a dip also, but he still has money in the bank and everything seems fine. More time passes, his investments continue to grow, he continues to pay his bills in a timely fashion, so he feels he has earned the right to have a bigger more expensive car. Once again, he dips into his invested funds to buy the car, investments drop and Unearned Income takes another dip.

Roger recalls a neighbor who asked him how to get started investing in rental properties. Roger showed him how to buy his first house. A few months later the neighbor was talking about buying a second house and kicking his investment program into second gear. Roger drove by his house one day, and he was in his front yard hosing down a huge motor home. "Why would you buy this?" Roger asked him. "You were doing so well investing." His neighbor told him, "I really wanted to buy that second home, but I saw this motor home and I wanted it even more!" As they drove away, Roger's son John, who was six at the time, said, "Now that was dumb!" If a six-year-old can understand the concept, it can't be that hard! As our friend Jim Rohn says: "Don't buy your second car until you've bought your second piece of real estate. Because cars go down in value, while real estate goes up."

This same scenario plays out over and over again in Mr. Ordinary's life. If it's not a boat or a bigger car, it's a vacation, a bigger house, a country club membership, an airplane, a vacation home, you name it. As this continues, Mr. Ordinary is viewed as a prominent member of the community, a person of means and one who lives life to the fullest. He likes this newfound feeling of importance, which makes it easier to continue his behavior. It's not until the latter stages of his working career that he looks at his situation and realizes that death or Social Security is going to precede financial independence. Not a very pleasant realization!

Yes, Mr. Ordinary has some unearned income at retirement, but not enough, even with Social Security added, to sustain the lifestyle he has been accustomed to living. Now he starts making excuses. He says to himself,

"I'm retired now and I really don't need this big a house anymore," so he downsizes. He says, "I'm not working anymore so I don't really need three cars," so he sells two. And so it goes, as his lifestyle shrinks to fit his meager retirement income.

Believe it or not, those who develop the Weekend Millionaire Mindset and live the Lifestyle of Success actually get to do more in retirement than they did during their working years, and often get to retire much earlier than Mr. Ordinary, and you know why? Because they learned the secret of the Lifestyle of Success, and yes, we can graph this secret as well.

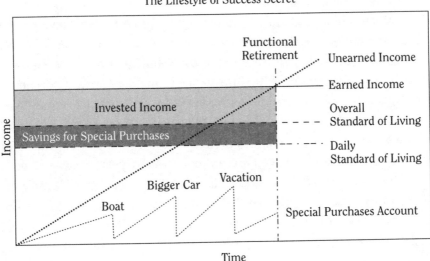

The Lifestyle of Success Secret

Figure 5

When you see it on a graph, it's pretty simple, isn't it? The secret is to segregate your funds and understand that your standard of living comes in two parts. One is the Daily Standard of Living, or what it takes to live from week to week, and the other is the Overall Standard of Living, which takes into consideration large periodic purchases in addition to day-to-day living costs. Mr. Ordinary fails to plan for this second part, and has to dip into retirement funds for the big purchases.

In Figure 5 you can see that with the exception of the Special Purchases Account, the graph is the same as one of the Lifestyle of Success in Figure

1. The difference is understanding how big purchases fit into your overall standard of living. "Standard of living" is what it costs you to live today. If you live in a big house, drive a fancy car, have a boat or airplane, the cost of all these things figures into your Overall Standard of Living and has to be paid from your Earned Income before you can set aside money to invest to achieve financial independence.

Delayed Gratification

About now you're probably thinking, "How can I have the things I want and still plan for financial independence?" It's called "patience," and with few exceptions, patience does not mean going out and financing these purchases. It requires setting up separate accounts to accumulate money for large purchases and another to accumulate funds to produce the unearned income required to achieve financial independence. One guides you in determining when to buy that new car, take an expensive vacation, buy a boat, or make any other large expenditure that improves your standard of living today. The other account is untouchable!

To do this you have to become a master at deferred gratification! Let's face it; we live in a "want it now" society. When Roger went to work for Montgomery Ward, they constantly repeated the slogan: "Want it! Charge it!" Easy credit was the way they built their markets. Not only were they making 18 percent interest on charge accounts, they were building a mailing list of people who could walk into their stores and say: "Charge it!" Roger was horrified at this massive effort to get people to go into debt, and eventually the federal government put some brakes on it and passed a law that said if you're going to offer credit, you must make the terms of the credit clear in your advertisements.

Deferred gratification means training yourself to think, "I want it but I don't need it." Thinking this way isn't easy because American marketers are masters at getting us to want stuff that we don't need. That almost sank the U.S. auto industry in the 1970s. We became so good at marketing cars that we didn't have to build good cars anymore. Americans would buy anything. General Motors could say to their advertising agency, "Can we stick a Cadillac emblem on a Buick and call it a Cadillac?" "Sure," the geniuses on Madison Avenue would tell them, "we can sell that!" The problem was, the Japanese were making better and better automobiles and holding prices down. Soon they offered a much better value and were selling us what we wanted to buy, not what Madison Avenue wanted to sell us.

No question about it, we are being bombarded by experts in getting us to spend money. Delayed gratification is not easy. Here are some suggestions on how to achieve it:

- Don't be tempted by TV commercials, even if you have to get a TiVo device or record programs on your VCR so you can fast-forward through them.
- Skip the advertisements in magazines and newspapers by turning the pages to avoid them.
- Don't make going to the mall your recreational activity. Climb a hill or take a walk in the woods instead.
- Avoid expensive restaurants. A barbecue in the backyard with friends and family can give you just as much enjoyment.
- Learn to walk through stores like Wal-Mart and say to yourself, "Look at all the stuff in here that I don't need!"

Delaying gratification is hard work at times, but if you make a hard and fast rule that you're not going to dip into your investment savings no matter how strong the urge, you will be rewarded handsomely in the long run.

Notice how the line for the Special Purchases Account in Figure 5 goes up and down and up and down without having an effect on the Unearned Income line. Money accumulates in this account until there is enough to buy the boat, the purchase is made, and the account drops down. The same holds true for the bigger car purchase, the vacation, and any other major expenditure. At least that's the way it works for people with a Weekend Millionaire Mindset—those living the Lifestyle of Success.

How Patience Pays

Let's look at the role patience plays in building financial independence. Would you believe that you can drive a Chevrolet or a Cadillac for the same money? That's right! You read correctly! You can drive a Chevrolet or a

The Lifestyle of Ordinary

Cadillac for the same amount of earned income. Want to know how? Well, look at the chart in Figure 6.

Chevrolet or Cadillac? The Power of Patience!

Month	Payment	Principal	Interest	Balance	Payment	Interest	Balance
	A $22,000 Chevrolet Financed for 60 Months at 10% Interest				The Same Payment Invested at 8%		
1	$ 467.43	$ 284.10	$ 183.33	$21,715.90	$ 467.43	$ 3.12	$ 470.55
2	467.43	286.46	180.97	21,429.44	467.43	6.25	944.23
3	467.43	288.85	178.58	21,140.59	467.43	9.41	1,421.07
4	467.43	291.26	176.17	20,849.33	467.43	12.59	1,901.09
5	467.43	293.69	173.74	20,555.64	467.43	15.79	2,384.31
6	467.43	296.13	171.30	20,259.51	467.43	19.01	2,870.75
7	467.43	298.60	168.83	19,060.91	467.43	22.25	3,360.44
8	467.43	301.09	166.34	19,659.82	467.43	25.52	3,853.39
9	467.43	303.60	163.83	19,356.22	467.43	28.81	4,349.62
10	467.43	306.13	161.83	19,050.09	467.43	32.11	4,849.16
11	467.43	308.68	158.75	18,741.41	467.43	35.44	5,352.04
12	467.43	311.25	156.18	18,430.16	467.43	38.80	5,858.27
24	5,609.16	3,943.65	1,655.51	14,486.51	5,609.16	735.34	12,202.76
36	5,609.16	4,356.61	1,252.55	10,129.90	5,609.16	1,261.93	19,073.85
48	5,609.16	4,812.82	796.34	5,317.08	5,609.16	1,832.24	26,515.24
60	5,609.16	5,317.08	292.08	–0–	5,609.16	2,449.85	34,574.26

Figure 6

This chart is divided into two parts. We'll refer to the left side of the chart as Mr. Ordinary and the right side as Mr. Financial Independence. Mr. Ordinary buys a $22,000 Chevrolet and finances it at 10 percent annual interest for 60 months. (We know, you're thinking that you can finance a new car at zero percent interest; if that were the case, why would you have the option of zero percent financing or a large "cash back bonus"? The reason is simple; the price of the vehicle is inflated to include the interest you aren't being charged when you finance at zero percent, but if you pay cash, they will give it back to you.) Anyway, we'd prefer to be upfront about it and show you that Mr. Ordinary's payments are $467.43 per month for 60 months, which includes interest.

Mr. Ordinary's side of the chart shows the monthly breakdown of each payment during the first year; what portion goes to reduce the loan balance (principal) and the amount that is interest. As you can see, the balance declines after each payment only by the amount of the payment that is principal. The amounts shown opposite 24, 36, 48, and 60 months are the totals at the end of year 2, 3, 4, and 5. Each year Mr. Ordinary has to take 12 times $467.43, or $5,609.16, from his earned income to make the payments.

The right side of the chart shows what Mr. Financial Independence does with his money. Like Mr. Ordinary, he takes the same $467.43 per month, $5,609.16 per year, from his earned income, but rather than making payments on a car, he invests the money. In this example, he earns an 8 percent return on his investments. This is the money that shows up in on Figure 5 as the Special Purchases Account.

So, here we have two people, both of whom have committed $467.43 per month of their earned income, but at the end of 60 months, what does each have? Mr. Ordinary has a five-year-old worn-out Chevrolet and no money. Mr. Financial Independence has $34,574.26 and can go pay cash for a new Cadillac. Big difference! If you look at what each got for the effort it took to earn $467.43 per month for five years, the difference is staggering. Mr. Ordinary got a $22,000 automobile that started dropping in value the minute he drove it off the lot. Mr. Financial Independence started earning income from the very beginning and continued to do so for the entire five years. As a result, if he chose to buy a new car, he could get one that was $12,574.26 more expensive than Mr. Ordinary for the same effort. That's the price of impatience, a price that Mr. Ordinary rarely ever figures out, which is why he remains ordinary.

"But," you say, "what did Mr. Financial Independence drive while he was investing his $467.43 per month?" The answer is, he drove the cheapest thing he could get by with in order to put himself in a position where he could drive a nice car for the rest of his life, without ever having to pay interest. Mr. Ordinary chose to drive a nicer car in the beginning than Mr. Financial Independence and unknowingly locked himself into a cycle of financing car after car for the rest of his life; a cycle he will repeat with nearly every major purchase he will make during his lifetime.

Remember when we asked you in the beginning of Chapter 2 why you can find neighbors, living side by side, both earning the same income, yet one has a lovely well-maintained home, nice clothing, new cars, and all the trappings of success, while the other lives in a house that needs painting, wears hand-me-down clothing, drives an old clunker, and is always broke? Could it be the cost of impatience; the combination of interest paid for the use of a lender's money to finance large expenditures coupled with the lost income that could be earned if money was saved for these purchases? We're not saying that interest paid on consumer debt is the only difference between the Lifestyle of Success and the Lifestyle of Ordinary, because other factors like lack of planning and impulse buying play a role as well. But for Mr. Ordinary, there are few things that hinder his ability to achieve financial independence as much as interest on consumer debt.

Now that we have defined the different lifestyles that people follow, and we're writing about how to develop a Weekend Millionaire Mindset, the next step is to define wealth as we use the term. In the next chapter, we'll go into detail on this subject and share what we feel constitutes wealth.

Key Points from This Chapter

- Ordinary people live well and pay their bills, but that doesn't mean they're building wealth or will ever be financially independent.
- Dipping into retirement savings to make major purchases is a sure way to lose the compounding effect that builds wealth.
- Separate retirement investment money from savings for large purchases and have the discipline to keep them separate.
- Deferred gratification will allow you to drive a Cadillac for the same money ordinary people spend on a Chevrolet.
- Train yourself to resist temptation. Saying, "Look at all this stuff I don't need," when you go shopping is a good way to start the training.

5

What Constitutes Wealth?

Ask 100 people to define wealth and you'll probably get 100 different definitions. It seems that wealth means something different to everyone. To some, wealth is having good friends and being well-liked, to others it is close family ties, to still others it is a loving relationship, good health, education, or the feeling of being appreciated. One might say that wealth is having an abundance of whatever is important to you. We won't argue or disagree with that definition, but since this book deals with achieving financial independence, we feel we should define wealth as it relates to your financial condition.

One reason so many people think of wealth in subjective terms is because to most people the idea of becoming a millionaire is so far beyond their imagination that it seems a dream. Why? Could it be because they have been conditioned by society to think in terms of "earning" a living? When they sit down with a calculator and figure out that they would have to "earn" at $12.50 per hour, 40 hours per week, 50 weeks per year, for 40 years just to "earn" $1 million dollars, they see the goal of becoming a millionaire as impossible. Many working people don't earn $12.50 per hour on their jobs, and that's before taxes. When they have to pay living expenses from what's left over after taxes, they struggle just to exist.

Even people who make $40 to $50 per hour find that becoming a millionaire is a daunting task. Although this seems like a good wage, after it is reduced by taxes they would still have to set aside more than 30 percent of their income to save $12.50 per hour. Practically no one is willing to do this, which is why so many people define wealth in subjective terms that have nothing to do with money. Not believing it's possible to become wealthy financially, they define wealth in other ways, which can't be measured. But for those who want to reach financial independence, wealth is measured in terms of money or the monetary equivalent of assets that generate money; in other words, things that can sustain and improve your standard of living.

When we talk about wealth, a lot of people get nervous because they view money as the root of all evil. Perhaps that's rooted in biblical teachings. A few years back, Mike was in Asheville, North Carolina, where he lives, when he came upon a street preacher who had drawn a sizable crowd in a downtown park. The preacher was pounding his Bible and shouting at the top of his lungs as he extolled the virtues of being poor. Mike stopped for a few minutes to listen to his sermon, which he closed with the quote, "It's easier for a camel to pass through the eye of a needle than it is for a rich man to enter the kingdom of heaven." With messages like this being delivered in the name of God, no wonder many people have problems with money.

In fact, money is not the problem, it's what some people do in pursuit of money or do with money after they get it that causes problems. Money is not the root of all evil, it is just a tool, a common means of exchange. What causes problems are greed, laziness, dishonesty, deceit, fraud, corruption, cheating, trickery, and other human flaws that lead to the unscrupulous quest for money.

Before the advent of money, the common means of exchange was barter. People would trade labor or something they could grow or produce directly with others who had what they needed. (They might trade vegetables they grew in their garden for milk, butter, and cheese produced by a dairy farmer.) The problem with barter was that people who had what you needed might not have needed what you had to trade, so eventually humans devised a system whereby every product or service could have a value as measured in some form of currency. In more primitive times things like beads, feathers, precious metals, or stones were used as a common means of exchange. Today this common means of exchange is money, which is generally defined as currencies issued by the various governing bodies of the world.

Building wealth is not about working for money, it's about money working for you. Wealth is not measured by what you own; it's measured by the degree to which what you own can enrich your life. In other words, wealth is an income stream; an income stream for which you don't have to work. You may think you want to be a millionaire, but being worth a million dollars is far less important than the income a million dollars can generate. Let us give you an example.

Suppose you have a million dollars worth of gold locked in a safe deposit box at your bank. Technically you are a millionaire, but what is the gold doing to enrich your life? Suppose you took the gold out of the vault, turned it into money, and used the money to buy 10 houses costing $100,000 that would rent for $1,000 per month each. Now you would still be worth a million dollars, but the million dollars would be generating $10,000 income per month, every month for the foreseeable future; an income that would grow as inflation pushed prices up. In this scenario, can you see how your invested money could enrich your life every month without depleting your million dollars? On the other hand, if you kept the gold locked in the vault, inflation would gradually erode its buying power, and other than the satisfaction of knowing you had it, the million dollars would not enrich your life at all.

With this in mind, let us once again say that we define wealth as an income stream for which you don't have to work. When most people see others living in a big house, driving luxury cars, wearing expensive clothes and belonging to a country club, they think these people are wealthy. Maybe, maybe not! The true measure of wealth is how long these people can sustain that lavish lifestyle if they suddenly can't work and earn money. Let us give you a couple of contrasting examples.

Early in Mike's business career, he was in the sign business. One of his clients was a man named John who owned a popular restaurant. John drove a new Cadillac, lived in a beautiful home, and had a ranch where he raised show horses. His child attended an expensive private school. He owned a big motor home and had all the appearances of wealth. John rented signs from Mike to advertise his restaurant, was one of Mike's best customers, and always paid his invoices promptly. Eventually they developed a personal friendship and took hunting and fishing trips together.

John had been in business just a few short years longer than Mike, yet he seemed to have everything he wanted, while Mike was struggling to keep his door open. When they took trips together, John always had a big roll of cash in his pocket and made it a point to let Mike know how well he was doing. Mike would pay his share, but he had no money to spend frivolously the way John did. Mike liked spending time with John because he was very impressed with John, and if the truth be known, even somewhat envious of John's success. He hoped he could learn from John, and that some of John's good fortune would rub off.

Several years passed in which Mike struggled and pinched pennies in order to put money back into his business to make it grow. He never seemed to have any excess money to blow. All the while, John seemed to be on a roll. He bought a new Cadillac every couple of years, traded up to bigger and more elaborate motor homes, and even opened a second restaurant. It seemed he could do no wrong. He was obviously earning a very nice income.

Then one day Mike received a phone call. His friend John had been taken to the hospital, suffering dizziness and a headache. As soon as he received the call, Mike went to the hospital, but by the time he arrived, the doctors had already sent John to intensive care. He had suffered a massive brain aneurism and his outlook was doubtful. Although John was only 48 years old and had a wife and small child, he failed to make it through that night, and his death set in motion a tragic turn of events that had a lasting impact on Mike.

When news of John's passing broke, talk seemed to center around the fact that he had been so successful financially but had not lived to enjoy his success. Some even commented that all he thought about was making money. Visitors at the funeral home and attendees at his funeral were united in their expression of sympathy to his family, and everyone commented that at least his financial success would assure they would be cared for after his death. But as the days passed following his funeral, John's darkest secret began to surface. He had spent everything he made as he went through life, and in death he left his family in debt.

His family ended up having to sell the restaurants, the ranch, the motor home, the Cadillac, and the family home. Even the life insurance they thought he had carried had been canceled. For Mike this was not a lesson in greed, corruption, or any of the other human flaws that lead to unscrupulous quests for money. John was a man who earned his money honestly and paid his debts timely; he just failed to plan for the future. This is a characteristic that keeps ordinary people ordinary, and discovering it provided Mike with a lesson he never forgot and a lesson that played a big part in developing the Weekend Millionaire Mindset.

Throughout their friendship, John always spent more than Mike, but that was because he was spending all he had. Mike just didn't know that at the time. On the other hand, Mike was more frugal and continued to invest part of his money in assets that would provide future income. That meant he did without some of the things John was buying, but his assets and income were steadily growing. In the beginning, he was investing in the construction of billboard signs to rent, but his accountant eventually advised him to diversify his investments, so he began to invest in rental real estate. He made it a point to reinvest at least 20 percent of his income in assets that would produce passive income; income for which he didn't have to work. John never enjoyed any passive income.

The shock of learning that John had left his family in a desperate state of affairs strengthened Mike's view of planning for the future. Although he was still a young man and believed that living well today was important, Mike also understood that unless he planned for his family to be cared for if something should happen and he couldn't work, or planned for himself if he should live to a ripe old age, he wouldn't be able to enjoy the peace of mind he wanted. This kept him investing 20 percent and more of his earned income into his business, plus investing a few hours each week of his spare time trying to find and structure real estate deals that would add to his passive income.

One important step he took was to set up a special bank account into which he deposited all of the income and paid all of the expenses from his rental properties. In the beginning this account contained very little money because the new purchases he was making had little cash flow after expenses. Gradually, however, as funds began to build up in this account, instead of taking the money out and spending it, Mike would reinvest it by purchasing more income-producing properties. Throughout the 1980s he kept looking for more deals he could purchase with little or no money down, and he continued to reinvest his positive cash flow.

Back in the late 1970s, when he first started investing in real estate, Mike set an initial goal of $1,000 per month income. He reached this goal fairly quickly and then set a new goal of $10,000 per month income from his investments. This goal was also achieved within a few short years. By now he was beginning to understand the power of real estate investing, and even though he was still working a full-time job, he set a new goal of $100,000 per month. This was a huge goal, but he knew that if he could reach it, he would be able to retire from active work with a standard of living far beyond anything he'd ever imagined possible when he was a young man.

The 1990s opened very strongly, with Mike well on his way to reaching this latest goal, when fate dealt him an unexpected setback. Almost exactly a decade after the death of his friend John, and just days prior to his forty-fourth birthday, Mike was flying home from Florida in a private plane when he began experiencing severe pain in his lower abdomen. Fortunately he was not the only pilot onboard, so Mike insisted on continuing the flight all the way back to Asheville. When they landed, he was suffering such intense pain that his friend helped him off the plane and rushed him to the emergency room at a local hospital.

Upon initial examination, the doctors thought he was suffering an attack of kidney stones, but tests proved this not to be the case. For days his condition continued to worsen. The doctors ran test after test and brought in various specialists to try to determine the cause of his problem, but he kept slipping further into a state of infirmity. Things were becoming critical as his condition worsened.

Eventually, one of the doctors decided to perform a heart catheterization to determine if his coronary arteries had suffered a blockage. This produced a very traumatic development for his wife. A few years earlier, her father had suffered a massive heart attack and died having the same test. She became distraught and refused to allow the test to be performed until she could bring their two young sons, ages five and seven, to visit their father. She felt she was bringing them to say good-bye, and it produced one of the most memorable moments of Mike's life.

When his children arrived, his son Jason, who is known for verbalizing whatever is on his mind, quickly came to the side of the bed and took Mike's forefinger in one little hand and his pinkie finger in the other. As he stood there squeezing his father's fingers, a big tear came into his eye and he said, "Daddy, are you going to die?" As sick as he was at the time, the impact of this straightforward question from his son forced Mike to recall how his friend John had left his family in dire financial straits when he was suddenly taken from them.

Mike turned his head and looked into those innocent little blue eyes filled with tears and told Jason, "No, buddy, I'm going to be fine." When he said it, his resolve to get well skyrocketed, but he also knew that if he didn't make it, his wife and children would not have to worry about the future. All those years in which he had spent less than he made and invested the difference suddenly became the most important thing he'd ever done. The peace of mind it gave him—that his family would be financially secure—confirmed the decisions he had made over the years. This allowed him to begin his recuperation knowing that they would be able to sustain their standard of living even if he could never work again.

Fortunately, the heart catheterization was uneventful and revealed no problems; however, subsequent tests revealed that Mike was suffering from a renal infarction. A clot was blocking the flow of blood to his left kidney and the tissue was dying. With the problem diagnosed, the doctors immediately ordered intravenous anticoagulation therapy. After several weeks in the hospital, Mike experienced a full recovery.

The lesson from this experience came several weeks after Mike had returned to work. He was in his office when the lead doctor who had cared for him during his nearly three-week hospitalization called. After making the obligatory inquiry as to how he was doing, the doctor asked Mike if he could take him to lunch one day. Mike thought this was unusual, especially since their offices were several miles apart, but he agreed and they scheduled a date.

On the appointed date, Mike's doctor drove to his office, picked him up, and drove them to a nearby Mexican restaurant. As they ate and made small talk, Mike's curiosity nearly got the best of him. He couldn't understand why his doctor wanted to treat him to lunch, but he held his tongue and waited as they talked. Finally, the doctor got to the purpose of the luncheon when he looked up and said, "I'd like to ask you a question, and if you don't feel comfortable with it, you don't have to answer, but I'm really curious: Do you have a strong faith in God?"

Thinking this was a somewhat bizarre question, Mike responded with, "Yes, I'm a believer in God, but I'm curious as to why you ask."

"Well," replied the doctor, "I've been treating sick people for quite some time, but I've never seen anyone facing the possibility of death deal with it as calmly and self-assuredly as you did. I just wondered if it was because you had a strong faith and had put your life in God's hands."

As he pondered his doctor's comment, Mike closed his eyes, looked inward and did some soul-searching. Yes, he had been calm and self-assured throughout his illness, and yes, he had been aware, especially in those first few days, that he might not pull through. But why? As he sat there searching for an answer, it suddenly hit him. He opened his eyes and said to the doctor, "I guess the reason I felt the way I did is that there is nothing I have wanted to do in life that I haven't done or was in the process of doing when I got sick. In other words, I feel like I have lived a full life up until this point in time. Sure, I've made mistakes, but I learned from them and they made me a better person. I also didn't have to worry about my family because I knew they would be provided for if I didn't make it. I guess if I had to be perfectly honest about it, I wouldn't change anything, including getting sick. That tear in my little boy's eye when he asked if I was going to die made getting well mandatory. I didn't want that to be his last memory of me."

Many people believe that wealth is having a good job and a high income. As you can see from these contrasting stories involving Mike and his friend John, there is big difference between earning a living and building wealth. Perhaps the stress and pressure of trying to maintain John's high standard of living may have contributed to his untimely death. Possibly, the tranquility Mike enjoyed helped him to recover from his illness and enabled him to watch his sons play sports, finish school, and become outstanding young men. What's not speculation is the fact that the small sacrifices Mike made by living within a more modest standard of living while he was building wealth contributed to the serenity he benefited from during this trying time, and that it played a huge part in his development of the Weekend Millionaire Mindset.

Key Points from This Chapter

- Wealth can be defined in many ways, but for the purposes of this book, we're going to focus on wealth as measured financially.
- Don't shy away from the goal of becoming wealthy because it may seem impossible to attain.
- Money is not the root of all evil. Only lowering your ethical and moral standards to get money is evil.
- Wealth is not what you own or the size of your salary; wealth is a passive income stream that can ensure your standard of living.
- Learning to live within your means and making a habit of regular investing will produce life-changing results.

6

Debt: Constructive or Destructive?

Has debt got you down? Are you struggling to make all those payments that come due each month? Do you sometimes get the feeling that no matter what you do, you just can't seem to get ahead? Do you hope for a raise so you can use the extra money to work your way out of debt? Or do you feel that the only way to improve your life is to change jobs, move, inherit money, hit the lottery, or find a get-rich-quick scheme that really works?

If you responded positively to any of these questions, then you are experiencing the effects of destructive debt. For many people, the mounting pressure of debt creates problems with spouses, significant others, friends, coworkers, or simply drives them crazy.

Destructive debt is a terrible thing. It is debt to acquire items that are consumed prior to being paid for or that go down in value after their acquisition, without generating income to service the debt. Examples are debt to pay for food, fuel, clothes, entertainment, gifts, recreation, personal care items, telephone, electricity, water, cable television, and any similar items that people charge to credit cards. Don't misunderstand us: There's nothing wrong with using credit cards to pay for these items if you pay the bill in full when it comes due. As a matter of fact, we both regularly use our credit cards for normal monthly expenses and enjoy the convenience of only having to write one check or make one automatic bank draft for the payment. It does not become destructive debt until it carries over to the next month.

Debt to acquire cars, boats, campers, motorcycles, furniture, or other large ticket items that are not used to generate income are additional examples of destructive debt. As we saw in the example in Figure 6 in Chapter 4, the cost of financing the purchase of these large ticket items can be significant. In today's world, more people ask themselves, "Can I make the payments?" than ask, "Can I afford to buy?" Why? Why do so many people succumb to impulsive buying urges? Could it be because we are continuously bombarded with advertising messages that make it seem like the "cool" or "in" thing to do?

As you begin to develop the Weekend Millionaire Mindset, you will find overcoming these impulses increasingly easier and you'll make more informed buying decisions. Building wealth is more about managing money than about making money, but that's not what our education system teaches. Mike once presented a program to a high school economics class in which he described the Lifestyles of Success, Failure, and Ordinary. After his presentation, the teacher asked if he would be willing to present the same program to another of her classes after lunch. He agreed, but at this second presentation he noticed several adults had entered the classroom and were sitting along the back wall. Following his presentation, the teacher invited him out into the hallway, where she introduced one of them as her husband. She told Mike that part of the reason she wanted him to present the program again was so she could call and ask him to attend. He also learned that the other adults were faculty members who had heard about the program during their lunch break.

Considering that most high school graduates leave school without knowing how to balance a checkbook, prepare a family budget, or fill out a financial statement, is it any wonder so many people get in financial trouble? It should also come as no surprise that many college freshmen become addicted to destructive credit card debt before they complete their first year of higher learning, and the sad part is, they usually don't realize they're addicted until they are so far in debt it will take years and years of sacrifice to get out of the hole.

But all debt is not bad. You've heard it said that it takes money to make money: To most people, this means working harder and earning more, but to the Weekend Millionaire, it means getting money to work for you, and it doesn't have to be your money. That's where constructive debt enters the picture. If you could borrow money for 6 percent interest annually and invest it in assets that would pay you 10 percent or more annually, how much would you want to borrow? Would you agree that this kind of debt could eventually make you wealthy?

Isn't this exactly what banks do? When you deposit money into a savings account or certificate of deposit, the bank is borrowing from you. For the bank, your account is debt, and it shows up as a liability on its financial statement. When the bank loans your money to another customer at a higher interest, this loan is an asset for the bank; an asset that is expected to pay the bank more than the bank is going to pay you for the use of your money. In this example, your deposit account is constructive debt for the bank.

Now let's take this a step further. If you borrow money from the bank, the loan is a liability, but if you take that money and invest it in something that will pay you much more than you're paying the bank, whatever you invest in is an asset and the bank loan becomes constructive debt. If; however, you borrow the money from the bank by charging daily activities to your credit card, you have to go to work and earn the money to pay it back. The money you borrowed may have allowed you to have a little more fun or enjoy yourself a little more while you were doing it, but the burden it puts on you when it comes time to repay is what causes it to become destructive debt.

Following the Great Depression of the 1930s, most people developed a great fear of debt—any kind of debt. During this period, so many people lost everything they owned that wasn't paid for free and clear that debt became something to fear. For decades afterward, debt was viewed by ordinary people as a tool of the Devil, to be shied away from at all cost. They thought that only the foolish went into debt. Without going into the cause of the Great Depression and its overall effects, let's just agree that the generation of people who grew up during the 1930s and 1940s lived very frugally, and that they focused more on saving than spending. If they did go into debt, it was rarely for something other than to purchase a home to live in.

Following Franklin D. Roosevelt's New Deal and World War II, the country gradually began a period of recovery and debt started to lose its stigma. Returning GIs, who had endured a time of great sacrifice, came home to a changed world. Modes of transportation were more advanced and travel became popular, new modern conveniences such as kitchen appliances and washing machines placed increasing pressures on family budgets, and buying things on credit that they couldn't afford to buy for cash became more accepted. During this time, retail stores frequently offered their customers the option to pay over time when they made large purchases.

Although metal cards giving deferred payment privileges to good customers date back to as early as 1914, it wasn't until 1950 that Diners' Club issued the first credit card as we think of them today. It was invented by Diners' Club founder Frank McNamara and was set up to use for restaurant charges only. American Express followed suit in 1958, and during that same year Bank of America issued the first bank credit card, Bank Americard, which was the forerunner to today's VISA card. By 1966 the success of these credit cards prompted a group of U.S. banks to form an association to exchange information on credit card transactions, and in 1967 they introduced Master Charge, the forerunner of today's MasterCard.

By this time the Baby Boom generation was beginning to come of age, and it took to credit like ducks to water. Almost all of them wanted to give their children more than they had experienced growing up. Credit was a quick and convenient way of doing this. Merchants soon learned that people usually spent more when they purchased with credit cards than when they had to pay cash, and the banking industry discovered a huge new source of revenue from the much higher interest rates they could charge on credit card balances. The race to obtain new customers became so heated that banks were actually mass mailing active credit cards to people who had not even requested them. Fortunately, this was curbed by Congress in the mid-1970s when it banned the practice.

As economists had learned, it was spending, not saving, that ultimately pulled the U.S. economy out of the Great Depression. It was forced spending by the federal government in the form of hundreds of billions of dollars worth of defense contracts during World War II, not the attempted reorganization of the economy under the New Deal, that built factories, boosted production, and put people back to work in meaningful jobs that set us on the road to prosperity.

The advent of the credit card and the ease of credit for consumer purchases kept the economy growing, but at a price. The payments consumers were making on this easy credit was coming from the cash they were earning on their jobs, trading labor for money. What made this debt so destructive was the fact that a sizable portion of the payments was interest, which bought them nothing. This meant that part of the money they earned was merely being transferred to people with money to loan, and as a result, the rich got richer and the poor got poorer.

To illustrate the effect of this destructive debt, back in 1929, at the start of the Great Depression, the top 20 percent of American society controlled just over 50 percent of the nation's wealth and the bottom 20 percent controlled about 5 percent. But by 1997 things had changed dramatically; just the top 10 percent controlled over 72 percent of the wealth and the bottom 40 percent controlled less than 1 percent. Now can you see why we say that consumer debt is destructive debt? Every working person in America who is making payments on consumer debt from the money they earn on their job is transferring wealth to the wealthy, not improving their own standard of living with the new toys they are buying. Your true standard of living is determined by what you can purchase with the money you earn working plus the income produced by your investments. Financial independence does not occur until your investment income will fully support your lifestyle. Nothing more, nothing less!

So, if this is the case, how can any debt be used constructively? The answer is very simple! Don't borrow money unless you can put it to work and have it earn more than it costs you to borrow it. While that answer may be simple, the execution is not. You don't just run out and borrow money and then look for a place to invest it. You have to be patient, creative, determined, and committed. You need patience to sort through all the opportunities that present themselves in the marketplace if you expect to find the ones that have real potential. You have to use your creativity to develop opportunities with potential into investment-quality possibilities. Then you must have determination in order to convert possibilities into probabilities and make a commitment, if you expect to turn probabilities into performing investments. This is a process we will go into as we take you on your journey toward developing the Weekend Millionaire Mindset, but first let's discuss how you can use debt constructively.

Using Constructive Debt: A Case History

In Chapter 2 we mentioned that Mike set a goal to become a millionaire by 30 and retire by 50. When he set this goal, he was a young man 20 years old, married and living in an old rented house. He had just been laid off, or as we would say today, "downsized," from his $80 per week factory job and his total assets consisted of an old car on which he was making payments and $300 in severance pay his former employer had given him when he was released. Even the most optimistic of people would have to stretch to see him as millionaire material.

But having this goal, and being committed to it, caused a transformation in Mike that started him down the road to developing a Weekend Millionaire Mindset. The first thing the goal did was help him understand that he would never become a millionaire by looking for another $80 per week factory job. At $80 per week, it would take over 240 years just to earn a million dollars, let alone be worth that much. If he was going to become a millionaire by age 30, he would have to build his net worth by an average of $100,000 a year for 10 years, a task that would seem impossible to the ordinary person. But Mike chose not to be ordinary. He started asking himself, "How can I?" instead of resigning himself to saying, "I can't."

When he was working his factory job, Mike had earned extra money by using his artistic talents to paint signs for the plant. Since he now had no job, and a huge goal, he decided he would start his own business painting signs for others. He used his $300 severance pay to buy an old van and a few supplies and started making calls on local businesses. He soon learned that there was much more to the sign business than he had experienced at the plant. With youthful naiveté, he visited a local sign shop that had been in business for several years, said he wanted to start a sign business, asked the

Debt: Constructive or Destructive?

owner if he would tell him what kinds of materials to use and to show him how to lay out the sign copy so it would be properly positioned. The shop owner, Dave Cheadle, who is now in his late 70s and still in the sign business, shared his knowledge and expertise with Mike and allowed him to come back any time he had questions. Dave's kindness and generosity was never forgotten, and he and Mike remain friends to this day.

With this humble beginning, Mike started his business. But he soon learned that painting signs and selling them was not much different from working the factory job; he was still basically trading labor for money. Mike was patient, and worked very hard, but after a full year in business his total income had only reached $3,400 and he realized that either he didn't have enough time, or people weren't willing to pay enough for what time he did have, to reach his goal of becoming a millionaire by age 30. He knew there was potential in the sign business, but that he would have to be more creative to turn it into an investment-quality possibility. As he pondered his options, one nagging thought kept entering his mind: "When I sell my work, where is my investment?"

Then he thought about the wealthy people he knew and saw that they all had one thing in common: They owned stuff; stuff that made money for them. Although he had a sign business, he didn't own anything that generated income. The only income from his business came from the sale of signs that required his labor to create. Once the sign was sold, he had to make another one in order to earn more income.

One day, Mike was having lunch with one of his good customers who wanted him to build a large roadside sign, but he wanted to rent the sign, not buy it. In his head, Mike quickly figured that it would take more than $500 to buy the materials and another $500 worth of his labor to paint and erect the sign, plus he would have to pay a landowner rent for permission to put the sign on his property. When Mike said he didn't have the money, his client offered to sign a contract to rent the sign for $50 per month for five years and suggested to Mike that a bank would probably loan him the money based on the contract. This lunch conversation gave Mike an idea on how to turn the potential of his business into a real investment possibility.

Little did he realize it at the time, but this would become his first experience with constructive debt. What he discovered when he went to his bank to get a loan was that his banker had never heard of financing a sign. He wanted to know where Mike planned to put the sign, did he own the property or have a lease for the land, how would the sign be constructed, how long would it last, what kind of maintenance would it require, how creditworthy was the customer, and what kind of contract did he have for the rental.

Mike hadn't thought about any of these things. When he went to visit his banker, he had prepared a proposal showing how a loan for $1,200 would pay for the materials, his labor, and the first three years of projected ground lease rental. He showed the banker that if the $1,200 was financed for three years at 10 percent interest, the payments would be $38.72 per month, and his monthly lease rental of $50 per month would more than cover the payments. Then he explained that after the first three years, the entire $50 per month would be his for the next two years, and that at the end of five years he would still own the sign and could either renew the advertising contract or rent it to another business. He thought this was a slam dunk!

As it turned out, the banker agreed it was probably a good deal, but in spite of Mike's enthusiasm, he had trouble determining how to make the loan. What was the collateral? Was it the ground lease, was it the advertising contract, or was it the sign structure itself that had the value? In the end, Mike assigned them all to the bank to obtain this first $1,200 loan, a process he would repeat frequently over the next several years.

As his business grew, if one bank wouldn't loan him more money, he would go to another and another until he got what he wanted. Eventually he was able to borrow millions, which he invested constructively in sign structures. It was this determination and commitment that brought him the financial success that allowed him to attain the $1 million net worth mark and reach the first part of his goal by age 28.

As his assets grew, so did his problems. In the early 1970s, Lady Bird Johnson, wife of former President Lyndon Johnson, successfully lobbied Congress for passage of the Highway Beautification Act, and numerous states, counties, and local municipalities jumped on the bandwagon and began regulating signs.

By the late 1970s, after listening to concerns from his bankers, lawyers, and others, Mike's accountant at the time, John Kledis of Asheville, North

Debt: Constructive or Destructive?

Carolina, suggested that he consider diversifying his investments. He suggested rental real estate as a possible alternative to signs. The problem was, all of Mike's assets were invested and he was struggling to borrow additional money to keep his business growing. He didn't have any extra money to invest, but he took his accountant's advice and began exploring real estate anyway. He soon learned that renting houses was very similar to renting signs, but it was much easier to obtain the financing.

He began spending a few hours of his spare time, mainly on weekends, looking at properties and making offers. In the beginning he had to make offers that would require little or no cash to complete. It took him nearly a year to make his first purchase, but with it he discovered a new way to use debt constructively. The next year, he purchased two houses, the third year four, and the rest is history. It was the energy with which he tackled this new endeavor that ultimately led to his phenomenal success and the accomplishment of his goal to retire by age 50. This success story is chronicled in our best selling book *The Weekend Millionaire's Secrets to Investing in Real Estate: How to Become Wealthy in Your Spare Time* (McGraw-Hill, 2003).

While Mike found success by borrowing money to constructively invest in billboards and real estate, other successful people discovered different avenues to wealth. One friend of Mike's invests in video games and vending machines; as he sleeps, people are filling them full of quarters. Another friend invests in coin laundry machines that are located all over town, including in apartments owned by Mike. Yet another invests in automobiles that he leases, and another is involved in private mortgages. These are all ordinary people who have found ways to invest borrowed money in assets that generate enough to pay back the loan plus make a profit. These are true investments, because these people do not have to work a job to earn the money to pay back the loans.

Wherever you live, if you look around you will see people who have found ways to constructively use debt to build wealth. This is probably where the statement "It takes money to make money" originated. Borrowed money can be a great wealth-building tool, but as Henry C. Alexander, who effectively changed the way Morgan Guaranty Trust did business, said, "Increased borrowing must be matched with increased ability to repay. Otherwise we aren't expanding the economy; we're merely puffing it up." It doesn't matter whether it's the economy of a nation or the economy of an individual, when you borrow money to invest in income-producing assets, your wealth will grow and your standard of living will eventually improve. On the other hand, if you borrow money and spend it to live better today, your standard of living will improve for the moment but will surely decrease over time.

When you learn the difference between destructive debt used for daily living and constructive debt to wisely invest, you will be well on your way to wealth. When statesman, lawyer, and orator Daniel Webster said, "Credit has done a thousand times more to enrich mankind than all the gold mines in the world," he definitely wasn't talking about consumer credit. Although Webster died in 1852, prior to the advent of today's credit card, his comment is just as valid now as it was back then—but it only applies to constructive debt, not destructive debt.

Let's hold that thought as we move to the next chapter and get you started on your journey to financial independence.

Key Points from This Chapter

- Using credit cards to purchase items that you can't pay for when the monthly statement comes is the most common way people create destructive debt.
- Financial independence comes more from knowing how to manage your money than it does from learning how to earn more money.
- Constructive debt is created when you borrow money that you can invest in something that earns more income than the money costs to borrow.
- Learn to embrace constructive debt but fear destructive debt.
- Use constructive debt to build wealth and increase your income.

7

Beginning the Journey to Financial Independence

Having read this far, you know that we've discussed financial independence but haven't applied the term to everyday living. We've discussed how people who enjoy the Lifestyle of Success embarked on a course that led to them creating an ongoing stream of income that was enough to maintain their lifestyle without having to work. We've explained that it takes patience and the discipline to delay gratification in order to live better in the long run. We've also shown you the devastating effects of overspending and consumer debt. But up till now we've just been conditioning you to begin your journey toward financial independence.

As with all journeys, there has to be a starting point, and the distance between your starting point and your ultimate goal determines the amount of time and course of action needed to reach it. Where are you in relation to your financial goal? If you're 25, college educated, have a great job, have already started accumulating some savings and investments, and your goal is to reach financial independence in 30 years at age 55, your course of action will be totally different from someone who is already 55, broke, out of work, and wondering how they're going to make it to the end of the month. But the one thing you both have in common is time. Young, old, rich, or poor, everyone has 24 hours in a day and seven days in a week. What you do with your time determines how quickly, if ever, you reach financial independence.

No matter what you've done up until now, you have already embarked on your own personal journey through life. You may have never thought about it in the way we're about to discuss it, so before we ask you to determine where you currently are on your journey, let's talk about the journey itself. The following chart illustrates a simple fact of life.

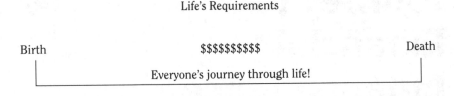

Life's Requirements

Birth   \$\$\$\$\$\$\$\$\$\$ Death

Everyone's journey through life!

Getting from birth to death has a cost!

Figure 7

As you can see in Figure 7, everyone's journey through life involves getting from birth to death, and the cost associated with doing so. How much is that cost? Who knows! It all depends on the length of the journey, how you conduct yourself on the trip, and when you pay for it. Some people only live for the moment and never worry about tomorrow. They take the approach that we have no guarantee of tomorrow; therefore, why not enjoy today to its fullest? If these people die young, but they've spent everything they've made having fun and enjoying themselves, they win. On the other hand, if they live to a ripe old age and end up spending the last half of their life in misery because they didn't plan for the future, they lose.

Other people spend their entire working lives living very frugally, saving, investing, and planning for retirement. They don't take vacations or live in fine houses, drive luxury cars, or enjoy any of the other pleasures money can bring, because they want to be sure they will be able to live well in retirement. Then, if they make it to retirement age, although they are financially well off, they're so used to doing without or are in such poor health that they can't enjoy it. If they happen to die before retirement, they leave behind a nice nest egg for their heirs to enjoy, but they didn't get much pleasure out of accumulating it.

Unfortunately, some of our brightest and most energetic people end up becoming road kill on life's economic highway. Granted, there are people born with problems such as physical defects or mental incapacities from birth that they can't do anything about. Some contract contagious diseases or have unfortunate accidents that limit their abilities, which may necessitate seeking help from others, but these aren't the people we're talking about. All of us who enjoy good health, education, and the ability to care for ourselves should find the generosity to help those less fortunate, but we should never lose sight of the fact that our primary goal is to take care of ourselves first so we don't become a burden on society. If you want to help the poor, start out by determining not to become one of them. They certainly don't need the competition. The decisions we make day to day determine the amount of joy or pain we experience on life's economic journey.

Financial success means many things to many people, but financial independence is the same for everyone. Financial independence is the point at which you can continue to live your chosen lifestyle from the income generated by your investments. It's the "chosen lifestyle" that varies, not the definition of financial independence. Whether your chosen lifestyle requires $3,000 or $30,000 or $300,000 or $3 million per month, you cannot be financially independent until you have an adequate stream of income from your investments to sustain whatever lifestyle makes you happy. Keeping this in mind, let's take another look at life's requirements.

As you can see from Figure 8, what you spend today pays for the days starting at birth and moving toward death. What you invest today pays for days moving from death back toward birth. With this in mind, can you see how life becomes a balancing act? Can you see that by spending too much on today you risk having a good life tomorrow, and if you invest too much for tomorrow you reduce the quality of your life today? That's what developing a Weekend Millionaire Mindset is all about. As we said in Chapter 1, this mindset is rooted in little decisions, those small day-to-day decisions that position us to make better big decisions when the time comes.

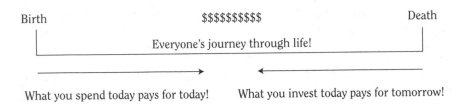

Life's Requirements

Birth $$$$$$$$$$ Death

Everyone's journey through life!

What you spend today pays for today!   What you invest today pays for tomorrow!

Buy retirement days now, while you're able to work!

Figure 8

To achieve the goal of financial independence, you have to start by determining the kind of lifestyle you want to live. In Mike's case, when he set his goal in the 1960s to become a millionaire by age 30 and retire by age 50, he obviously knew that he wanted a higher standard of living than what he was living at the time. His dilemma was how to divide his earnings between improving his current standard of living and investing for the future.

Isn't that a decision we all make consciously or unconsciously every day? Do we eat out tonight, or save money by cooking at home? Do we buy that new pair of sneakers, when we have a perfectly good pair, just because our friends have the new style? Do we trade cars now and get that new one that smells and looks so good, or do we wait a year or two and invest the savings? Do we buy that Sea-Doo this summer and finance it, when we know our time at the lake will be limited, or do we wait until next year or the year after, when we can pay cash for it and have more time to enjoy it? How many decisions like this, big and small, are you faced with every day? Do you realize that a day's income invested today could pay for several days 20, 30, or 40 years from now? Do you have the three Ds: the *discipline* to invest now, the *dedication* to keep it up long term, and the *desire* to one day live your chosen lifestyle without having to worry about money? If so, keep reading!

Look back at Figure 8. Notice how the lines with the arrows pointing from birth and death are about the same length. Don't be misled by this. The length of each arrow will be in direct relation to your standard of living. If you live the Lifestyle of Success we discussed in Chapter 2, start early enough in life, live an overall standard of living reasonably below your earned income, and invest wisely, your arrows may meet near the middle. In this case, you will be able to retire early, not have to reduce your standard of living, and enjoy your retirement years, no matter how long they may last. By the same token, if you live the Lifestyle of Failure we discussed in Chapter 3, you will have to keep earning all your life, suffer through dramatic swings in lifestyle, and probably have to settle for whatever standard of living you can manage on Social Security. And finally, those of you living the Lifestyle of Ordinary we described in Chapter 4 can look forward to a comfortable lifestyle, but one that will most likely have to be pared down in retirement because you won't have enough income to continue living the way you were while working.

Let's now begin to explore what you can do to start developing the Weekend Millionaire Mindset. As we mentioned at the beginning of this chapter, we all have 24 hours in a day, seven days in a week, so let's analyze this time and determine what we do with it.

Everyone's Week

Day 1	Day 2	Day 3	Day 4	Day 5	Day 6	Day 7
8 Hours	8 Hours	8 Hours	8 Hours	8 Hours	8 Hours	8 Hours
8 Hours	8 Hours	8 Hours	8 Hours	8 Hours	8 Hours	8 Hours
8 Hours	8 Hours	8 Hours	8 Hours	8 Hours	8 Hours	8 Hours

Three 8-Hour Blocks of Time, 7 Days a Week

Figure 9

Figure 9 is a graphic representation of what everyone's weeks look like. For ease of demonstration, we have divided each day into three blocks, each consisting of one eight-hour block of time. In this regard, everyone is equal. Time is a commodity of which we are all granted the exact same amount. You cannot save time, hoard time, bank time, or accumulate time. You cannot acquire time, purchase time, inventory, or collect time. You can only spend time. It's how you spend time that determines what you accomplish in life. There are many ways to spend time. You can spend it usefully, constructively, beneficially, creatively, efficiently, positively, productively, and wisely; or you can spend it wastefully, foolishly, frivolously, extravagantly, lavishly, carelessly, and inefficiently. If you think about it, you can come up with hundreds of other ways you can spend time, but not a single way to get more of it.

So, if you can only spend time, what can you do to become more successful? The answer is simple: You improve yourself. Through education and practice, you learn how to produce more in the same amount of time. For example, if you're a typist and you type 40 words a minute, you can become twice as valuable by increasing your typing speed to 80 words per minute. This is done with practice. If you take a medical first responder course, you may be able to get a job with an ambulance crew, but if you're willing to dedicate years to intense study, you can become the doctor who treats the patients the ambulance crews bring to them. We don't need to tell you how much difference there is between the compensation of a doctor and that of an ambulance crew member. This is due to education. In both of these examples, we're talking about ways to make the time you spend more valuable, not have more of it. Unfortunately, most people try to get ahead by spending more time rather than by improving the output of time spent. Let's look at a typical work week.

The chart in Figure 10 shows how ordinary people spend their time. They typically spend five of their eight-hour blocks of time working, seven of them sleeping, and have nine left over as discretionary time, which we call spare time in the chart because "discretionary" won't fit in the box. But seriously, work and sleep are mandatory for most people, but what you do with your discretionary or spare time is up to you ... or is it? What you earn with your work time has everything to do with what you can do with your spare time. If your knowledge and skills at work hours can earn you $2,000 per week, you will be able to enjoy your spare time much more than if they only earn you $200 per week, which brings us to the biggest secret to developing a Weekend Millionaire Mindset. There is something you can do with time other than spend it: You can invest it!

Beginning the Journey to Financial Independence

A Typical Work Week

Work One 8-Hour Block of Time, 5 Days a Week
Sleep One 8-Hour Block of Time, 7 Days a Week
Nine 8-Hour Blocks of Spare Time

Figure 10

If you have a typical work week, like most people, you have 72 hours of discretionary time. Let's analyze how most people spend this time. You might spend two hours per day—some people spend more—getting up, getting dressed, and getting to and from work. Based on a five-day work week, that uses up 10 hours, but leaves you with 62. You may not do it, but a lot of people spend another couple of hours per day, every day, lying in bed sleeping, or just doing nothing. Whether or not you do this, let's allocate the time anyway, which takes up another 14 hours per week, but still leaves you with 48. Throw in another couple of hours per day for eating, bathing, grooming, and now you're down to 34, but everyone has other things they need or want to do, so let's allocate three more hours per day, every day, to things like watching television, playing video games, golf, tennis, jogging, housework, laundry, or other chores around the house, and suddenly you only have 13 hours remaining. Of this time, let's allocate eight hours to your church, civic, or charitable activities, and now you're down to just five hours per week. Granted, in our description, we've painted you as spending a good portion of your spare time doing nonproductive things. We realize that you have the discretion to change how you use many of these hours, but indulge us for the benefit of this example, because even if you live just as we've described, we're going to teach you how to "invest" these few remaining hours to become financially independent.

Before you start thinking thoughts like, "I don't lie around in bed doing nothing," or "I only sleep six hours a day," or "It only takes me 30 minutes a day to get ready and get to and from work," or "I have a two-hour commute each way to work, plus the time it takes me to get ready," or any of a hundred other circumstances that explain why our example doesn't apply to you, stop and think about what you do. If you don't need as long to get ready and get to work, great, but what else are you doing with the time? If you have a two-hour commute each way, isn't that your choice? The key point here is how you invest that commuting time. Do you waste it listening to a shock-jock on the radio or listening to country and western music? Or do you slip in an educational CD and invest the time in learning knowledge and skills that will raise your earning power? Isn't our example just a series of discretionary things that you choose to do with your time? But this isn't a time management course; it's a book about developing a mindset that will encourage you to manage your time, your money, and your life.

The amazing thing about the Weekend Millionaire Mindset is that it doesn't require you to live like a pauper while you're waiting for your ship to come in. It won't make you feel like you have to devote all your spare time to building wealth while sacrificing the fun times in life that everyone needs. What it will do is help you identify your strengths and weaknesses, show you how to rely on your strengths while you strengthen your weaknesses, and help you to become a well-rounded, confident, and financially secure person.

You have already completed part of your journey through life; the ensuing parts of the book will help you determine where you are on this journey and how much further you will need to go. Now let's move on and position you to complete your journey to financial independence.

Key Points from This Chapter

- Financial independence means creating an ongoing stream of income that is enough to maintain your lifestyle without having to work.
- The decisions you make day to day determine the amount of joy or pain you experience as you travel down life's economic highway.

Beginning the Journey to Financial Independence

- What you invest today while you still have strong earning power determines how well you will be able to live in retirement when you aren't earning as much.
- Time is the same for everyone. What you do with it determines the kind of future you will have.
- Investing part of your spare time in education is the best way to increase the earning power of your work time.

PART II

The Formative Years

Everyone's life is a series of experiences; some good, some bad, and some that come and go with little thought one way or another. The interesting point about these experiences is the number of them that contain important life lessons but that we let pass unnoticed. In this part and the two that follow, we will be describing a number of events from our own lives that implanted strong life lessons in our subconscious minds, even though we failed to recognize it at the time. It was not until years later that we were able to look back, analyze the events, and understand the impact they had on our future.

As you read the chapters in this part, think about your own life. Look back to incidents from your childhood and try to recall events that changed the way you act or react today. Keep in mind that all of these changes may not be positive; in fact some of them may have produced strong negative reactions. It's the events that left lasting impressions, both good and bad, on which we want you to focus. While you're reading, if an incident comes to mind, stop and jot down a note to help you recall it later. As you read our stories, be sure to write down any events that come to mind, no matter how insignificant they may seem. Don't try to look for the lessons in your life experiences as you make these notes. We will ask you to refer back to these notes later, after you learn how we discovered the lessons embedded in some of our seemingly insignificant experiences.

We will be sharing our stories to help you see how we used these life experiences to guide our growth and development, but it will be the events from your own life that you will use to develop your Weekend Millionaire Mindset. We will not be getting heavily into psychoanalysis by trying to convince you that you aren't where you want to be in life because someone stole your doll or football when you were four years old. What we will be doing is helping you examine your cumulative life experiences to see if you missed some lessons that may have been embedded in them. If so, we will help you learn how to discover and implement these lessons to improve your life in the future and reach financial independence.

Developing a Weekend Millionaire Mindset is a journey, not a destination. It is a personal journey, because everyone's experiences are different. Opportunities abound, but if you aren't ready and aren't prepared, you will fail to recognize them when they arise. You'll join the ranks of those who whine and complain about how other people have all the luck. When you aren't prepared for an opportunity that comes your way, someone else will grab it and you will be talking about how lucky they were.

The formative years are those years when you're like a sponge—young, innocent, and willing to soak up everything that comes your way. The problem is, it's just as easy to soak up bad information as good. If you soak up too much bad information, it can turn you from a sponge that soaks up knowledge into a rock that resists all change. But even if you've already become a rock, we encourage you to take a second look at those times when you soaked up bad information, because we're going to teach you how to expunge the negative from your mind and become a sponge once again. Greed, jealousy, hate, envy, bitterness, mistrust, and suspicion are all negative thoughts and emotions that come from bad experiences. Hurt, anger, and resentment can devour you like a cancer if you don't get rid of it.

You'll see from the stories in this part that we didn't always react well when things didn't go our way, but it was up to us to choose whether we let disappointment and failure get us down or teach us a lesson. We learned that some of the best lessons life teaches us are what *not* to do. It's the choices we make when things happen that have an influence on our lives. Yes, there is a cause and effect to almost everything. Life deals two people a lemon; one complains about the sour deal he got, while the other makes lemonade. Why? Why do people have such differing reactions to the same event? Why do some people let negative emotions destroy them while others use the same emotions to get stronger? These are all part of what we will be exploring in this part and the two that follow it.

Before you continue on to Chapter 8, get a pad and pencil so you can make notes as you read. We know that the stories and events that follow will trigger memories from your past that will help you have a better tomorrow. We also know that if you don't jot these down as you read, by the time you finish the book, many of them will be forgotten. You must understand that it's your stories— not ours—that are the building blocks of your Weekend Millionaire Mindset. The more of them you have to work with, the easier your journey to financial success will be.

8

Going to War

As a young man, Mike grew up poor, but didn't know it at the time. Other than memories of fishing with his grandfather when he was a toddler, his first memories of growing up involved the hard-luck town of War, West Virginia, and a stepfather he thought physically abused him. His move from the loving, nurturing surroundings of his grandparents' home to the hostile and foul environment of the coalfields of southern West Virginia left an impression that would impact on Mike's life forever.

Psychologists say that most of our view of the world is well developed by the time we're seven years old. By that age we have developed a paradigm or a mental map of the way the world operates. As you read this story of Mike's early years, think about how your early life may have affected your view of the world.

Shortly after he was born, and for reasons that were never discussed with him until after he was an adult, Mike's mother left his father and returned home to live with her parents in Abingdon, Virginia. His grandparents' home was a loving and safe setting surrounded by relatives and friends. His grandfather, whom he fondly called Pop, would take him on fishing trips to South Holston Lake and to nearby rivers where, with incredible patience, he would sit by the water's edge as Mike ran around, made noise, threw rocks in the water, and did almost everything imaginable to scare the fish. In spite of his rambunctious behavior, they always managed to catch fish.

When they returned home, Mike would run in first to get everyone to come and look at their catch of bluegill, bass, trout, or other fish. Pop would always say that Mike caught them all, which everyone knew wasn't the whole truth, but Mike would swell out his little chest and feel great when everyone bragged about what a good fisherman he was becoming. He and Pop would then take the fish to the basement and dump them in an old laundry sink where they would clean them and get them ready to be cooked. Pop taught Mike how to scrape the scales from the fish, but for safety's sake he would handle the knife and do the cutting while Mike watched and learned. When it came time to eat the fish, his grandmother would prepare a great meal of corn bread, beans, potatoes, and other vegetables. The big table in the dining room would be set and the whole family, including aunts and uncles, would gather round for dinner.

After the food was blessed, his grandmother would make it a point to let everyone know that their meal centered around the fish that Mike had caught and she would ask him to tell everyone how he caught them. As you can imagine, the tales coming from him as a three- or four-year-old could be quite colorful at times, and naturally there was always the big one that got away. These were the good times.

Pop was a conductor with the Norfolk & Western Railroad and his work required him to be away most of the week, but when he returned home, Mike would be the first to greet him, and before he could even get into the house, he was asking if they could go fishing. This was like a marriage made in heaven, because Pop liked to fish about as much, maybe even more, as Mike did. How could the rest of the family begrudge him taking his grandson fishing?

Week after week they would make trips to the nearby lake and rivers. Mike soon learned that by calming down a bit and being more patient, he could usually catch more fish. Pop always seemed to find a place on the lake or a pool in the river where the fishing was good, and Mike would sit on the bank for hours watching the float bob on the water, waiting for it to go under so he could give his pole a big jerk and hook another fish. But this joyous time was to come to an abrupt end.

In June 1950, Mike's mother remarried and moved with her new husband to the small coal-mining town of War, West Virginia. They took Mike to live with them. Nestled in the heart of the Appalachian Mountains, War, which is the southernmost town in West Virginia, must have been the place Johnny Cash was talking about in his song "A Boy Named Sue," when he told his son that the reason he gave him that name was because he knew "he would have to get tough or die." Back then, War was a place where differences were settled with your fists, and Mike can recall the Klu Klux Klan burning crosses at night. It was an inhospitable place where the drinking water smelled like rotten eggs from the sulfur it contained. There was no sewer system in the area, and when those with indoor plumbing flushed their toilets, the waste was piped directly into the rivers. Several times a day steam locomotives would roll through town belching black smoke and stirring up jet-black dust from the coal that spilled from the rail cars hauling bituminous coal from the numerous mines throughout the area. War was a filthy place.

During the heyday of the coal boom, jobs were plentiful in the dark, cold underground mines, but many workers would breathe in the coal dust that would later develop into deadly black lung disease. For most young men, the future held little promise other than following in their fathers' footsteps and taking jobs working in the mines. That was the world Mike was suddenly introduced to when his mother remarried.

Eventually, the mines began to close, jobs were lost, and today War is a place lost in time. It is home to around 2,000 people, the majority of whom receive some form of public assistance. Most of the stores have closed, and people still live in houses with cracks in the walls and leaks in the roofs, and children still wake up hungry with no hope for the future.

Homer Hickham's book *Rocket Boys* (Delta, January 2000), which inspired the movie *October Sky*, describes what life was like in War in the 1950s. Homer grew up in Coalwood, another small mining town just a few miles away, but he attended Big Creek High School in War, where his rocket building science project led to him winning the West Virginia State Science Fair. His determination eventually pulled him out of the dismal area, and he later became a scientist with NASA. Although he was a couple of years older, his accomplishments in the 1950s were an inspiration to Mike and helped him realize there was more to life than a job in a coal mine. Today, Homer's writings about life in the coalfields of southern West Virginia bring back many memories of what it was like going to War.

Mike's earliest memories of War consist of trying to adjust to life with a new stepfather, Paul, a strict disciplinarian who believed in the old adage, "Spare the rod and spoil the child." Paul was the oldest of 12 children. His father had died just after the youngest was born, and he was left to assume the role of helping his mother raise his younger siblings. This experience is probably what made him a strong believer that children should earn their keep around the house.

Paul was 40, 10 years older than Mike's mother, when they married. His whole life, with the exception of military service during World War II, was centered in War. When he took Mike and his mother to live there, it was for Mike a far cry from those wonderful days of loving grandparents and sitting on the bank of the lake with Pop catching fish. He suddenly went from being nurtured and pampered to a hostile place where he always seemed to be in the way. Today we'd call this a traumatic experience. It was then too!

There were always chores to do before he could play, and the "Thank you" he got was the privilege of staying there and having something to eat. Getting paid was unheard of, and allowances were out of the question. Little did he realize it at the time, but this experience started him on his journey to develop a Weekend Millionaire Mindset. The experiences that followed this traumatic situation and circumstance are what molded Mike's character and propelled him to success.

Throughout this part of the book, we will describe some experiences that illustrate how we learn even when we don't realize we're learning. So read on, and when these stories trigger the recollection of memorable events from your past, make notes about them, because you will use these notes later when we discuss how to develop your own Weekend Millionaire Mindset.

Key Points from This Chapter

- Life can hand you difficult situations, but these don't have to ruin your life.
- Childhood memories, both good and bad, can be used to build character.

9

Everyone Is Not Equal, but Opportunities Are

In his book *All I Really Need to Know I Learned in Kindergarten*, Robert Fulghum writes that wisdom was not at the top of the graduate school mountain, but there in the sand pile at kindergarten. After outlining the things he learned, he continues by saying, "Think what a better world it would be if all—the whole world—had cookies and milk about three o'clock every afternoon and then lay down with our blankies for a nap." That's a nice thought, but unfortunately, that's not the way it works in the real world.

People don't always share everything nor do they always play fair. They do occasionally hit each other and don't say they're sorry. They often take things that aren't theirs and fail to put them back where they found them or clean up their own messes. In fact, people sporadically violate each and every one of the things Fulghum says he learned that would make the world a better place; and of course, they also violate most of the Ten Commandments too.

What we want you to learn from this book is how to get along in the real world, a place where people don't always live by playground rules or follow God's laws. We come into this world as innocent children with eyes wide open and filled with wonder. We're like sponges that soak up what we see and hear, and these perceptions shape our lives. Isn't it amazing how children playing on a playground make up rules and settle differences without missing a beat until the adults show up? Have you ever noticed that when parents arrive and start giving advice, problems that seemed insignificant before suddenly become major arguments?

Moms and dads have their own ideas about what's fair and what the rules should be, based on their own life experiences. When they inject these ideas into their children, it often results in the children losing their innocence and seeing things in a different light. When left alone, it's amazing how children seem to know who is best and who struggles at a particular sport. Watch them make allowances for these differences. They have a unique ability to handicap the players in ways that evens the competition.

We remember, for instance, when choosing sides for playing games, that everyone agreed on the best two players and then let them alternate, choosing from the rest to make up teams that were fairly even. We would agree upon the length of a game, and if the sides seemed too unbalanced after the first game, we'd trade a player or two to balance the sides. Sometimes we would let the two worst players be the captains and pick the teams. The bottom line is, we had great fun, played hard, and everyone went home happy. As we grew older, however, priorities changed and our individual wants and needs took us down different paths. The games we played became more serious and the consequences of losing more dramatic.

By far the most important game we will ever play is the game of life. How we deal with the defining moments with which we're presented is what determines our success or failure in the game of life. Mike lived in War, West Virginia, from when he was four until when he was 12, and as you will see from the story that follows, he is a testimony to the old saying, "Character is formed in the crucible of hard times." At eight he faced a situation that provided him with several defining moments, and the life lessons he learned from this incident are the subjects of the next several chapters.

For Lack of a Bicycle

In the years that followed Mike's mother's remarriage and the move to War, he developed a close friendship with a neighbor boy named John Allen. The two of them became practically inseparable. The Allens owned Western Auto, one of the few stores in town, and they were constantly bringing home new things for John to play with. Mike felt that John's parents must be rich because they owned a store, but this never presented a problem with their friendship because John always shared everything with his best friend.

When his family got the first television in town, he would invite Mike over to watch cartoons and western movies. They would roam the neighborhood together, and usually wherever you would find one, the other would not be far away. John's parents even gave him a big part of their yard to do with as he pleased, and he and Mike would dig holes, build roads, and play with toy trucks and bulldozers for hours. Mike was envious of the fact that they could dig in John's yard because he had to keep his mowed with an old push mower, but this never came between the two boys. It was not until John's parents got him a new bicycle, which was also sold at their store, that Mike experienced his first memorable life lesson.

Suddenly, John was able to ride all over the neighborhood, but Mike still had to walk. This was the reality of life; John's parents could afford things that his couldn't. Try as he might, Mike could not talk his mother and stepfather into buying him a bicycle. He could have wallowed in self-pity and let jealousy eat at him while his best friend rode his new bicycle, but that was not Mike's nature. Although they scraped to get by financially, his mother never complained. Looking back today, Mike realizes that his mother is the most positive person he ever knew. She lacked many of the things other women enjoyed, but she never let it affect her happiness. Although he didn't realize it at the time, the way she reacted to his wanting a new bicycle taught him his first life lesson: *Everyone is not equal, but opportunities are*.

She took Mike aside and told him, "Honey, I'm sorry we can't afford to get you a bicycle, but if you really want one, I'll bet you can find a way to get it." Of all the compliments Mike could pay his mother, probably the greatest is the fact that she never discouraged him. Throughout his life, each time he sought her advice or guidance about some new idea or about whether to try something he had never done, she would just say, "If you think you can do it, I'll bet you can." This was basically what she did when she told him that if he wanted a bicycle, she believed he could find a way to get one.

The Formative Years

Throughout his years in War, Mike was always a very industrious child. Since he received no allowance, his choice was to do without or do something about it. He soon learned that he could scour the riverbanks and roadways to find discarded soft drink bottles or scrap metal that he could sell to earn spending money. He learned that he could walk the railroad tracks and pick up coal that fell from the trains, which he could put in sacks and sell for a few cents. It was always exciting when he could earn a quarter because this was enough to get in to see a movie, buy popcorn and a soft drink, and still have a nickel in change.

When Mike's mother told him that if he really wanted a bicycle, he'd find a way to get one, she probably didn't realized just how much she was empowering him to achieve success later in life. It wasn't until he reached adulthood and began reflecting on this experience that he realized that what she'd given him was an opportunity instead of a handout; however, it was up to him to take advantage of it. He could easily have just given up, but he wanted that bicycle. Mike thought that since he had always been able to make a few cents when he wanted to buy an occasional toy, a candy bar, or to go to a movie, why couldn't he earn enough to get a new bike? While he and John were not equal in the things their parents could buy them, Mike was blessed with a mother who gave him something that money couldn't buy. She gave him confidence and taught him that opportunity—in his case, being able to pick up bottles, scrap metals, and coal to earn spending money—was equal for everyone.

While the opportunity was equal, their level of desire was not. John had his bike; why should he have to scrounge around trying to earn money? Mike didn't have a bike, but he wanted one badly. As a result, he considered doing things John wouldn't in order to get one. In the process he learned the effect of desire, one of the three Ds of success. Without realizing it, his intense desire for a bicycle like John's started Mike down the road to developing the Weekend Millionaire Mindset he enjoys today. As you will see in the chapters that follow, this road was filled with potholes, bumps, curves, and obstacles, but its journey was filled with life lessons that brought much success.

Key Points from This Chapter

- Life isn't always fair—bad things do happen occasionally.

Everyone Is Not Equal, but Opportunities Are

- When life isn't fair, you can either complain about it or do something about it.
- A key step in developing the Weekend Millionaire Mindset is learning to create strong desire. What do you want so much that you'd overcome almost any obstacle to get it?

10

It Takes Planning to Be Successful

I f it's going to be, it's up to me!

That must have been the thought running through Mike's head when he left home that morning in 1954 without telling his mother or anyone else and headed into town. He was on a mission. He wanted that new bicycle and he thought he had come up with a way to get it, so he was on his way to see John's mother at the Western Auto store.

When he arrived at the store, Mrs. Allen, who was a large woman, saw him walk in and promptly asked, "What are you doing here by yourself?"

"I came to talk with you about buying a bicycle like the one you got John," he said.

Mrs. Allen, who was always kind to Mike, leaned down and said, "Honey"—that's what she called Mike—"does your mother know you're here? You know I couldn't sell you a bike without her permission. Besides, where did you get the money to buy a bike?"

"No, Mom doesn't know I'm here, but she told me that if I wanted a bicycle, I would find a way to get one. Since she told me that, I've been thinking about it, and here's what I've come up with. If you will let me have a bicycle, I'll pay you a dollar a week until I get it paid."

"Honey, where are you going to get a dollar a week, every week?" she responded.

Mike hadn't thought about that. He knew that he'd been able to collect soft drink bottles, scrap metal, and coal to make a little spending money, but he'd never made even close to a dollar in a week. That was a lot of money for an eight-year-old to think about earning in 1954 in War, West Virginia, so he didn't have an answer to Mrs. Allen's question.

When she saw his head drop and his shoulders slump, Mrs. Allen pulled Mike to her and said, "I know you would like a bike, honey, but you don't always get everything you want. I'll talk to John and see if he will let you ride his when he's not using it."

"But, you don't understand," Mike said with a tear in his eye, "I want to ride with John so we can do things together. I don't want to ride by myself."

"I'll tell you what," Mrs. Allen replied. "You show me how you can earn a dollar a week, and I'll sell you a bicycle just like John's as long as it's okay with your mother."

With this statement, she taught Mike his second memorable life lesson: *It takes planning to be successful.* He had gone to her with a suggestion that met his desire, but it offered her no reason to accept it. He had approached her with an intense desire to have a new bike, but with no plan for how he would make the needed dollar a week. Although he didn't comprehend it as such at the time, this experience taught Mike that people do things for their reasons, not yours. As much as Mrs. Allen empathized with him, he was not her child and it was not her responsibility to see that he got a bike.

It would have been very easy for Mike to have left the store that day feeling defeated, but Mrs. Allen's comments encouraged him. When he returned home, he told his mother about the encounter and asked her if she had any ideas about how he could earn the dollar per week. Her advice was the same as before: "If you really want the bike, you'll find a way to make the money."

Since the only way he'd made money in the past was collecting bottles, scrap metal, and coal, he went to work immediately. He scoured the town looking for the usual items he could turn into cash. He didn't go to the extremes of ripping up railroad tracks to sell, as Homer Hickham and the

Rocket Boys were portrayed as doing in the movie *October Sky*, but he did work at it diligently. He wanted to see if he could find enough stuff in a week to earn a dollar. Sadly, his valiant effort only led to earning about 45 cents, and although it was more than he had ever earned in a week before, it was far short of a dollar.

Discouraged, but not defeated, Mike talked with his neighbors, his schoolteachers, his friends, and anyone else who would listen, but no one had any suggestions as to how an eight-year-old could earn a dollar a week. He even took a stack of old magazines his mother had saved and went around the neighborhood trying to sell them for a nickel each, and a few people who probably felt sorry for him bought a magazine.

But it was what he discovered while alone in his room one night that changed his fortune. He was lying on his bed feeling a bit sorry for himself and flipping through one of the old magazines when he saw an ad with the headline: KIDS—EARN EXTRA SPENDING MONEY. It was an advertisement for people to sell a weekly newspaper called *Grit*. The ad explained that it was a large, nationally circulated newspaper that offered young people an excellent opportunity (there's that word again) to earn money. The ad explained that the papers sold for a nickel; they cost three cents and the other two cents was profit. Bingo! Here was the answer Mike had been looking for.

He ran in, showed the ad to his mother and told her that he was going to sell newspapers to make the money to get his new bike. She read the ad and finally looked up and said, "See, I told you that if you really wanted it, you would find a way to get it."

He was so excited he could hardly sleep that night. He couldn't wait to go see Mrs. Allen the next day to get his new bike. Promptly at 9:00 A.M. when the doors opened, Mike was the first person in the store. He ran up to Mrs. Allen waving the ad in his hand and with a big smile and youthful enthusiasm he exclaimed, "Look, Mrs. Allen, I found a way to make a dollar a week." He handed her the ad and continued, "I'm going to sell *Grit* newspapers. They sell for a nickel each, and I get to keep two cents from each one. All I have to do is sell 50 papers each week and that will give me the dollar a week I need to pay you. Can I get my bike today … pleeeease?"

Since it had been a few weeks since he first approached her, Mrs. Allen was caught off guard by Mike's enthusiasm. She vaguely recalled telling him to show her how he could earn a dollar a week and she would sell him a bike, but she had no idea that he would follow through and come up with a plan to do it. Not wanting to dampen his enthusiasm, but looking for a way to buy some time, she asked him, "What makes you think you can sell 50 newspapers a week? That's a lot of papers."

He hadn't thought about that. He couldn't answer her question. Thump! He'd just hit another pothole on the road to developing his Weekend Millionaire Mindset. He had been so focused on how many papers he would have to sell to earn a dollar a week that he completely failed to consider how he could do it. Although she had no intention of bursting his bubble, Mrs. Allen had just hit him squarely between the eyes with a dose of reality. Making a plan involved more than just talk.

Was this another opportunity to quit? Absolutely! Did he let it get him down? Absolutely not! This experience exposed Mike to another of the three Ds of success, which is Dedication. He really wanted that new bike; he had demonstrated his desire by continuing to look for ways to make the money he needed to get it, and now was faced with having to find the dedication to keep moving toward his desire.

We'll continue this story in the next chapter, where you will learn what Mike did to overcome this obstacle and keep moving forward. But before we move on, we want to remind you again that you've probably had similar experiences in your life. You may or may not have learned from them as Mike did, but that's not a problem. We're going to teach you how to look back and reflect on your reactions, and help you start defining the actions you can take from today forward to develop your Weekend Millionaire Mindset.

Key Points from This Chapter

- Being successful takes more than positive thinking; you need a plan as well.
- People do things for their reasons, not yours.
- Another key step in developing the Weekend Millionaire Mindset is being determined. Determination is what keeps you going even when obstacles get in your way.

11

Ideas Must Be Implemented to Be Valuable

We've all heard it said that good ideas are a dime a dozen, but implemented ideas are priceless. Mike's plan to sell 50 papers a week was a good idea, but Mrs. Allen's question about how he would sell them exposed a fundamental flaw in the plan. He had an idea, but he hadn't thought about how to implement it. Isn't that what happens time and again to people who come up with great ideas, only to keep them to themselves until they see someone else implement them?

An eight-year-old growing up in the coalfields of Southern West Virginia in the mid 1950s didn't have a clue about how this high-powered psychology stuff was supposed to work, but what we have discovered is that Mike had at least two of the three Ds of success: Desire and Dedication. It was these two characteristics that kept driving him to succeed.

As you can imagine, when Mike left Western Auto that day, he was extremely disappointed. He had gone to the store expecting to ride home on a shiny new bicycle, but instead found himself walking back feeling dejected, yet having learned his third memorable life lesson: *Ideas must be imple-*

mented to be valuable. He had a great idea about selling papers to earn the money to buy a bicycle, but hadn't thought about how to put it into practice. Later, in his adult years, Mike found a quote by William Benton, a former U.S. senator from Connecticut, that fits this situation perfectly, and one that still guides him in business today: "The rewards in business go to the man who does something with an idea." The same could be said about life in general. Wow! So simple, but so true!

Mike wanted that new bicycle and wasn't about to let this new obstacle stop him from getting it. Once again he talked with his mother and his friends, but it was his favorite teacher who pointed him in the right direction. Ora Ann Hash had taught Mike in the second grade, and he'd been a rowdy and rambunctious student who started the year full of mischief. By the year's end, however, he was her favorite student and she was his favorite teacher. A particular incident early in the school year endeared them to each other in an unusual way. It was an incident she considered her most memorable, and it provided a story she was still telling long after she retired.

While the story has nothing to do with Mike getting the bicycle, but it's so humorous, and it gives an insight into the type of child Mike was in his formative years. We hope you'll find it worth the few lines it takes to include in this text.

A Barrel of Laughs

Ora Ann Hash was an excellent teacher and a kind and generous young woman, but very gullible. Early in the school year Mike discovered that he could put thumbtacks in her seat and she would sit down on them without ever looking. He could make obscene noises and she was never able to tell where they were coming from. Once, he even put a big water snake in the pencil drawer of her desk, and when she opened it she nearly fell over backward trying to get out of its way. But the most memorable incident occurred when she had finally had enough of his antics and she made him go to the blackboard, which was directly behind her, draw a circle on it with chalk, and then stand there with his nose in the circle.

For Mike, all of his tricks and clowning around were done in fun, but having to stand in front of the class with his nose in a circle was just too embarrassing. He wanted to get even with her, so he started to peek around to either side when she was standing at her desk instructing the other students. On one of his peeks he noticed that she merely stood up from her chair to talk and then sat back down when she finished. He also noticed the trash barrel sitting next to him directly behind her chair. What an opportunity!

If you can imagine this trash barrel, it was made of heavy pasteboard with a smooth metal ring around the top that had been used at one time to secure a lid. It was a squatty container about knee high, but considerably wider than a normal waste basket. Mrs. Hash was a rather large woman, with a healthy derriere just about the same size as the trash barrel.

You guessed it; the next time she stood up to talk, Mike quietly switched her chair with the trash barrel. True to form, she spoke for a couple of minutes and then sat down … right in the barrel. Now picture this: She initially caught herself near the top, but with each movement her plump bottom slipped farther into the barrel, until it eventually wedged all the way to the bottom. Her knees were pulled directly up under her chin and her calves and arms hung over the sides of the rim, which fit neatly up under her knees and armpits. This left her in quite a predicament … especially since she was wearing a dress.

Completely stuck in the barrel and unable to move, she screamed at Mike to go get the principal. Scared nearly to death, he ran down the hall to the principal's office, knowing he was going to get the paddling of his life, but returned minutes later with the principal in tow. Poor Mrs. Hash; she was wedged tightly into the barrel totally unable to move, and all the students were huddled around with worried looks on their faces.

As soon as the principal saw her—not knowing at the time that Mike was responsible for her predicament—he lost all restraint and burst out laughing. "Ora Ann, what on earth are you doing in that barrel?" he howled.

By now she had determined that she was not hurt, just stuck so tightly in the barrel that she couldn't move. When the principal laughed, it dawned on her what the scene must look like to him and she started laughing too. She was notorious for her loud high-pitched laugh. It could be heard all over the small school, and when she started, it got all the children laughing too. This raucous noise brought other teachers running, and the instant they saw the situation, they too began to howl with laughter. It would be nearly impossible for the best screenwriters to produce a more hilarious scene.

Eventually, with the help of the principal, the custodian, and two other teachers, Mrs. Hash was extricated from the barrel. One got her by the legs and another by the arms and they lifted her up while the other two pulled and tugged at the barrel. When she was finally out, she told the principal what Mike had done. He grabbed Mike by the arm and started toward the office, but she stopped him. "This laugh has been too good to paddle a child over, let me deal with him."

She felt the scare he had received was adequate punishment, and she was right. Following that act of kindness on her part, Mike vowed to never pull a prank in her class again, and he didn't. In fact he ended up becoming a model student. She called him her favorite student and even let him occasionally spend time at her home helping her with chores. The loving relationship that developed between them was what led Mike to seek her advice in finding a way to convince Mrs. Allen that he could sell 50 papers a week.

Mrs. Hash's Good Idea

Mike had a long discussion with Mrs. Hash. He told her about John getting the new bicycle and how badly he wanted one too. He explained how his mother had told him that if he really wanted one, he would find a way to get it, and he told her about his trips to see Mrs. Allen and how she wouldn't let him have a bike until he could prove to her that he could earn a dollar a week to pay for it.

Mrs. Hash opened her desk drawer and pulled out a small notebook. As she held it in her hands, she said, "I'm going to give you an idea, but it will require a lot of discipline on your part to make it work. I'm going to give you this notebook and I'm going to put my name in it first and agree to buy a paper from you each week. All you have to do is find 49 more people who will agree to buy a paper each week and get them to sign up under my name. If you can do this, it will give you something to take back to Mrs. Allen to show her who is going to buy your papers."

With this statement, she introduced Mike to the third of the three Ds of success: Discipline. Throughout life he would come to realize that these three Ds—Discipline, Dedication, and Desire—are like the legs of stool. With all three you have stability and almost anything is possible, but if you're lacking any one of them, it's difficult to maintain balance and success is much harder, if not impossible, to achieve. The question was: Did he have the discipline to go out and find 49 more people who would agree to buy *Grit* each week?

Filled with enthusiasm, Mike immediately paid a visit to other teachers in the school and got six more of them to sign up. Then each day after school he called on nearby neighbors, where he got another 12 to sign up. Gradually he started working his way farther from home, and after nearly two weeks of calling on anyone who would talk with him, he had over 60 people signed up to buy. Now it was back to see Mrs. Allen.

When Mike walked through the doors of Western Auto this time, nearly three months had passed since his first visit. While many would have given up long before, maybe even after the first disappointment, Mike's desire for a new bicycle, his dedication to finding a way to get one, and the discipline he demonstrated by sticking with it until he found over 60 people willing to buy a paper from him each week, set him apart from most.

This time when he sat down with Mrs. Allen, she was impressed. "I can't believe you've put all this work into getting a bicycle," she told him. "Now that you've shown me how you are going to pay for it, I guess I don't have any choice except to sell you one." Mike was bursting with excitement when she took him to the area of the store where there were several bikes to choose from.

"Pick out the one you want and we'll work out a payment arrangement," she said. "I talked with your mother a couple of weeks ago and she said you were out signing up people to buy the paper, so I've been expecting you."

"You mean I can pick out any one I want?" he asked.

"Yep," she said. "With all the work you've done to show me how you are going to pay for it, I'll let you get any one you want, even one that's more expensive than John's."

"No, I want one just like his," Mike said. "The only thing different I want is a basket on the front so I can carry the papers in it when I deliver them."

Ideas Must Be Implemented to Be Valuable

That day, Mike concluded his first entrepreneurial transaction and learned that his mother was right: If he wanted something badly enough, he would find a way to get it. What would have happened if his mother and step-father, knowing how much he wanted a bicycle, had simply given him one? No gift could have taken the place of the life lessons he learned from this experience. Imagine the problem-solving skills, the feeling of accomplishment, the growth in confidence, and the self-esteem he would have been denied.

As he peddled home on that shiny new bicycle, his chest swelling with pride, little did he realize that he had just completed his first leg on the journey to becoming a Weekend Millionaire. Everyone has experienced situations in life like these; the problem is that only a few have the Discipline, Dedication, and Desire to see problems through to a successful conclusion. It's always easier to find fault, complain, and commiserate about the tough times life hands us than it is to stand up and do something about it. As we continue with this part, we will analyze more stories like this one and point out the life lessons embedded within them.

Twenty-five years later, when Roger was president of one of California's largest independent real estate companies, he discovered that there was a question he could ask job applicants that, if answered correctly, could virtually assure them of success as real estate agents. The question was: "How old were you when you first started earning money outside of your family?" You'd be amazed at how the answers to that question would vary. Some, like Mike, would say, "When I was eight, I started my own business delivering newspapers." Some would say, "When I graduated from college and I was 22." It turns out that there is a remarkable correlation between a person's level of initiative and the age at which they started earning money outside of the family. We found the same reaction when we wrote about investing in real estate in *The Weekend Millionaire's Secrets to Investing in Real Estate*. Readers who had started making money early in life had a high degree of initiative and were almost certain to do well.

We hope you are following our earlier suggestion to make notes about your memorable life experiences that are triggered by our stories, because whether you realize it or not, you have learned from these experiences. If what you've learned has been more negative than positive, by reflecting on the choices you made and the results you received from these choices, you will be able to improve your decision making and start developing your own Weekend Millionaire Mindset.

Key Points from This Chapter

- Ideas don't make you rich, implementing them does.
- A good sense of humor, even in difficult situations, makes life more enjoyable.
- The three Ds of success—Discipline, Dedication, and Desire—are equally important to achieving success.
- The age at which you first started earning money outside of your family can be a good indicator of your degree of personal initiative.

12

People Help Those Willing to Help Themselves

When Mike peddled away from the Western Auto store, the proud owner of a beautiful new red Western Flyer bicycle, he left knowing that he had committed to pay Mrs. Allen one dollar a week for 34 weeks. The sense of pride he felt knowing that she trusted him to fulfill this responsibility was enormous. She had graciously agreed to wait three weeks before the first payment would be due in order to allow him time to place his first order for papers, have them shipped to him, and give him time to get them sold.

It turns out that Mike was about to face another defining moment. Like most kids his age, all he was interested in back then was riding the new bike home to show to his mother and his friends. The last thing on his mind was the thought that he had just been given an opportunity that would teach him one of the most important lessons of his young life.

He had a new bicycle and was bursting with the pride of accomplishment that came with having successfully met a challenge, but Mike had something even more important: He had a big responsibility. Now that he had the bike, he had to pay for it. While Mrs. Allen had given him three weeks before the first payment would be due, he still was committed to paying her one dollar a week for 34 weeks. That might not seem like much today, but in 1954 in War, West Virginia, earning a dollar a week for a child about to turn nine was a huge undertaking.

With help from his mother, Mike immediately placed an order for his first 60 papers. When they arrived, he mounted his new bike, put a load of papers in its basket, and headed out to deliver them. With each stop, he handed over a paper and collected a nickel. Several of the people who had signed up to buy a paper told him that they didn't really think he would follow through and actually deliver to them. It made Mike feel good when people complimented him on his fortitude and commitment. As the nickels in his pocket increased, so did his feeling of accomplishment.

By the time the final paper was delivered that first week, two more people had signed up for delivery starting with the second week. Mike increased his order to 62 papers and repeated the process the following week. As word began to spread about how this young man was working to pay for his bicycle, more and more people signed on for delivery. Within six weeks his paper route had grown to 73 customers and he had religiously paid Mrs. Allen a dollar each week.

People all over the small town were talking about this young boy who each week spent his spare time working to pay for the bike he had purchased on credit. This may well have been the first evidence that one day he would develop a Weekend Millionaire Mindset, which says you can convert spare time into financial independence. It also taught Mike something very important about credit. He learned that credit, when used to purchase something that earns money or can be used to earn money, is good debt. He was using the bicycle, purchased on credit, to deliver papers to earn the money to pay for the purchase. This was a criterion he would maintain into adulthood.

After a few weeks in which more people bought the paper each week, Mike again visited Mrs. Hash, who had given him the original idea of signing up people for regular weekly delivery. He wanted to tell her about his success. As he explained that he was now earning enough to pay Mrs. Allen the dollar a week he had promised plus earning an extra 35 to 40 cents per week, she asked him what he was doing with the extra money. He said he was putting it in a jar in his bedroom.

She now gave him some additional advice that would end up playing a big role in Mike's later success. She advised him to accumulate two or three dollars and put them away, to have in case something happened and he couldn't earn a full dollar one week. She explained that if he did this, he would always be able to meet his obligation even if he had an unexpected problem. Little did he know back then that what she was advising him to do was set aside reserve funds to use in case of an emergency. But in spite of these wonderful lessons he learned from buying his bicycle, the biggest lesson was yet to come.

Preparation Meets Opportunity

One of the customers to whom Mike delivered the paper each week was the manager of the Western Union telegraph office in War. After observing his commitment to delivering papers for over a month, when Mike came by with the current week's issue, the manager asked him to step into his office. He directed him to a chair next to his desk and asked him to have a seat. Mike's first thought was that the man had decided to stop buying the paper, but to his surprise the manager started out by saying, "I've got a problem that I'll bet you could help me with if you're interested."

"What kind of problem?" Mike asked.

The manager began, "I've been observing your commitment to delivering the papers each week, and I've talked with Mrs. Allen, who tells me that you haven't missed a payment on your bike since you got it. That's remarkable for a youngster of your age; in fact, it's not a bad record for any age, and it shows me that you are a responsible young man. For that reason, I have a proposition for you. We get several telegrams each week that have to be delivered. I've been doing this myself, but it's a real headache because I need to be here at the office most of the time. Since you know nearly everyone because of your paper route, if you're interested, I'll pay you 25 cents each to deliver the ones here in town. What do you think?"

"Wow!" Mike said. "How many are there each week?"

"Some weeks there are three or four; others there may be 10 to 15," the manager replied.

Understandably, this excited Mike. "What would I have to do?" he asked.

"Just come by the office after school. If any come in that day, I'll let you deliver them. When you give the telegram to the person to whom it is addressed, you will need to have that person sign a receipt for it. Bring back the signed receipt and I'll pay you. That's all there is to it."

With that, Mike began a new job and learned one of the most important lessons of his life: *People help those willing to help themselves.* The Western Union manager saw him as a responsible young person and gave him an opportunity he had never given a youngster before. Mike didn't ask for the opportunity, it was just offered. Some people would say, "Oh, that was just luck," but a careful analysis of the situation would reveal that this was merely an example of preparation meeting opportunity. As we mentioned in the preface to this part, if you aren't prepared for an opportunity that comes your way, someone else will grab it and you'll be talking about how lucky they were.

In this case, Mike was prepared. He knew the town, he knew the people, and he had the bicycle. As a result, he got the extra job and was able to pay off his bicycle in just over three months instead of the eight months he was expecting it to take. He also had extra spending money to do other things. Throughout his life he would find that the better prepared he made himself, the bigger were the opportunities presented to him. I guess you could say he was pretty lucky.

But back in War, his paper route kept growing and he continued delivering telegrams. This continued until 1958, when he moved with his family to the big city (or at least it seemed like a big city, compared to War) of Bluefield, Virginia, where he would continue his formative years.

Key Points from This Chapter

- The more you demonstrate responsibility, the more opportunities you will be given.
- Borrowing to purchase something that makes you money can be good debt.

People Help Those Willing to Help Themselves

- Create an emergency fund to see you through difficult times.
- People notice people who are industrious and are trying to help themselves.
- The better prepared you are, the luckier you get.

13

Patience and Persistence Are Unstoppable

Mike's move to Bluefield, Virginia, in June 1958 was like a breath of fresh air after living with the black coal dust, open sewers, and putrid-smelling drinking water of War, West Virginia. But it also brought additional challenges and life lessons. While in War, the family had grown from three to six with the birth of two half brothers and a half sister. The home they moved to in Bluefield was like a palace compared to the one in War. It was a new three-bedroom, one-bath home on a large two-acre parcel in a subdivision. Mike still had to share a bedroom with his two half brothers, but he didn't mind.

During their years in War, his stepfather Paul had sold insurance. He was employed by People's Life Insurance Company, for which he worked a weekly route, called a "debit," covering several small coal-mining towns, including War. He would leave home each morning to sell life and accident policies to miners who hoped the insurance would provide for their families if they were injured or killed in the mines. He kept a route book in which he posted the weekly premiums he would collect in person by visiting the miners' homes. Each day when he returned from work, he put away the money he collected that day, and every Thursday night he prepared a report that he would deliver to the company's offices in Bluefield, West Virginia (the town straddled the Virginia–West Virginia state line) on Fridays. Paul was a man of impeccable honesty and with a strong work ethic, and it had paid off for him. When the position of sales manager became available, the company promoted him and moved Paul and his family to Bluefield to work out of the district office.

During their years in War, Mike's relationship with Paul gradually deteriorated. Whether this was the result of Mike feeling slighted at the birth of Paul's natural children, or because of his frustration that he was unable to learn anything about his real father, is hard to say. In any case, Mike became more withdrawn and resentful of the busy-work that Paul always seemed to find for him to do. He resented the fact that he never received an allowance or was paid for any of the things he did around the house. Paul always said, "You live here so you have to earn your keep."

The only work for which Mike can remember getting paid occurred during the winter before the move to Bluefield. The old house where the family lived had a coal-fired furnace for heat. One day Paul had a large truck-load of coal delivered to the house. The truck backed up and dumped its load in the yard beside a small window that opened to a coal chute that went into a bin in the basement. When Paul came home that evening, he informed Mike that his job was to shovel the coal into the coal bin. He explained that he would need to shovel the coal into the chute until the center of the bin filled up and then he would have to go inside the bin and shovel it to each side to make room for the rest of the load.

When Mike came home from school the next day, he changed into old clothes, found a shovel, and went out to the side of the house where the pile of coal awaited. He was small for his age, so as he stood beside the pile that towered over his head, he knew it would take days to complete the job. Because of his size, he could only lift the shovel when it was about half full. With each partial shovel of coal, his resentment grew. It took two days to fill the center of the coal bin, then another day inside working in a cloud of black dust to shovel the coal to each side. When breathing became difficult, he would blow his nose and fill the tissues with jet-black mucus stained that way by the coal dust. With each shovel of coal, Mike would ask himself, "Why me? Why can't I go play like all the rest of the kids my age? Why do I always have to work?"

It took days, but he finally completed the job. When he had all of the coal in the bin and the yard cleaned up, his animosity toward Paul had reached an all-time high. Paul must have sensed this, because he took Mike aside, put his arm around him and said, "You did a good job. Here!" and handed him a dime. A dime! He couldn't believe his stepfather was being that cruel to him! He had been earning 25 cents per delivery from the telegraph office and over a dollar a week from his newspaper route. A dime! It seemed more of an insult than a reward; and that was the only money Mike remembers ever receiving from him.

We tell this story to give you a better understanding of the feelings that existed between Mike and Paul just prior to the family's move. To say it graciously, the pent-up emotion Mike felt was a seething hostility lying just beneath the surface, waiting to erupt. What transpired after the move did nothing to ease the tensions.

More Tribulations

The new home they moved into was located on top of a rolling hill in a new subdivision. There were few homes in the area; in fact, hunters regularly hunted rabbits and quail in the undeveloped fields throughout the subdivision and only the main road was paved. The rest were dirt, some of them even single-lane dirt roads. One of these single-lane tracks, cut into the side of the hill in front of the house, provided access to their new home. The driveway branched off it and went up and around the hill to the back of the house, where it ended with a turnaround at a basement garage door.

The house had a full basement that included a single car garage that opened to the turnaround at the top of the driveway. The yard consisted of a small level area that extended away from the house for a few feet, but most of the land sloped sharply away down the hill in all directions. There were six lots with the new house, which gave it about two acres of yard. Guess whose job it became to keep it mowed? You got it! Mike had to keep the yard mowed in the summer and the snow shoveled off the driveway in the winter, but the event that brought things to a head with him was an earth-moving project.

With very little level land around the house and just a single-lane dirt road leading to it, Paul decided it would be a good idea for Mike to dig into the bank along the road in front of the house and haul the dirt up the hill in a wheelbarrow. That way, he could build a terrace so his mother could have a level place for a clothesline while also widening the road. It was a brilliant idea for everyone except Mike, who would have to do the work. Each day, Paul assigned him a number of loads of dirt to haul up the hill and dump. He was not allowed to spread the dirt out until Paul came home, so he could count the loads to see if enough had been hauled that day. Every day when it wasn't raining or snowing, Mike would have to haul his assigned loads of dirt before he could play with his friends. You can imagine how this made him feel as the other neighborhood kids rode bikes or played ball. Often they would come by and make fun of him, calling him "dirt digger," "wheelbarrow jockey," and other names as he worked beside the road.

For two years Mike dug into that bank with a pick and mattock, shoveled the dirt into a wheelbarrow and hauled it up the hill to build the terrace. The days when he didn't haul enough loads, Paul would send him back out after dark to finish his assigned work. It was not a fun time, but it was a learning experience. Gradually, he grew stronger and improved his techniques for digging and shoveling dirt. He learned that by striking the same spot repeatedly with the pick or mattock, he could drive the blade deeper into the bank, thereby loosening larger amounts of dirt with less effort. He discovered that a pointed shovel could be pushed into the dirt easier than a flat shovel. He learned to use his feet and legs to push the shovel into the dirt instead of his back. He tried several different ways to push the wheelbarrow up the hill and in time learned that by keeping his body erect, moving up between the handles, and letting the weight rest on his fully extended arms he could get up the hill with larger loads without hurting his back.

These dirt-digging and hauling techniques may not seem important, but like so many other experiences in Mike's young life, he learned valuable lessons from them. First, he discovered how practice, with a focus on improvement, could make him better at whatever he was doing, even if it was simply digging and hauling dirt. During the two years he worked on this earth-moving project, he constantly focused on ways to haul the required number of loads with less effort and in less time. By the time the project was finished, he was able to do the same amount of daily work he was doing in the beginning in less than half the time and with less exhaustion. And by seeking out better and more productive ways to do the work, he learned that it gave him additional time and energy to do other things he wanted to do for himself.

Throughout this project, Mike didn't haul a single load of dirt up that hill without his resentment toward Paul growing. The name-calling he experienced from the kids in his neighborhood gradually made its way to the high school he attended. One day he was seen working in a light rain, and for the next month, he became known as "Mud Dauber" at school. All these things took their toll on his psyche, and by the start of his junior year of high school Mike was contemplating leaving home. But something else was happening at the same time.

As the road widened and the terrace grew and Mike began to see the results of his efforts, he discovered another real life lesson: *Patience and persistence are unstoppable*. Slowly, with just a few loads of dirt a day, spread out over time, he had changed the landscape around his house. The road was now wide enough for two cars to pass, and his mother had a new clothesline on the wide terrace he had built in back of the house. The work was hard, but it hadn't killed him. True, his resentment toward Paul was at an all-time high, but the pride of accomplishment he felt was even higher. It was not until later in life, when he was reflecting on this experience, that he realized it was the event that taught him that patience and persistence could literally move mountains, or as the old saying goes, "A mouse can eat an elephant if you give him long enough."

As we have mentioned several times already, these stories and experiences from our lives are included to stimulate your thinking and help you recall events from your own past that contain lessons to help you develop a Weekend Millionaire Mindset. Hopefully you still have your note pad and are writing down these thoughts as you read. In our case, the more stories we wrote, the more we recalled. To include them all would take several volumes, and since this book is not an autobiography, we have distilled our stories down to just those that taught us significant life lessons and helped us develop our Weekend Millionaire Mindsets.

Now let's move on to Part III, where we will continue to share events that played major roles during our learning years.

Key Points from This Chapter

- With change come challenges, but these can make you stronger.
- Harboring resentment and hard feelings only makes work more difficult.
- Practice improves performance, even if you are simply digging dirt.
- Tasks that may otherwise seem daunting become doable when you break them down into small pieces; think one shovelful at a time.

PART III

The
Learning Years

We consider the learning years to be the transition years between childhood and adulthood. These are the years between the time when you first start making decisions for yourself and the point in life where you become established on a steady career path. Some people have more of these years than others; in fact, it could be said that some people never get beyond the learning years, because they never get established on a steady career path. These are also the years when you begin trying to apply lessons learned during your formative years and are often the years where people run into problems. We call these the learning years because they are the years in which you discover that you don't know everything, after all.

We're sure you've known young people who dropped out of school with great career aspirations only to run head on into the reality that life doesn't always deal the hand you expected. Even those with high school diplomas or college degrees often face unforeseen setbacks that change their direction in life and set them on different courses than they thought they would take. Whether we want to admit it or not, money and the need to earn a living alter the lives of nearly everyone in some way or another.

Unfortunately, our public education system concentrates so much on preparing students to get a "job" that it inadvertently diminishes or kills the entrepreneurial spirit in many young people. Guidance counselors and other academic advisors show students the average difference in income between school dropouts, high school graduates, college graduates, and those holding advanced degrees as a way to encourage them to advance their education. Don't get us wrong, we certainly don't mean to imply that education is not important. Education puts tools in your toolbox, and the more of them you have, the better ... most of the time.

Where we feel public education falters is in its application of the tools. High school students are taught math and science, English and foreign languages, but very few graduate with the ability to balance a checkbook or prepare a family budget, nor do they understand how critical these things are to success in life. Mike once hired a man for a manual labor job who was in his mid-30s and held a doctorate degree in geology. When Mike questioned the man as to why he was applying for such a menial job, he said, "Because I can't find a job in my field and I need to work." Mike soon discovered the man's problem: He had a great education but didn't have a clue how to apply it.

The learning years begin when you get out on your own and start trying to apply what you learned in school and from your childhood experiences to situations in the workplace. During these years, many people become frustrated because what they learned as theory doesn't always work when applied to practical situations. It's like a person who takes a sales job, goes through the company's training program, and learns to make a great sales presentation, only to call on prospects that didn't attend the same training program. Unless they come to the realization that it's not how good the presentation is, but whether the sale is made, they only become more and more frustrated, until they leave that job and go looking for something else to "try."

The stories in this part, like those ones in the previous part, are designed to help you understand the role common sense plays in developing a Weekend Millionaire Mindset. Once again, we urge you to keep a note pad handy to jot down memorable situations from your life that may be triggered as you read these chapters, experiences that you can delve into and examine to find the building blocks you need to achieve success.

You may be thinking, "I don't have any experiences like yours." But you do! No, they won't be the same experiences we've had, because everyone is different, but you have had experiences that contain hidden life lessons just like we have, and what this book is all about is learning how to find these and apply the lessons they contain. We share our experiences to help you see how we distilled the key learning points out of our experiences, even the ones that weren't always pleasant or comfortable. What's important is that you keep making notes as you read and are reminded of events from your life. In time you will begin discovering things you missed at the time—things that will help you make better decisions in the future. You will also see that the decisions you make determine your success or failure in life.

Now let's move on to discuss the learning years in more detail.

14

Growing Requires Stretching, Getting Out of Your Comfort Zone

We closed the last part by mentioning that Mike's building animosity toward his stepfather as he started his junior year of high school had him dreaming of leaving home. Throughout that school year their mutual hostility grew, until they actually exchanged physical blows. Mike was headstrong, stubborn, and toughened from growing up in the crucible of hard times. Paul was just as determined to have things his way. By late spring the situation reached a point where Mike refused to listen to any more criticism or be given any more orders by Paul.

One day Paul was in a bad mood and Mike caught the brunt of it. "You're so stupid, you don't have the sense God gave a dumb goose," Paul yelled at him.

"Oh yeah, we'll see about that," Mike yelled back as he swung a fist at Paul. His defiance was met with a sharp slap across the face that knocked him into a corner, and then Paul stomped and kicked him until Mike apologized and agreed to succumb to his demands.

Growing Requires Stretching

With rage boiling inside him, Mike crawled to his room and made the decision that enough was enough. He would leave home. But with no money and nowhere to go, he knew he would have to bide his time and wait for the right moment to leave.

That moment came in June 1962, shortly after the school year ended and the family was paying a weekend visit to his grandmother's house in Abingdon, Virginia. The afternoon they were to depart for the return trip to Bluefield, Mike slipped out the back door and ran. He didn't know where he was going, but he knew it was not back to Bluefield. He ran until he reached a nearby swamp where thick brush and cattails would conceal him from view. As he hid crouched in the muck and mud of the swamp, he knew he'd made a decision from which there would be no turning back.

This would become the first life-altering decision of Mike's learning years, and with it came a rapid series of life lessons. Knowing there would be no turning back, he was forced to learn the importance of making a decision and then making it work; of finding a way, not an excuse. This attitude would stick with him for the rest of his life. When he walked out that back door and ran, he knew he would never return to the life he'd known before. Was he scared? Absolutely! Did he know what the next day would bring? No! What he did know was that he had made a decision, he was committed to it, and he would find a way to make it work.

The rest of that afternoon was a tense time for him. In the rolling hills there was little ground cover. The swamp upstream from the dam, at an old grist mill, was the only area for miles around where he could hide. Mike knew that Paul would be looking for him, so concealment became his first order of business. Sure enough, within an hour Paul was driving up and down the road next to the swamp, yelling as he passed by, "I know you're in there somewhere; either get out here now or you'll wish you had."

Mike had worked his way deep into the swamp to ensure that Paul could not see him. But as the car drove up and down the road and he heard Paul calling out to him, the fear that the color of his clothes would make him stand out in the brush and cattails caused him to slip into the water up to his neck to be completely concealed. Despite the water snakes, muskrats, turtles, and other swamp creatures that he saw swimming around him, he remained in the water until after dark, when he felt it was safe to move.

When he crawled out of the swamp, his skin was wrinkled like a prune from being in the water so long and he was covered with thick smelly mud. He had no other clothes, so all Mike wanted to do was get the mud off and try to clean up a bit. He made his way along the opposite edge of the swamp from the road until he reached the dam that backed up the stream. He carefully made his way down to the bottom of the dam, stripped naked, stepped under the edge of the spillway and let the water rushing over the dam wash him off. He stood there for several minutes letting the water rinse the mud from his body then washed his clothes in the spray until they were relatively clean. Shivering from the cold water, he wrung out his clothes, put them back on, and sat down on a rock to contemplate his next move.

There was an old mill next to the lake created by the dam. As he sat there, he thought, "What have I done?" He was wet, cold, tired, and hungry, and he didn't have a clue what to do next, but he knew he had made the right decision. He decided to look around the old mill, which was still in operation then but has long since been torn down, to see if he could find something to eat and maybe a place to rest. It was Sunday night and the mill was closed; there were no houses around, so he felt comfortable exploring the grounds. When he came around the building to the parking lot, he noticed a truck backed up next to a loading dock. Upon closer examination he discovered that it contained vegetables, which were probably bound for market. He lifted a couple of tomatoes, a cucumber, and two potatoes from the truck, went back to wash them in the water, then sat down on a rock to eat.

The raw vegetables curbed his hunger, and after eating them, he looked for a place to rest until morning. On the uphill side of the mill, near the dam, there were several corn cribs and other small storage buildings. He tried a number of them before finding an unlocked crib. It contained several feet of dried corn, still on the cob, and scattered around the crib were several empty burlap sacks that had probably held corn at one time. He gathered up several of the sacks and crawled into the crib with them to create a makeshift bed in the corn. By now his clothes were nearly dry, and he curled up on the sacks and immediately fell asleep. He didn't wake up until the following morning, when he heard birds chirping as the sun began to rise.

Growing Requires Stretching

At first Mike didn't realize where he was, but when he opened his eyes and looked around, it dawned on him that this would be the first day of a new life for him. He sat up, stretched, and let his mind sort through thoughts of what he should do next. He knew the mill would open for business soon, so he wanted to be gone before the employees arrived. He also knew he would be welcome at his grandmother's house, but he was concerned that Paul might have stayed overnight and would be waiting for him to show up. As daylight was beginning to break, he decided to make his way back to his grandmother's to see if Paul's car was still in her driveway. He wanted to get there before people in the house awakened.

He left the mill and cut through the fields away from the road until he arrived at the edge of his grandmother's neighborhood. He made his way through people's yards and quickly crossed streets until he was close to her house. He approached from the back along a high hemlock hedge that hid the next door neighbor's lot until he could see her driveway around the corner of the hedge. To his relief, it was empty; Paul's car was not there. He eased into the edge of the hemlocks and sat down where he could keep his eye on the driveway yet still be concealed from view. He wanted to be sure Paul wasn't just out looking for him again, to try and force him to return to Bluefield.

One hour passed, then two, then three. The sun climbed higher in the sky, the dew evaporated, and as the temperature began to climb, the reality of his situation settled in. He had no money, no clothes other than what he was wearing, and no idea what to do next. The only thing he was sure about was that he was not going back to Bluefield. As he sat there pondering his next move, he recalled the time when he lived in the town of War and wanted a bicycle. He recalled his mother saying to him, "If you really want one, I'll bet you can find a way to get it."

When he thought about the obstacles he had encountered and the things he'd done to overcome them in order to get that bicycle, it dawned on him that this was just another challenge. Although he had no idea at the moment how he would survive, he knew he would find a way. He was anxious and a bit nervous, but he was not afraid. Although he couldn't define it as such back then, this was a learning experience, and one of many that would teach him that *growing requires stretching, getting out of your comfort zone.*

The Learning Years

Mike's decision not to return to Bluefield was a leap of faith … a stretch. Spending time submerged in a smelly swamp, showering with cold water pouring down from a spillway, eating stolen food, and sleeping in a corn crib, all in less than 24 hours, definitely took him out of his comfort zone. These were short-term inconveniences, though, that he was willing to endure to build a better life. As he sat there huddled in the hemlock hedge, facing life with no shelter, no money, no job, no transportation, no education, and none of the necessities even an abusive home could provide, it was scary and quite a stretch. He kept staring at the empty driveway and getting hungrier and hungrier. Finally he got up the courage to go to his grandmother's house to see if he could get something to eat and talk with her about his future.

He came in the back door and found her sitting at the kitchen table having a cup of coffee and staring out the window. When she saw him, she jumped up, ran over, and threw her arms around him. With tears in her eyes, she said, "Oh, I'm so glad to see you. I've been up all night worrying. Where have you been?"

"Where's Paul?" he asked.

"He and your mother and the other children went home last night," she replied. "He was so mad at you; I hope he didn't take his anger out on your mother or the children. Why did you run off like that?"

"I just couldn't take it anymore. Nothing I did pleased him. He called me stupid and dumb; he said I didn't have the sense God gave a dumb goose and stuff like that. It made me so mad I just finally had enough of it. I made up my mind before we came over here that I would not go back to Bluefield and live like that anymore. When they were getting ready to go home yesterday, I knew that the only way I could keep him from forcing me to go back was to run away and hide. That's why I left."

"I understand how you feel," she said, "but what are you going to do? You haven't even finished high school."

"I don't know," Mike replied. "I don't know what I'm going to do; I was hoping I could talk with you about that and make some decisions. The only thing I know for sure is that I'm not going back to Bluefield. I've been thinking about it for hours and I was hoping you'd let me stay here and finish my last year of high school, and after that I'll get a job and take care of myself.

Growing Requires Stretching

If you'll let me stay here, I'll earn my keep, I promise. I'll mow the lawn, trim the shrubs, and do anything else you want; I just need a place to stay for a year until I can finish school."

"Honey, you know you're welcome here anytime, but your mother is worried sick about you. She called last night when they got home and has already called this morning to see if I've heard from you. Let's give her a call so we can at least put her mind at ease, okay?"

"You can call her, but I'm not going back," he said. "Yesterday was one of the most miserable days of my life. I spent the afternoon up to my neck in swamp water and mud, washed myself and my clothes in a cold creek, ate stolen food for dinner, and slept in damp clothes in one of the corn cribs down at the mill, but as bad as that was, it was better than going back to Bluefield."

That exchange began a year-long roller coaster ride that swept Mike out of his formative years and into his learning years. It was a year in which he would solidify his ability to make decisions and then make them work; a year when he would focus on the future without looking back or second guessing himself. It would be a difficult year of growing and stretching.

His grandmother called his mother and relayed his feelings about returning to Bluefield. She told her that he would be staying with her for his senior year of high school. They made arrangements to have his clothes packed and put on a bus to Abingdon, where they arrived the next day.

During that summer, Mike mowed and trimmed his grandmother's property just as he promised. He also did numerous other things to earn some spending money to help pay his way. He caught small painted turtles in the swamp and sold them to a local pet shop for 25 cents each; he cut cattails and sold them to flower shops for a dollar a dozen; he mowed lawns, trimmed shrubbery, cleaned gutters, painted, and did any other odd jobs he could find.

Toward the end of summer, he enrolled at Abingdon High School for his senior year. The first day of school, he didn't know a single person, and even worse, no one seemed to be interested in meeting him. He tried to make friends, but with little success. He was soon labeled a pest by the students and considered a disruptive student by the teachers. By Christmas he had been sent to the principal's office numerous times, and the guidance counselors had begun to realize there was more to his disruptive behavior than showed on the surface.

The first week after the holiday break, his guidance counselor called him in to discuss his behavior and try to help him get the second half of the year started on a better footing. Mike told her that he realized he had a chip on his shoulder that was causing him problems, but he didn't know what to do about it. She told him that she knew a good psychiatrist, and asked if he would consider meeting with him to see if he had any suggestions that might be helpful. At this point Mike was willing to try almost anything, so he agreed to go.

The guidance counselor took him to Bristol, Virginia, for the meeting. Mike only attended one session, but what he learned during that session resulted in some enormous personality changes and started him on the road to developing a Weekend Millionaire Mindset. He quickly opened up to the psychiatrist, revealing his feelings about his childhood, his life with Paul, and his resentment and bitterness toward him, and the emptiness he felt about never having met his real father. As his emotions poured out, he broke down into tears and cried, "Why can't I just have a life like everyone else? Why does everything have to be so hard?"

The psychiatrist allowed him to regain his composure and then gave him some advice that stuck with him the rest of his life. He gently laid his hand on Mike's arm and said, "Son, nearly all the problems you've described are your fault. Now before you get upset at me, let me explain; whenever something happens to you, whether it is good or bad, you have the choice as to how you react to it. When something good happens, it's easy to react in a positive way, but when something bad happens, it's much more difficult to feel or act positively. Let me explain something. Have you ever noticed how when you react negatively to something someone does that it always seems to make matters worse? You end up saying things you shouldn't say, doing things you shouldn't do, and acting in ways that bring negative responses from other people. Once you perform a negative act or utter hurtful words, they can't be taken back, and this causes people not to like you."

As Mike sat there listening, he was mentally playing back his responses to criticism, directives, and other actions he hadn't liked. The longer the psychiatrist spoke, the more he realized that he was right on target. He couldn't think of a single time when he hadn't reacted negatively to things that didn't go his way. Suddenly it became clear that he had brought much of his anger and disappointment upon himself.

As the session neared its end, the psychiatrist said, "Let me give you a challenge. When you go to school tomorrow, the first time someone says or does something that bothers you, stop and mentally say 'positive, positive, positive' to yourself three times before you make a comment. While you're doing this, think of something good to say or don't say anything at all. Remember that how you react is your choice no matter what other people say or do. If you can't think of something good to say, then just choose not to say anything. Try this for one week and see if it doesn't make a big difference."

This was all new information. Like so many young people, at this stage of his life all Mike knew was to retaliate in kind to negative words or actions. When people would pick on him or make fun of him, he wanted to get even. This "get even" attitude was especially damaging because his small size made him an easy target to be picked upon. As late as his junior year of high school, he was the smallest student in the class, standing less than five feet tall and not weighing 100 pounds. Even the girls were all bigger than he was.

Although he experienced a huge growth spurt after leaving home, and by the start of the school year was no longer one of the smallest students in school, he still had a chip on his shoulder about being picked on. When the psychiatrist explained that the way he had reacted was probably bringing on most of the treatment he hated, Mike listened. He left the counseling session determined to accept the psychiatrist's challenge and agreed that if he faced adversity during the coming week, he would either respond positively or not at all. At least it was worth a try.

His first opportunity to try out this new commitment to not meet negative with negative came very quickly. When he got on the school bus the following morning, his biggest nemesis tried to trip him going down the aisle. He stumbled but didn't fall, and even though several of the other kids laughed, he just continued to an empty seat near the back of the bus and sat down. The trip to school was otherwise uneventful, but as he got off the bus, the boy who had tried to trip him was waiting.

"Didn't you see my foot when you were getting on?" he asked in a cocky tone. "What were you trying to do, step on my foot on purpose?"

Positive, positive, positive, Mike thought before answering. Then he responded, "No, I wasn't trying to step on your foot. I saw that shirt you're wearing and I really like it. I guess I was looking at it and didn't see your foot, I'm sorry."

This was a big change for Mike. Before the counseling session he would probably have responded with something like, "If you hadn't stuck your damned foot in the aisle trying to trip me, you wouldn't have gotten it stepped on." And that would have led to an altercation that probably landed both of them in the principal's office. But to his amazement, this boy who had picked on him all year, simply said, "You really like the shirt? Thanks! My girlfriend gave it to me for Christmas and today is the first time I've worn it."

"It's really a neat shirt," Mike replied. "I wish I had one that nice."

And with that, a grin came on the boy's face and he again said, "Thanks!" as he headed off to class. Mike stood there for a moment, stunned. Wow, maybe this positive stuff really does work, he thought as he headed to class. He couldn't help but think about the kind of altercation the incident could have turned into if he had responded in his usual way. Without even realizing it, Mike was well down the road to developing a Weekend Millionaire Mindset.

It's very difficult to make dramatic behavior changes, but in spite of the fact that he never made a return visit, the more Mike practiced what the psychiatrist had told him, the more surprised he was at how differently both students and teachers were treating him. By the end of that trial week, he could see some real benefits from thinking positively. By the end of January, following the same positive regimen, he was feeling much better about himself. And by the end of February, in spite of experiencing a few minor slips, his confidence was growing, his spirits had lifted, and he was beginning to look forward to the future. He felt better about himself than he could ever recall.

But though he was experiencing positive effects from his changed behavior, nothing could have reinforced the power of his new approach more than what happened in March. All winter his grandmother had been telling him that she wanted to get in the attic as soon as the weather improved and throw away a bunch of old stuff that had been stored there for years. Now, finally, Mike was in the attic helping her. For several hours they went through boxes of old clothes, shoes, toys, and other things that get stored away in most homes. Mike was going up and down the stairs carrying boxes to be thrown away when, on one trip back to the attic, he noticed an old cigar box lying off to one side. He picked it up, opened it, and his life changed forever. Inside the box was a single envelope addressed to his mother, and the return address on it was from Lee Summey, his biological father.

He sat there holding the letter; his hands were trembling and his heart racing as an overwhelming feeling of anxiety swept over him. All the problems he'd had with his stepfather—the anger, hurt, animosity, and disruptions in his life—had been coupled with an intense longing to learn about his real father, though he had no idea where his real father was. This was the first evidence he'd ever found that might help him locate his father. His mother's breakup with his father had been a bitter one, and as a result, no one in the family would talk to him about it.

He wasn't sure if he should tell his grandmother about what he'd found or hide it and look at it later. But she knew what he'd found, because she said, "Honey, I saved that letter to give to you when you were old enough to understand. It was a letter that came to your mother when they were in the process of getting divorced. I forgot about it being up here with all this junk."

Mike's grandmother was always the one person he could turn to for support. She was a small woman who insisted that all her grandchildren, nieces, and nephews call her by her first name, Sallie. She would stand up for him when she was around Paul, and Mike felt that she was the only one who understood his plight. His one big problem with both his mother and Sallie was that they would never tell him anything about his father. Now he had a letter with an address—albeit sixteen years old—that he could write to and maybe get a response.

That's just what he did. That very night he sat down and wrote a letter that would change his entire direction in life. Figure 11 shows a copy of the front of that letter:

Figure 11

Mike found this old letter in 2004 while cleaning out his dad's house after he passed away. You can see the note he put on the front of the envelope that reads, "Address 16 years old forward if possible."

Several days passed after he mailed the letter, and deep down inside, Mike doubted he would receive a response. But on Tuesday, March 26, 1963, as he stepped off the school bus a little after 3:00 P.M., he saw Sallie standing on the front porch waiting for him. In her hand was a letter, and when he got to the end of the walk and started up the steps, she reached out and handed it to him. She didn't say a word; she just gave it to him. When he looked down and saw it was from his dad, the first thing he noticed was that the handwriting resembled his. He dropped his schoolbooks on the porch and sat down on the steps with the letter. This was one of the most emotional moments of his life. Sallie must have sensed that because she sat down beside him and put her arm around his shoulders.

"Go on, open it," she said.

But Mike was afraid. What if he was remarried? What if he had other children? What if he didn't want to see him? What if he did? These and a dozen similar thoughts ran through his mind as he sat there holding the letter. He wanted to open it, but he didn't. The anticipation about what it contained was so great it almost overwhelmed him. He sat there looking at the envelope for what seemed an eternity before he finally took out his pocketknife and slit it open. He took out the single sheet and unfolded it. The letter was brief, but it contained everything he hoped it would.

"I've thought about you many times over the years and wondered how you were doing, but due to the circumstances under which your mother and I separated, I didn't feel like I could contact you," his dad wrote. "I'm not much for letter writing, but I'd love to talk with you. Please call me collect after 5:00 P.M. at ... " and he listed the telephone number. Mike had just turned 17 in January, and for years had longed to have a dad like the other kids around him. Now he was less than two hours from talking with his father for the first time in his life. What would he say? What would his dad say? What would he sound like? What kind of job would he have? Would he want to see him? Mike's head was spinning. A thousand thoughts rushed through his mind in a blur of mixed-up feelings and emotion.

If growing requires stretching, getting out of your comfort zone, this was one huge growing experience. As he waited for five o'clock to arrive, he paced the floor. He wanted to scream at the top of his lungs with excitement, and at the same time wanted to sit down and cry. He couldn't tell you why he felt either way; he just did. The closer it got to the time, the more nervous he became. Sensing his discomfort, Sallie tried to comfort him and assure him that everything would be all right, but for Mike, the wait was gut-wrenching. Finally, at 5:02 he picked up the phone and dialed the operator.

He gave her the phone number and told her he wanted to place the call collect from Mike Summey. On the second ring, a man answered, "Hello!"

"Sir, I have a collect call from Mike Summey, will you accept the charges?"

"Yes, absolutely," the man answered.

"Go ahead, sir, your party is on the line," the operator said.

"Dad, is that you?" Mike asked.

"Yes, it's me, boy. It's sure good to hear your voice," his dad replied. "How are you doing?"

And this started a phone conversation that lasted over an hour. Mike learned that his dad, Lee, was remarried to a nice lady named Madge. He even spoke to her on the phone and learned that they did not have any other children and she would love for him to come for a visit. She also informed him that it was his dad's forty-fourth birthday and this was the best present he could ever have gotten.

Everyone agreed they wanted to meet each other, and the sooner the better. The problem was, they were several hours apart over twisting mountain roads. Mike was in Abingdon, Virginia, and his dad was in Asheville, North Carolina. Lee suggested that Mike hang up and call the bus depot to find out when bus service was available between the towns, and then call him back with the information.

Mike made the call and learned that the only service available left Abingdon at 8:30 in the evening and arrived in Asheville at two in the morning. The next bus was less than two hours from leaving. He immediately called back and advised his dad of the schedule.

"Can I come tonight?" he asked with great anticipation. "I don't think I can wait another day."

"Sure," his dad replied. "If you can catch the bus, Madge and I will meet you at the bus station."

"I'll catch the bus, one way or another," he replied.

"What will you be wearing, so we'll be able to recognize you?"

"I'll be in blue jeans and a plaid shirt, but I have a red baseball cap. I'll wear it so you can spot me easier," Mike said.

With that, Mike threw a change of clothes in an old grocery bag, grabbed the few dollars he had been able to save, and ran nearly three miles to the bus station. He had just enough money to buy a one-way ticket, and he hoped his dad would cover the cost of a return ticket. That began a larger journey that would take Mike from the hills of southwestern Virginia to the mountains of western North Carolina, where he still lives today. The trip was a leap of faith, because when he stepped off that bus, he had little more than the clothes on his back and two dollars in his pocket and was coming alone to meet a father he had never known. Talk about getting out of your comfort zone!

His visit lasted from early Wednesday morning until he reluctantly returned the following Sunday afternoon. During that trip, he learned that he had a whole family in Asheville—aunts, uncles, cousins, and a grandmother who was the matriarch of the entire clan. His dad wanted Mike to go back and finish high school, but also wanted him to come to Asheville to

Growing Requires Stretching

live with Madge and him following graduation. This was what Mike had hoped for, and he couldn't wait. Finally, good things were coming his way, and coming in bunches. On the bus trip home, he closed his eyes and wondered if all his good fortune could be the result of the positive attitude he had developed after seeing the psychiatrist.

When he returned to school on Monday, he had some explaining to do about the days he had missed the previous week, but everyone in the office could sense his enthusiasm and see his excitement as he told them where he had been. He was granted excused absences for the days and allowed to make up his missed work. As each new day dawned, he faced it with renewed vigor and growing self-assurance. He could sense that he was turning his life around and doing it on his own. There really did seem to be something to this positive thinking stuff after all, but he still wanted to put it to another test.

Throughout the year Mike had kept his eye on what he considered to be the prettiest girl in the school. Donna Woodward was a gorgeous little girl in the junior class who was just under five feet tall and weighed less than 100 pounds, but she had the voice of an angel. She would sing the national anthem at school events and always got the singing parts in school plays. He had been infatuated with her from the moment he first saw her, but so were most of the boys in the school. With his newfound courage, Mike decided to ask Donna to be his date for the Junior/Senior Prom; another stretch in the growing process, especially since he had never had a date before.

It took him several days to find the opportunity to get her aside so he could ask her, but when he did, she readily accepted. He couldn't believe it. Now what was he going to do? He had no car, no nice clothes, and no one he could turn to for help. Once again his mother's words came back to him: "If you really want it badly enough, you'll find a way to get it." And taking Donna to the prom was something he really wanted to do.

With only a few weeks to go before the big dance, he was nearly in a panic. There was no way he was going to tell her he couldn't go after she had accepted his invitation. He would find a way! So he did anything and everything he could to make money. He trimmed shrubbery, cleaned gutters, washed and waxed cars; anything to earn a dollar or two. Finally he had enough to buy a new suit to wear to the prom, but he still had to get there.

That was going to be a challenge. He kept working and saving, and by the time the big day arrived, he'd saved enough to afford a taxi to take them to the prom.

Mike had never mentioned to Donna how they would get there, and she probably assumed he would have a car, so when he showed up at her house in a taxi, her mother was nearly in shock. She wasn't about to let her daughter go to the prom in a taxi. She was, however, gracious when she took Mike aside and told him to send the taxi on its way. She would let them drive her car. June Woodward is to this day one of the kindest, most understanding people Mike has ever known, and he remains grateful to her for making it possible for him to have a wonderful prom to cap off an otherwise tumultuous roller coaster year in his life.

We have only touched upon a few of the emotional problems Mike faced from June 1962 until June 1963, when he encountered enough obstacles that would have ripped most people apart. The first half of the year was a dismal downhill slide that focused on negative thoughts and deeds, while the second half focused on the power of positive thoughts and actions. Everyone faces problems, but as Mike learned, it's how you respond to them that determines your success or failure in life. Reflecting back on that year, the biggest lesson he learned was that you don't develop a Weekend Millionaire Mindset with a head full of anger, resentment, and negative thoughts. Positive, positive, positive is the way to go.

Now we'll move on to the next chapter and pick up with additional life lessons he learned following his move to North Carolina.

Key Points from This Chapter

- It takes commitment to change your life; the kind of strong commitment that Mike had when he wanted to change his life so bad that he ran away from home.
- Life gets better when you get better; learn to take charge of your actions.
- You can't control what happens to you, but you can control the way you react to what happens to you.

Growing Requires Stretching

- When bad things happen, think positive, positive, positive before you respond.
- When you experience difficulties, think of them as growing pains—the kind that comes from stretching and getting out of your comfort zone.

15

The Grass Isn't Always Greener

The day after graduating from high school, Mike packed his few possessions into a cardboard box and boarded a bus for Asheville, North Carolina, to live with his father. Although he had learned how thinking and acting positively could improve his situation, he still had deep-seated emotional wounds that needed to heal. He carried with him high hopes and dreams for a better life. The move represented a fresh start in a new town with a new family, and a chance to establish a promising future. He was thinking positive, positive, positive.

Mike quickly learned that his dad was not a man of means but he liked to play the part. He was a bookkeeper for a small coal and oil company and lived in a modest three-bedroom, one-bath block house that had been constructed by two of his brothers who were in the building business. He drove a new Buick and always wore a suit and tie ... even when mowing the lawn. He dabbled in the stock market and owned a few utility stocks, but loved to give the impression he was a heavy hitter. This all seemed strange to Mike, because he had grown up in a family where discussions of money centered more on what they didn't have than what they did.

From the first day they met, Lee Summey wanted to impress Mike with how smart he was and how much he was worth. From that first visit, he'd learned that Mike hadn't grown up in an affluent family, and it seemed that Lee wanted to be sure he appeared better off financially than his ex-wife. He was now married to Madge, a wonderful Polish lady from Texas whose family owned a farm with several oil wells on it. Her parents had arranged for the oil royalties to be split between themselves and all their children. Although the monthly check was only a few hundred dollars, Lee never missed an opportunity to talk about the oil wells he had in Texas.

As soon as he arrived in Asheville, Mike went to work with his dad's brothers building houses. For the first time in his life he had extra spending money, from the $40 he made each week. Over the next few months, he borrowed his dad's car and used part of his newfound money to take out a few dates and buy some new clothes. He also purchased three $25 U.S. savings bonds as a way of setting aside some money for the future. Eventually, his dad helped him buy a 1959 Studebaker Lark for $300, and Mike moved on to a new job as a lab technician, where he matched dye colors in a textile factory at the big salary of $60 a week.

The longer he lived with his dad, the more Mike came to realize that there was a vast difference between the two of them. Lee was an ultraconservative person who was extremely reluctant to try new things or take risks in his life. The salary he made at his boring job keeping books for the small coal and oil company, coupled with the monthly oil royalty check they received from Madge's family oil wells, provided them with a comfortable but modest living. When Mike asked his father why he didn't look for a better job, Lee would go into a long dissertation about how well he was doing financially and how comfortable he and Madge were going to be when he retired because they would have the oil checks to go with his Social Security income.

Mike, on the other hand, had spent his entire life facing one challenge after another. Taking risks was nothing new or frightening to him. Lee believed that Mike should get a job, stick with it, and not dream about whether it provided him with the things he wanted from life. Mike, however, lived with the belief that if he wanted something badly enough, he would find a way to get it, just as his mother had always told him. These different outlooks on life began to cause problems between them. When Mike said he was thinking of quitting his factory job to go to work with an encyclopedia company making door-to-door calls, it escalated the problems.

Mike had seen a help wanted ad in the classified section of the local newspaper offering $80 a week for individuals to call on families in order to place encyclopedias in their homes. He answered the ad and arranged to come in after work for an interview. There, the manager explained that they needed people to make the calls in the evening, to families with children, asking the adults if they were willing to accept a free set of encyclopedias. In exchange, they would agree to write an endorsement the company could use in its marketing efforts. All the recipient family needed to do was subscribe to the company's research services. There was no mention that this was a sales job. The manager explained that the pay would be $80 per week during the training period, and then as long as one set per week was placed, the pay would continue to be $80 a week or more. Mike said he was interested but asked for a few days to consider the offer.

When he tried to discuss this job with his dad, it precipitated a series of lengthy discussions and heated arguments over several days. Lee viewed the job as having lots of risks and no guarantees beyond the training period. Mike viewed it as an opportunity to make more money, and he had the self-confidence to believe he could do it. The more they talked, the more their differences came to the surface, until the argument escalated to the point where Lee told Mike, "If you're foolish enough to give up a secure factory job to go sell encyclopedias, then just move out because you're not going to stay here and live off me."

This lack of support surprised Mike, and hurt his feelings as well. If he had confidence in himself, why couldn't his dad have confidence in him too? What had seemed like such a rosy future with his dad a few months before had turned into a shouting match and an uncomfortable coexistence. The more he tried to get his dad to understand his feelings, the madder Lee became. At one point Lee even picked up an ashtray and threw it at Mike.

It taught Mike a valuable lesson: *The grass isn't always greener on the other side of the fence.* He could not believe that the promising relationship he'd had with his dad could have deteriorated so badly. All he wanted to do was find a job where he could make more money; one where he wasn't just paid for his time, but could be rewarded based on what he accomplished. He never dreamed that such a job would be so intimidating to his father that he'd be ordered out of the house if he accepted it.

He was faced with a difficult decision. Did he follow his heart and pursue something he felt sure he could do, or did he allow his dad to dictate his future? Each time he tried to bring up the subject, it only made matters worse. Mike decided that if his dad wouldn't support him in this endeavor, he would probably not support him in others, so he began to look for a place to live that he could afford. He eventually located a two-room furnished apartment in the attic of an old house in downtown Asheville that he could rent for $50 a month. The price included the utilities, so all he would have to pay was rent. The problem was, the landlord wanted a $50 deposit plus the first month's rent before he could move in, and Mike only had money for the rent, not the deposit.

He had the three $25 savings bonds he'd purchased, but when he tried to cash them in, he discovered that he hadn't owned them long enough to be able to redeem them without penalty. Since he had decided to take the new job with the encyclopedia company, and his dad had said he would have to move out if he did, Mike went to him and asked to borrow the money for the deposit. Lee refused! Mike never knew if Lee was trying to discourage him from moving out or just trying to dissuade him from changing jobs.

Mike's request led to another heated argument in which he yelled, "Whether you loan me the money or not I will find a way to get it and I will move."

Lee retorted, "You're moving out to take a crap job like that and you want me to loan you money? What do you think I am, stupid? All you're going to do is make a fool of yourself and then come crawling back here wanting to move in again, plus I doubt if you'd ever pay me back even if I did loan you the money."

That comment cemented Mike's determination. He looked Lee directly in the eye and said, "I know you don't think I can do the job, but I know I can and it pays a lot more than what I'm making now. I'm going to get my own place and I'm going to take the job. I wish you would support me, but if you won't, so be it, I'll do it on my own. I wouldn't have asked to borrow the money if the bank would have let me cash in my savings bonds, but don't worry about it, I'll find a way."

"What savings bonds are you talking about?" Lee asked.

"These," Mike said as he held out the three bonds.

"Where'd you get those?"

"I bought them with some of the money I've earned over the last few months," he replied.

"I'll tell you what," Lee said. "I'll loan you the money, if you will sign a note and let me hold those bonds as security so I will get paid back."

"That's a deal," Mike said, "but you have to promise that you will give them back when I repay the loan."

"You pay me back and you'll get the bonds back."

That was Mike's first experience with borrowing money. Lee sat down at the kitchen table and wrote out a loan agreement. When Mike saw it, he questioned the 6 percent interest the note contained. He was able to negotiate a zero percent loan (something he would do on a much larger scale later in life) as evidenced by the correction shown on the note in Figure 12 following. Mike signed the agreement, and Lee slid the paper across the table to Madge to have her witness his signature. Once the papers were signed and Mike gave him the savings bonds to hold, Lee gave him the $50 he needed for the deposit on the apartment.

This transaction took place on Thursday, April 2, 1964. On Friday, Mike paid the deposit and first month's rent, and he moved into his own place that weekend. This was another turning point in his life, because from that day forward, he would never rely on anyone else to provide him with a place to live, food to eat, clothes to wear, or anything else. With this move, he assumed total responsibility for himself. It had so shocked him that his own father would make him sign a note and put up security for a $50 loan that he knew he would never be able to rely on him in the future. As much as he regretted the break with Lee, he knew that if he was going to accomplish anything beyond mere existence in life, it was going to be up to him, not someone else.

We tell this story because of its significance in Mike's later life. We'll jump ahead a bit and explain that later, after he had achieved much success, a number of people who didn't know him during these years would assume

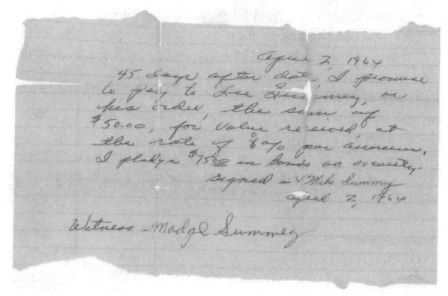

Figure 12

that he'd been born with a silver spoon in his mouth. This misperception was probably caused in part by his dad. For several years prior to his death, Mike heard reports from people that Lee had told them he had provided the money to help him get started. Out of respect, Mike never revealed the truth until after Lee died, but a big part of developing his Weekend Millionaire Mindset is depicted in Figure 12. You'll have to admit, it doesn't have any resemblance to a silver spoon.

His acceptance of the job with the encyclopedia company and move into the attic apartment were Mike's first steps into his learning years. Throughout the next several chapters, we'll share a number of other events that left lasting impressions and further established his Weekend Millionaire Mindset.

Key Points from This Chapter

- Building wealth involves believing in yourself and taking calculated risks, risks that even your closest friends and family may not support at times.

The Learning Years

- Lessons learned in early childhood can stick with you throughout your life. Positive lessons like the one Mike's mother taught him—that if you want something badly enough, you will find a way to get it—can guide you throughout the rest of your life.
- Changing your surroundings and meeting new people may give you good feelings initially, but it's your performance once you get there that determines what you get out of life.
- When you believe in yourself, don't let others—even family members—keep you from pursuing your dreams.

16

You're Rewarded for Performance, Not Promises

Mike moved from the security of his father's home into the small attic apartment and promptly gave a two-week notice to his employer that he would be leaving to take another job. Thoughts of starting a new job brought anxious feelings and caused him to have butterflies in his stomach. Could he have made big a mistake? Could his dad have been correct; would this be nothing but a crap job? These and other similar feelings ran through his mind, but not once did Mike doubt that he could actually do the job.

He arrived at his new office at eight o'clock Monday morning to begin the training period. He was surprised at how bare bones basic the furnishings were. There was a secretary's office, a manager's office, and a training room. He was ushered into the training room, which was filled with writing desks that reminded him of the ones he'd had in school. He was given several forms to complete so the company would have his personal information and tax status. Meanwhile, several other people arrived and were asked to fill out the same forms.

The Learning Years

Shortly after eight o'clock, before anyone had completed the forms, the well-dressed gentleman who had interviewed everyone walked in and introduced himself as the company's regional manager. After welcoming each employee individually, he explained that he was there to set up a new office to serve western North Carolina and upper South Carolina. He went on to inform the group that they were the company's first recruits from the area and would form the nucleus of the new office. He asked everyone to take their time completing the forms and to give them to the secretary when they were finished. He pointed to soft drinks, coffee, and a tray of pastries on a table in the back of the room and told everyone to feel free to help themselves to the refreshments. He said he would give them a few minutes to get to know each other and would return at nine o'clock to begin their initial orientation.

Promptly at nine he stepped into the training room, reintroduced himself, and asked the 12 people in the room to tell everyone their name and give the group a little information about themselves. At this point, he handed out adhesive-backed labels and asked them to write their name on one and stick it to their shirt. He said they would use name tags for the first couple of days, until everyone got to know each other better. Once the introductions were made and the name tags applied, he pulled up a stool at the front of the room and began to tell the group about their new jobs.

He began by explaining that the company was planning a major sales effort in the area within several months and the first phase of this campaign involved placing free sets of encyclopedias in a number of homes with children. All the families would need to do to receive the free books was sign up for a fantastic research program the company offered owners of their encyclopedias and be willing to write a letter of recommendation that it could use in future sales drives. Most of the rest of the morning was a discussion of how the research program worked and how fortunate it would be for a family with children to be able to subscribe to it without having to spend several hundred dollars to buy the encyclopedias first. The catch, if there was one, was that the subscription to the research program was several hundred dollars.

When the group broke for lunch, the new recruits went to a nearby fast food restaurant to eat, where they talked about the morning session.

"That guy must think we're stupid," one said.

"Yeah, what does he take us for, a bunch of fools?" another recruit said. "All he wants us to do is go out and sell encyclopedias and tell people they're getting them for free if they will sign up for their big fancy research program."

"You guys can go back and listen to more of that bull if you want," the first one said, "but I didn't take this job to be a door-to-door encyclopedia salesman. I'm going home and look for a real job."

"Yeah, me too," the second replied. "I'm not going back either."

"Don't you think you should at least give it a chance? Mike asked. "We've only been there half a day, and even if it is selling encyclopedias, what's wrong with that as long as we get paid?"

"Well, it's just not for us," the two responded in unison.

From this Mike learned a lesson that served him well in future years. Losers always move in the direction of doing nothing. Winners always move in the direction of doing something and making things work. Roger recalls learning the same lesson when he was 21 and a photographer on an ocean liner.

They had been at sea for four months and were returning through the Suez Canal to their home port in England. There was to be a gala dinner party to end the trip as they sailed through the Mediterranean. Roger told his two assistants that he wanted to make a real effort to get every passenger's picture at the gala and sell them to the passengers before the trip ended. His assistants both told him it would be a waste of time, everyone had enough pictures, and they would be too busy packing to buy them anyway. Roger didn't have the experience to know who was right but he insisted they cover the event. It was a huge success and they made a lot of money. From then on Roger would believe that losers argue to do nothing, and winners argue for action and to find a way to make things work.

At the encyclopedia company, the group returned from lunch, minus the two who decided to leave. When the regional manager entered the room, it was instantly apparent that something had happened. The level of enthusiasm that had been there during the morning session was gone. It felt more like a funeral wake than the first day of a new job.

"Okay, what's up?" the manager asked.

Everyone just sat there with long faces until Mike spoke up. "We were talking at lunch," he said, "and two of the guys said that this was nothing but a door-to-door encyclopedia sales job and it wasn't for them. They aren't coming back."

"Yeah, it looks that way to me too," said one of the other recruits.

"I can understand your concerns," the regional manager replied. "When I first came to work with the company, I felt the same way, but once I learned more about it, I had a better understanding of the company's program. You see, hardly anyone wants to buy a set of encyclopedias, but they will buy a research program that helps their children in school. So from that standpoint, yes, you will be selling, but it won't be encyclopedias. When you make a placement, you will legitimately be giving families a new set of encyclopedias and asking them to purchase the research program.

"Now here's the kicker—you aren't stupid and neither was I. We all know the company can't stay in business giving away its product. What we're banking on is that children will be able to find so much of what they need in the encyclopedias that they won't use the research program that much. And for every family that enjoys the books and sends us a nice testimonial letter, it gives us more credibility when we talk with new people.

"I didn't mean to get into this so soon, but let me show you something," and with that he brought out a big notebook filled with letters from satisfied customers and passed it around to the group.

"So, our jobs will be to make as many placements as possible, correct?" Mike asked. He was so determined (there's one of those three Ds again) that he wasn't interested in the overall marketing strategy, he just wanted to get started making money.

"That is true," the manager replied, "and so long as you make at least one placement per week, we will pay you $80 per week. Eventually, when you learn our system better, you will be given an opportunity to earn even more based on your performance."

"That sounds good to me," Mike said. "I'm ready to start learning."

The following day, two more of the recruits called in and quit, but this did not deter Mike. He threw himself wholeheartedly into learning the way the company operated and how they wanted him to present himself and their products to prospects. There were classes on how to dress, how to greet people when they came to the door, how to introduce himself, how to invite himself into their homes, how to build rapport, how to introduce the encyclopedias, how to present the research program, how children in school could use it, how parents could use it to help with homework, the importance of building the benefits of the program before discussing the cost, how to explain the various payment options, and how to write the agreement.

By the end of the two-week training program, two more of the recruits had left, but Mike had taken the training seriously. He'd worked at home memorizing the materials and had practiced over and over what he would say and how he would act. Now he was eager to get out in the field and go to work. Most of the remaining recruits were enthusiastic too, but cautiously hesitant at the same time.

On the afternoon of the final training day, the regional manager asked, "How many of you are sure you will be able to make at least one placement a week?"

All hands went up.

He continued, "As you recall from the first afternoon you were here, I said you would have an opportunity to be rewarded for performance if you wanted it. You've completed your training and are now ready to go to work. You've all raised your hands indicating that you are sure you will be able to make at least one placement per week. As you know, that's the minimum requirement for the company to be able to guarantee your $80 a week salary.

"If you would like to be *rewarded for performance, not promises*, here's the deal I'm going to offer you. You can choose to accept the $80 per week salary and have it paid to you regularly with the understanding that each six-week period you will be evaluated to see if you have made an average of one placement per week, or you can forgo this guaranteed salary and we will pay you $80 for each placement you make with no guaranteed salary. In other words, if you make two placements per week, you will make $160, but if you don't make any you won't get paid that week. This is totally your choice, so I'm going to leave the room for a few minutes and let you think about it before you make your decisions. Whichever choice you make, you will be able to change it later, but not until your six-week review comes up."

With that, he left the room and the newly trained recruits began to talk among themselves.

The Learning Years

"I'm going to take the fixed salary option for the first six weeks," one said.

"Me too," another said. "This all sounds good, but I want to wait and see how hard it is before running the risk of not getting paid some weeks."

"Well, I'm sure I can do it, so I'm going for the performance-based plan," Mike said. "If I can't make at least one placement a week, I don't need to be working here."

When the manager returned with forms for each recruit to complete indicating their choice of pay plans, Mike was the only one who chose performance over promise.

The following Tuesday would be their first day in the field. That weekend, he spent every available hour practicing and rehearsing what he would say and do when he started making calls.

Since it was required that both husband and wife be in attendance when a presentation was made, their actual "in the field" hours would be from six until nine o'clock in the evenings and all day on Saturdays. Sunday and Monday would be off days. The regional manager had brought in two sales managers from a different district to supervise the new recruits.

With only six of the original 12 new hires remaining, each sales manager was only responsible for three people. Tuesday afternoon the sales managers held a meeting prior to going into the field. They explained that each person would be dropped off in a neighborhood between 5:30 and 6:00 and then be picked up at the drop-off point between 9:00 and 9:30. Everyone should be at their pick point not later than 9:30.

Mike was the first one to be dropped off, and as it turned out, he ended up being the last one to be picked up. He didn't make it back to the pickup point until almost ten o'clock, and the sales manager was furious.

"I told you to be here by 9:30," he said. "You've kept everyone waiting nearly a half hour."

"What did you want me to do, walk out on someone who wanted the program without getting their order, just so I could get back here on time?" Mike replied.

"You mean you made a placement?" one of the new recruits asked.

"Yes," Mike said, "didn't you?"

"No," the recruit replied. "I must have knocked on 50 doors and I didn't even get to talk with anyone, not one presentation."

"Same here," the other recruit said.

"Well, don't worry about it," the sales manager said. "This was just your first night and it's always tough. Mike, let me see the contract you got for your placement."

"Which one?" Mike asked.

"You mean you made more than one?"

"Yes, I only got to call on seven houses, but I made placements in three of them."

"What!" the sales manager exclaimed. "Let me see."

Mike pulled the contracts from his briefcase and handed them to him.

"How did you do it?" the new hires asked.

"It was simple," Mike said. "I just did exactly what we were trained to do."

"But didn't you have people slam doors in your face?" one asked.

"Only one," Mike said. "But I think he was having a fight with his wife. I could hear them yelling at each other when I rang the doorbell."

"Mike, this is unbelievable," the sales manager said. "I don't think I've ever heard of anyone making three placements on their first night in the field. Tomorrow you're going to have to tell everyone how you did it."

Mike wasn't impressed with the fact that he might have pulled off a first; what impressed him was that he had earned $240 in a single night. That was as much as he made in four weeks at the job he'd left at the textile factory.

The next day he learned that of the five other new people, only one had made a placement. The other four talked about how many doors they knocked on and how difficult it had been to get to talk with anyone. Only two of them had gotten to make presentations, and in both cases it was just a single presentation. Everyone wanted to know what Mike had done.

The second night, Mike only made one placement. His third night, he made two. By the end of the week he had made eight and earned $640. By the time his six-week evaluation arrived, he made the list of the top 10 performers in the nation and had earned nearly as much as he would have earned in a whole year at the textile company. Three of the remaining people who started the same day he did had quit, two of them without making a single placement.

Mike was ecstatic. He had never made so much money, yet during the same six weeks, he noticed that all the other reps did was complain and make excuses. At his six-week evaluation, the company offered him a promotion to sales manager and asked him to help train new recruits. They explained that in this position, he would make $100 for each placement he made personally, plus $20 for each placement the reps under him made. Naturally, he jumped at the opportunity.

During that first six weeks, Mike continued to rehearse and practice in his spare time. Whenever he made a call that was not successful, he would make notes and try to determine where he'd gone wrong. His delivery and success rate continued to improve, but with the promotion came problems. Let's move on to the next chapter, where we will analyze another valuable lesson Mike learned after he was promoted.

Key Points from This Chapter

- Losers always move in the direction of doing nothing; winners move in the direction of doing something and making it work.
- Once you commit to a project, stay with it. You may hear 1,000 excuses for why other people aren't successful, but if you stay committed and look for ways to make it work, you won't have to make excuses.
- Don't sell yourself short by making other people's goals your goals. While the other recruits had a goal of one sale a week, Mike's goal was to make as many placements as possible.
- You get paid for performance, not promises.

17

The Ability to Do and the Skill to Manage Are Different

Although Mike had only been with the company for eight short weeks, including the first two that were training, everyone in the office was aware of his success. Prior to his promotion, the other representatives were constantly asking him how he did it. At the daily briefings, everyone waited for him to tell how he'd done the day before. They were envious of his ability to make placements nearly every day he was in the field, and those assigned to work under Mike were looking forward to learning from him.

Mike tackled his new sales manager position with the same drive and determination that he demonstrated as a field representative. As a sales manager, he would supervise four people. His first day on the new job, he called the representatives who would be working under him together for an initial meeting. He expressed great enthusiasm over his promotion and assured them he would do everything in his power to help them achieve the kind of success he had enjoyed. At his initial meeting he explained that in addition to conducting training classes, he would select one of them each day with whom he would make calls. That way he could evaluate their presentations in real-life situations, which would enable him to determine how best to help them.

Almost instantly, he sensed a feeling of uneasiness in the room. One of the representatives finally spoke up: "You mean we're going to have to make a presentation in front of you?"

"Sure," Mike replied. "There's a reason I want to do this. When we meet in the office and practice our presentations, it's not the same as giving them in front of a real prospect. Each of us—including me—makes mistakes or has weaknesses. Otherwise we'd all be making two or three placements a day. We're all different. What may be a strength for one of you is a weakness for another, and vice versa. By going with you, I can hone in on the specific areas I need to work with each of you."

"Okay, I understand," one of the reps said. "I think we were all afraid you just wanted to go along to criticize us."

"Not at all," Mike replied. "My job is to help you make more placements, not make you nervous. You have to realize that I make money when you make money. I just want to help you get better and become more productive."

Over the next six week period, Mike encouraged and helped them to improve their areas of weakness, and as a result his group performed remarkably well. Although his personal production fell off a bit because he was spending part of his time going on calls with his reps, his group's production was nearly three times that of the next closest group in the office. Both his income and his stature with the company grew tremendously. He had made more money in a fourteen-week period than he would have made in an entire year at the factory job he left, and he had waved a few of his checks in front of his dad to rub things in a bit. But what happened next surprised even him.

At his evaluation after six weeks, he was surprised to find both the regional manager and one of the company's vice presidents at the meeting. He had expected his review to be conducted by the manager of the Asheville office, to whom he directly reported, but here was the company brass sitting in on his review. His first thought was to wonder what he'd done wrong?

The meeting began with a glowing review of his accomplishments, both as a field representative and as a sales manager, and then the vice president dropped a bombshell on him.

The Ability to Do and the Skill to Manage Are Different

"Mike, we have offered the office manager here a transfer to a larger market and he's accepted. That leaves his position in this market open. Based on your outstanding performance, we want to talk with you about the office manager's job."

"I appreciate your vote of confidence," Mike responded, "but what does the job entail?"

"As you know, we are expanding here," the VP replied. "We now have five teams with four field reps and a sales manager in each team, that's 25 people. We would like to double that within the next year. The job would be to interview and hire the new recruits, supervise and assist a full-time trainer, and supervise the sales managers. It would also involve being responsible for all the paperwork and reports from this office, and making sure they're prepared accurately and timely. We will provide a secretary to handle the telephones and help with the paperwork. Of course, if you accept the job, we will be available to guide you while you're getting a grasp on the way things work, and we will always be available if you run into problems. We realize that you've only been with the company a short time, but you've done such a great job that we want to offer you this opportunity to grow with us and move into management."

"Well, I'm pretty happy as a sales manager and I'm making more money than I've ever made," Mike said. "What kind of opportunities will I have if I accept the job?"

At this point the regional manager spoke up. "As office manager, you won't have to make calls in the evenings like you do as a rep or sales manager. You'll be hiring people, training them, working with your sales managers, and in general making sure everything in the office runs smoothly. You won't have to go out in the field unless you need to fill in for a sales manager occasionally. The way you'll be compensated is by getting overrides on what everyone under you produces; that includes all the reps and the sales managers too. If you do as well as office manager as you have as a rep and sales manager, you could easily double what you're making now."

Mike accepted the office manager position and arrived at the office to begin his new job with the same enthusiasm and energy that had served him so well in the past, but this time he quickly discovered that *the ability to do and the skill to manage are very different*. The first morning, two of his sales managers quit with no notice, apparently upset by the fact that they were overlooked for promotion. The office secretary turned in her resignation as well, but at least agreed to work a two-week notice. She'd found another job paying more and had agreed to take it.

Before he could sit down behind his desk for the first time, Mike had a handful of problems and the sudden realization that he knew nothing about managing. He was in over his head and sinking fast. Although he tried everything he could think of, the situation only got worse. His limited education did not include organizational skills, people skills, communication skills, or management techniques. Sure, he was great at persuading people to let him place a set of encyclopedias in their home and getting them to sign up for the research program, but trying to get 25 people to work together was something else entirely.

Instead of increasing the size of the office from 25 to 50 employees, within a month he was down to just 14 people, and many of them were considering quitting. He'd hired a new secretary, who was answering the phones, but his ad in the Help Wanted section of the newspaper was only producing an occasional call. After two weeks of interviews, he only had six new recruits to begin the next training class, the least since he'd started with the company. New placements from the Asheville office had fallen to less than half what they were when he took the job. No matter what he did, things just kept getting worse.

Eventually, he started going out in the field at nights himself in an effort to make placements to improve the office's performance. But this only created more dissatisfaction among the field reps because they thought he was taking business away from them. As he neared his next six-week evaluation, Mike knew he had failed. He also knew that he didn't have the skills to repair the damage he had done. He could hardly believe how difficult it was to supervise an entire office, especially after doing so well with the four people he'd supervised as a sales manager.

We think it's important to point out here that, although he didn't realize it at the time, Mike had taken over the office manager's job with a huge impediment hanging over his head. His district had just lost its best sales manager when the company moved him into management. The leadership of the company had evidently not thought this through,

The Ability to Do and the Skill to Manage Are Different

which tells you that even smart, successful people sometimes make stupid mistakes.

Roger learned this lesson over and over when he was president of a large real estate company in California. Whenever an office manager's job opened up, invariably the top salesperson in the office wanted the job. But being a great salesperson doesn't mean you'll be a great manager. And taking over an office that has just lost its top salesperson has all the ingredients of a recipe for failure.

When Mike was a sales manager, he wasn't in management. He was more of an extremely productive coworker than a manager. His willingness to make calls with his reps and work individually with each one endeared him to them and made them feel like he was one of them. When he became an office manager, however, he was suddenly placed in a different role. He could no longer make calls with everyone, and he didn't know how to communicate this fact in a way that gained him respect. Instead of teaching his sales managers how to do the things that had made him successful in that position, he held classes with everyone, reps and manager alike, and didn't realize that this undermined his sales manager with their reps.

Although he didn't know it at the time, Mike was learning some valuable lessons. Management is getting things done through other people. Leadership is not jumping in front of a crowd and yelling "Follow me," it's being the kind of person others want to follow. His limited education prevented him from understanding these basic principles of management, and in total frustration he tendered his resignation from the company.

Suddenly he found himself down in the dumps, with that sinking feeling of failure: embarrassed, insecure, and without a job. As he sat in his apartment on his first day of unemployment, he knew it was only a matter of time until his dad found out and would say, "See, I told you so!" Fortunately, he had saved a little money when he was doing well so he wasn't broke, but he knew he'd need to find a job soon. He had a nice landlord, but who nevertheless insisted on being paid on time. He had enough money to make it about two months before he would run out. Swallowing what little pride he had left, he walked down the street to pick up a newspaper.

He returned to his apartment and sat down with the newspaper. There were several listings under the Help Wanted heading, but the only one that interested him was a listing for a lab technician at a defense plant. Since he'd worked as a lab technician at the textile plant before going to the encyclopedia company, he decided to try it. His call was taken by a receptionist, who gave him little information. But when he told her he had worked in a lab before, she asked him to stop by and fill out an application.

Mike endured a little over a month of unemployment before he received a call from the defense plant offering him the job. When he accepted it, he had no idea that it would transition him from plant worker to Weekend Millionaire. In the next chapter we will explore some of the events that started Mike on the road to clarifying and defining his Weekend Millionaire Mindset.

Key Points from This Chapter

- The ability to do things yourself and the skill to manage others to do them are very different.
- Even intelligent, successful people do stupid things. Act on your own judgment, not on the convictions of others.
- Know your strengths and your weaknesses.
- Accepting promotions for which you are not qualified before learning the skills needed to do the job may make you feel important in the beginning but it can also lead to failure.

18

Learning Is an Everyday Task

Stung by failure in his recent management position, Mike began his new job at Northrop Carolina Incorporated with doubts about his abilities for the first time in his life. He had never before failed at anything he set his mind to doing. When he reported to work that first day, it was with serious reservations. Did he have enough education? What would be expected of him? With the Vietnam War raging and the company a defense contractor, everything was so secretive. His first stop was the personnel office, where he spent the entire morning filling out forms with information that would be checked and rechecked during the process of obtaining "Secret" security clearance.

After lunch, he was introduced to Dr. John Godfrey, a brilliant Ph.D. chemist under whom he would be working. Jack—as he was called by his coworkers—was a heavyset, balding gentleman with a pleasant demeanor and a hearty laugh. He welcomed Mike to the company and then spent the rest of the afternoon showing him around those areas of the plant and lab he could visit without the security clearance and discussing the job he would be doing. By the end of the day, Mike felt much more comfortable about his new position.

He was still stinging from his failure at management, but the thought that kept running through his mind was, "Positive, positive, positive!" How could he make something positive out of such a dismal failure? The job paid $80 per week, which was $20 more than he had been making at the textile plant, but it was still far below what he had earned as a field representative and sales manager with the encyclopedia company. At first the only positive thing he could think of was the fact that he was making more than before he left the textile plant, but then it dawned on him that the most positive part of his failure was that it taught him the importance of learning.

When we talk about learning, we're not talking about formal education. Education gives you tools; learning comes from the application of those tools. Many highly educated people are functionally illiterate in everyday life. They have vast stores of knowledge but seem to lack the ability to put it to work in ways that produce meaningful results.

Roger remembers that when he was president of the real estate company they hired a new agent who had formerly been a scientist at an aerospace company until he got laid off. He was a brilliant person. He was the first person in the history of the state of California to ace the state real estate license test. He got all 150 questions right! He even got a letter from the state real estate commissioner congratulating him on his remarkable accomplishment. The problem was, being smart doesn't guarantee results; he never sold a thing and quickly got out of the real estate business.

On the other hand, there are people with little formal education but with extraordinary abilities to apply what they have. People like the brilliant scientist often suffer from the paralysis of analysis, making few mistakes and accomplishing very little, while those with less education but with the ability to apply what they have, are prone to make mistakes, learn from them, make corrections, and accomplish much. Becoming a Weekend Millionaire happens when you combine action and accomplishment with study and analysis. The Weekend Millionaire Mindset is the frame of mind that allows you to do this.

After receiving some of the large paychecks from the encyclopedia company, Mike knew that his new job would only be a stepping-stone, not a career. He would use it to pay the bills while he improved his knowledge. From the very beginning, he noticed something the Ph.D. chemists were doing that intrigued him. Every week, each of them would bring in a new word, give its definition, and then challenge the others to use it in conversation as often as possible. Mike asked to participate in their game.

To illustrate the power of applying what you learn, Mike still remembers the first word he learned: "vitiate," which means to make imperfect, faulty, or impure; to spoil or corrupt. Although it has been more than 35 years, he still remembers the first sentence in which he used the word.

"I'm going to vitiate that smile on your face if you don't get off my back," he said to another lab technician who was making fun of him for playing the bosses' game.

"Whatever," his coworker replied; obviously having no clue what Mike was talking about and too embarrassed to ask.

This exchange taught Mike a valuable lesson about the difference between education and learning. Although he knew the meaning of the word "vitiate," his coworker didn't, and it was obvious that no communication had occurred. Sure, he may have momentarily impressed the coworker with his vocabulary—after all, he was just playing a game—but he later learned that his coworker perceived it as a self-serving insult and a put-down.

This exchange became a defining moment in the development of Mike's Weekend Millionaire Mindset. It also helped him understand why he had failed so miserably in his management position. The lesson is so simple that most people completely overlook it: *The burden of communication is on the person doing the talking*. However, the communicator often blames the listener for not understanding. As the great American philosopher Archie Bunker would say, "The problem, Edith, is that I'm talking to you in English and you're listening to me in Dingbat."

It makes no difference how well educated you are, how great your vocabulary, or how well you can perform a task yourself, if you can't communicate with others in a way they can understand, you are handicapped. From that day forward Mike vowed to practice speaking at a level equal to or just below that of the person with whom he was talking.

Another observation that left a lasting impression on Mike was the way experiments were conducted. Since his job was in a research laboratory, there was a constant search for new products and for improvements to old ones. What impressed him most was how experiment after experiment would fail before finally arriving at the right combination to produce the desired results. He was amazed at Dr. Godfrey's patience when they were working on a new project. If an experiment failed, the chemist would merely sit down at his desk, fully document everything about the experiment, and then give Mike another assignment to try.

As he observed this calculated approach to developing new products, it subconsciously worked its way into Mike's mindset and began to direct the rest of his life. He found himself applying the approach to life in general, and rather than viewing failures like the one at the encyclopedia company as permanent, he started looking at them as simply obstacles he had to get past by going over, around, or through. What he learned from conducting these experiments was not the old "If at first you don't succeed; try and try again," but rather, "If at first you don't succeed, try it another way."

Although he had no background other than one high school course in basic chemistry, the longer they worked together, the more Mike learned from Dr. Godfrey, and the more curious he became. Unlike the other lab technicians who came to work, did their jobs, and went home, Mike was constantly questioning the chemist and asking for explanations of each experiment he performed. He wasn't content to just pour some chemicals together, watch them bubble, time the reaction, and then tell Dr. Godfrey how much if any precipitate was produced; he wanted to know what caused the reactions, what they produced, and why.

Eventually his barrage of questions resulted in Dr. Godfrey calling him into his office for a consultation. He began by praising the work Mike was doing and his interest in learning. He complimented Mike on the precision of his work and the confidence he had developed in his ability to carry out tasks correctly. Then he got to the real point of the meeting. He pointed out that each time he had to stop and explain something, it pulled him away from his work and lessened his performance. He explained that it had taken him many years of undergraduate and postgraduate studies to get his doctorate in chemistry and that no matter how long they worked together,

Learning Is an Everyday Task

Mike would never understand all of the chemical reactions without going back to school and studying chemistry.

He must have seen the disappointment on Mike's face, because he quickly shifted gears and assured him that he didn't have to learn all about the chemical reactions, because that was his job. He assured Mike that he was performing well above expectations and would be willing to help him learn as much as time would permit, but that they couldn't stop after every experiment for a chemistry lesson. Then he gave Mike the best advice he has ever received.

If you will read an hour a day about something you know nothing about, within five years you will be amazed at the impact it will have on your life.

Mike was young and impressionable, and he had tremendous respect for Dr. Godfrey. As a result, he left the meeting with a commitment to himself that he would do just that. Although it was difficult in the beginning, he finally settled into a routine of reading about 30 minutes before going to sleep each night and about 30 minutes after he awoke each morning; a routine that he still maintains to this day.

He reads everything from the *Enquirer* to the Bible. Nothing is off limits. Some reading is technical, some instructive, some just pure pleasure; but he tries to learn something new from each thing he reads. It may be what's happening in Iraq, a new medicine being tested, how to design and build a bird house, how to deal with difficult people, the differences between men and women, the plight of minorities, new law enforcement techniques, a love story, a murder mystery, or thousands of other seemingly unrelated bits of information. This has been a major contributing factor in the development of his Weekend Millionaire Mindset, one that proudly includes a Ph.D. in Life from the University of Hard Knocks.

Roger and Mike live in very different homes on different sides of the country. But if you visited them, you would immediately see something they both have in common. Their homes are loaded down with books; books on the floor, books all the way up to the ceiling, books on the nightstand, and books in the kitchen. We both remember thinking, "Wouldn't it be amazing if every thought man or woman has ever had were written and made available to the rest of rest of the world? Wouldn't that be something?" Then we realized that it has already happened. Every worthwhile thought (and a few not so worthwhile, frankly) is already recorded. All you have to do is pick up the right book.

Throughout the next several months, Mike became extremely resourceful and gradually gained Dr. Godfrey's confidence that he could accomplish virtually any task he was given. Whether it was finding the source for a particular piece of equipment, conducting specialized tests, or locating resources within other parts of the plant, Mike was very successful. It was during this phase of his development that he learned another valuable lesson: *Opportunity knocks, it doesn't kick the door down!*

One Monday morning Dr. Godfrey called Mike into his office and told him he needed to have three "Danger—Keep Out" signs made that he could put up at a test area he would be using. Mike called all of the sign companies listed in the phone directory, but none of them could meet the two-day turnaround time Dr. Godfrey needed. Rather than having to report that he was unable to get the signs, he used the opportunity to exploit one of his other talents. He had always been artistically inclined, and though he had never used this talent to paint signs, he was confident he could do an acceptable job. That afternoon, he met with Dr. Godfrey and explained the situation.

"I've called every sign company listed in the phone book," he began, "but none of them can get the signs done by the day after tomorrow. The best I've been able to do is get them in a week."

"Well, I've got several tests I need to run on Thursday," Dr. Godfrey said, "and I need to have the area sealed off and signs up before I can run them. Could you look around the plant and see if you can find any that aren't being used?"

"I have another idea," Mike replied. "We have plywood and paint in the company's store. If you would approve it, I'd be willing to work overtime and make the signs myself. I could go get the plywood and paint now, and then after work I could get it cut to the size you need and get one coat of paint on it so it could dry overnight. I could go by a paint store after that, pick up a small brush to letter with, and then come in early tomorrow morning and put on a second coat. It would dry throughout the day, and then I could stay over tomorrow after work to get them lettered. That way they would be ready when you need them, and what I would make in overtime probably wouldn't be any more that what it would cost to have a sign company make them."

"Do you think you could make them look professional?" Dr. Godfrey asked.

"If you aren't satisfied, you don't have to pay me for my time," Mike said, "how's that?"

"Well, go ahead and get started," Dr. Godfrey replied. "These experiments are time critical, and I can't do them without putting up the signs at the test area."

This was an opportunity that knocked, and Mike took advantage of it. Not only did he get to pick up some extra income, but it gave him an opportunity to show that he could produce a nice-looking sign. When he undertook the project, he had no idea that it would ultimately lead him down a life-changing path.

Dr. Godfrey was so impressed with the signs that he brought them up in a management staff meeting a few days later. Within days Mike started receiving requests from other departments throughout the plant to make signs for them. It seemed that the ones he made, while not perfect, filled the needs of the plant and cost the departments considerably less than having them made at one of the local sign shops. Before he knew it he was working several hours overtime each week and bringing in a considerable amount of extra money. Within a few months, what started as a small opportunity had turned into an extra income stream that allowed Mike to save a little money for the first time since he worked for the encyclopedia company.

Then, as often happens, Mike was dealt another blow. After more than two years of loyal service, Dr. Godfrey called him into his office and dropped another bombshell in his life. The employees in the plant were aware that with the Vietnam War winding down, the plant was struggling to obtain new defense contracts. This had already caused some layoffs and more were expected, but no one thought it would affect the research lab. Wrong! Dr. Godfrey praised Mike for the fine job he had been doing but explained that the lab's budget had been cut and they were going to have to lay off some lab workers. Since he had the least seniority, Mike was going to be the first one laid off. He offered his regrets but told Mike that he had no control over the situation. The only good part was that he could work for two more weeks and then receive $300 in severance pay with his final paycheck.

Mike was stunned! He had heard about layoffs in other parts of the plant, but never dreamed that he would be affected. What was most troubling to him was the fact that of his last two jobs, he lost one because he wasn't performing and now was losing the other in spite of the fact that he was performing exceptionally well. These are the kinds of life-changing experiences that provide the impetus that propels some people to greatness and relegates others to failure. As our friend W. Mitchell, a great motivational speaker, says, "It's not what happens to you, it's what you do about it."

In this case, Mike was dealt an unfortunate and unexpected blow, but it recalled the advice he had been given by the psychiatrist when he was in high school: "You always have a choice. Just think positive, positive, positive." But what could be positive about losing his job; his livelihood? It is at low points in life like this one that many people take on an "O woe is me" attitude and never recover from it. They fail to realize that just as a chain is no stronger than its weakest link, a life is no better than one's ability to handle difficult times. Anyone can do well when everything is going right.

Mike had a choice, he could let the experience drag him down—and make matters worse—or he could look for a positive way to learn from the experience and get on with his life. In the next chapter, you'll learn how he handled this adversity and how it contributed to his Weekend Millionaire Mindset.

Key Points from This Chapter

- Increase your ability to communicate by learning to use words and phrases that your listeners understand.
- Learn from scientific research methods. If what you're doing isn't working, don't give up; just keep making adjustments until you find a way that does.
- Daily reading on a wide variety of subjects will not only expand your knowledge, it will have an amazing impact on your life.
- Opportunities don't always jump out at you; the best ones are often embedded in what appear to be problems.

Learning Is an Everyday Task

- View problems as opportunities to expand your knowledge, your skills, and to improve your life.
- It's not what happens to you. It's the way you react to what happens to you that determines whether you succeed or fail.

19

Seek Positive Advice When Setting Life's Goals

Most people, when dealt a blow like the loss of a job or some other unexpected event, seek out those who are going through similar adversities because they think these people will better understand their plight. Although they tell themselves they are looking for advice, what they really want is sympathy. The problem is, sympathy doesn't solve problems; in fact, more often than not it exacerbates the problems.

When Mike first received word of his pending layoff—or his downsizing, as we would say today—he felt the same way most people in that situation would feel. His first reaction was to contact a couple of former employees of the plant who had been laid off to see what they were doing. As expected, what he got were tales of disappointment and woe. They had been unable to find jobs, their severance pay was running out, and so were their savings. Bills were piling up and they were at a loss as to what they would do. None of his conversations with these people gave Mike any hope or positive suggestions; in fact, they were downright depressing.

Seek Positive Advice When Setting Life's Goals

He remembered the advice Dr. Godfrey had given him months before, when he was just 19 years old, to read an hour a day. Since then, one of the books he had read was on goal setting. At the time he was reading it, it was dull and boring and wasn't of great interest to him. Now Mike was about to experience the first major impact the suggestion of reading an hour a day would have on his life. Facing the loss of his job and an unknown future, he recalled the message he had distilled from the book: *If you don't have goals you don't have direction.* Now when he asked himself, "What do I want out of life?" he realized that he had no idea!

This revelation was another turning point in Mike's life. Now, rather than think about where he could find another job, he was instead consumed with thoughts about what he really wanted out of life. Based on his limited work experience, he couldn't see working a job as anything more than providing him with a living. But he wanted more out of life than just a mere existence. He had dreams of living in a nice home, driving nice cars, taking exciting vacations, having a boat, and any number of other things people associate with wealth. The problem was, he couldn't see himself ever having these things if he continued as he had been.

Then he remembered what he had read: that goals, to be meaningful, must be specific, doable, and have a time frame for completion. And he began to comprehend that *wishes are not goals; goals are what make wishes come true.* What he needed were inspiring goals to guide him in life; goals that, once accomplished, would provide the things for which he wished.

The more he thought about it, the more aware he became that what he longed for more than anything was financial success. Although he was still young, he was already tired of worrying about where he would get the money for even his basic needs. He recalled the struggle he had gone through to get his first bicycle when he was just a child. He recalled many other times when people around him were able to purchase things he would have loved to have, or were doing things he would have liked to do. Now he was facing the loss of his job and the prospect of having to count his money before he could go through the checkout line at the grocery store. He didn't want to live that way.

The Learning Years

One night as he lay in bed pondering the impending financial difficulties facing him, he suddenly sat bolt upright and yelled, "Why can't I be rich?" As he sat there, with the words still echoing off the bare walls, it dawned on him that the biggest reason was he didn't have a goal to become rich. How could he expect to achieve a goal he didn't have? How would he even know if he made it if he had never defined "rich"? He stayed awake for hours pondering the future, and finally arrived at a simple statement that defined the goal and would guide him for the next 30 years.

He picked up a note pad and wrote: *I will become a millionaire by age 30 and retire by age 50.*

That's all it said; nothing fancy, no comments or suggestions about how to do it, just a simple statement about what he would do and when he would do it. He folded the note, put it in his wallet next to his money, got back into bed and went to sleep.

The next morning, he took the note out, unfolded it, and looked at what he'd written. *I will become a millionaire by age 30 and retire by age 50.* As he stared at the words and contemplated the possibilities, a chilling thought passed through his mind: "Is this really possible or am I just kidding myself?" When he thought of his $80 weekly salary, he took out a pencil and multiplied it by 52 weeks. It came to $4,160! That was his salary for a whole year. When he divided it into $1 million, he couldn't help but laugh at the result. Based on what he was making, it would take a little over 240 years just to earn a million dollars, let alone be worth that much, and for the first time he understood the power of goals. The written goal to become a millionaire by age 30 let him see that finding another $80 a week factory job was not the way to go. It didn't tell him what he should do, but it definitely showed him what not to do.

Recalling the advice his mother had given him as a child, "If you want it badly enough, you'll find a way to get it," Mike knew that if he wanted to be successful he would have to *learn from winners, not losers*. If his goal was to build wealth and become financially independent, he would need to seek advice from people who knew something about the subject. The only suggestion he received from the laid-off plant workers was to apply for unemployment. He needed to seek advice from successful people—people who had achieved success, or at least understood what success was. And he most assuredly wouldn't find these people in the unemployment lines.

During his final week of employment at the plant, Mike discussed his goal with Dr. Godfrey. When he showed him the paper where he had written down the goal, it brought a bit of a chuckle, and the comment, "Well, I wish you luck."

Mike laughed with him, but as he started out the door, he turned and said, "I didn't mean to bother you, but I'm going to have to do something other than what I'm doing now. Last night I figured out that it would take me over 240 years just to earn a million dollars at what I'm making here. I thought you might have a suggestion or two."

"Mike, having goals is great, but they need to be realistic," Dr. Godfrey replied. "Do you really believe you can become a millionaire by age 30?"

"I don't know," Mike said. "The idea came to me a few nights ago, I wrote it down, and now I'm looking for ways that can help me make it happen. I know it seems impossible right now, but until I give it my best effort, I'll never know for sure whether it's possible or not. Now, I'm exploring all my options and looking for the best way to get started."

"Have you thought of going into business for yourself?" Dr. Godfrey asked.

"No," Mike answered. "What kind of business could I go into?"

"Have you thought of starting a sign business?" he replied. "You've been making signs for the plant and they're quite good. Maybe you could do that for other businesses and create a good business for yourself. I don't know if it will make you a millionaire, but if you work hard and are successful, you can probably make more than you're making here."

That comment started Mike thinking. He had thought about continuing to make signs as a sideline to supplement his other income, but not about making that his full-time business. He decided to research the idea. The rest of that week, as soon as he got off work, he started visiting businesses throughout the area. He talked with the owners of restaurants, car dealerships, motels, real estate companies, and any other business owners who would spend a few minutes with him. All of them encouraged him to start a sign business and promised to give him work if he did. Finally, he called his mother in Virginia.

"Mom, I've got a bit of news for you," he said. "I've been laid off from my job. Friday was my last day, but don't worry, I think I'm going to go into business for myself."

"Doing what?" she asked.

"I've been making signs for the plant for the last several months, so what I've decided to do is start a sign company," he said. "They gave me $300 in severance pay and I've decided to use it to buy a van to work out of and a few supplies to get me started. I've talked with several business people and they all encouraged me and said they would give me work to do, but that's not the main reason for my call. What I'm more excited about is the goal I've set for myself."

"And what's that?" she asked.

"Mom, I'm going to become a millionaire by age 30 and retire by age 50," he replied. "What do you think of that?"

Then, just as Mike anticipated, she said, "That's a pretty big goal, but if you think you can do it, I'll bet you can find a way."

When he hung up with his mother, Mike placed one more call, this one to his father, to whom he had hardly spoken since he moved out to take the job with the encyclopedia company. He didn't call looking for approval for the decision he'd made; he merely wanted to inform his dad about what had happened with his job at the plant. The conversation was short and to the point. He told his dad about being laid off, and the response he received was not unexpected.

"So what are you going to do now?" his dad asked.

"I've decided to go into business for myself," Mike replied.

That brought the same question his mother had asked: "Doing what?"

"I've been painting signs at the plant for the past few months, so I've decided to go in business making signs for businesses."

"That's the biggest crock of &%#$ I've ever heard of," his dad yelled into the phone. "You'd better get a job and go to work. That's even worse than that stupid idea you had about selling encyclopedias."

And with that discouraging comment, Mike began a trek that would take him on a wild and sometimes frightening journey to becoming a millionaire. The contrasting opinions he had gotten from these back-to-back calls allowed him to see just how encouraging or discouraging other people's opinions could be. From that day forward, he vowed to never let negative people influence his decisions again. As a result, he would not talk with his father for more than three years.

Key Points from This Chapter

- Avoid people who spend their time complaining and griping; surround yourself with people who are inspirational.
- Set specific goals and let them guide you on your journey through life.
- Determine if what you are doing will get you where you want to go in life. If not, make adjustments.

20

Believe in Yourself, Cancel the Pity Party

When life deals unexpected disappointments, difficulties, hardships, adversities, and other suffering, it can be discouraging. When dreams are shattered, it can be a devastating blow if you let it. Everyone has bad things happen that they didn't expect. It may be the loss of a job, an accident, an illness, divorce, the loss of a loved one, or any of a thousand other unfortunate occurrences that disrupt their lives. It's up to each person, based upon his character, to decide whether that disruption will be temporary or permanent.

Some people have a run of bad luck and use it as an excuse to give up on life. They're easy to spot by their hangdog looks and lack of enthusiasm. The problem is, these people become so focused on looking backward that they run head on into new problems and disappointments that could easily have been avoided had they been looking forward. What has happened in the past cannot be changed. No matter how much you focus on past events, they will still be the same. The past is of no value unless you learn from it. Then its value only arises if you apply what you learn to make better decisions today, because it is today's successes that bury past disappointments and bring brighter futures.

As we've mentioned a few times already, we hope you're reading this with a note pad at your side. As we take you through some of Mike's experiences and the valuable life lessons he learned, we want you to make notes when these stories trigger thoughts about experiences from your past. This is an important exercise, because you are going to learn how to use the events from your life to develop your own Weekend Millionaire Mindset.

Mike's first year in business was difficult. He expended far more time, energy, and effort than he had the previous year. But after 12 exhausting months, he had earned only $3,200; considerably less than his annual salary at the plant. He was struggling just to keep food on the table. At this point, it would have been easy to give up and quit, especially after having failed in the management position at the encyclopedia company, been laid off from his last job, and now hit with declining income when he tried to start his own business. But Mike didn't think that way; although he wasn't aware of it at the time, he was gradually developing the Weekend Millionaire Mindset that would bring him later success.

Sure, his income was down, but his knowledge was up and his spirits were high; he decided to *believe in himself and cancel the pity party*. Unlike his last two jobs, he was in control of this one. He didn't have to worry about being fired or downsized; what he had to guard against was succumbing to the negative influence of other people. Had he been focused on the past, he might have been tempted to quit, but instead of being discouraged, he viewed this first year in business for himself as an investment, one that would pay dividends in the future.

The biggest lesson he learned was also one of the simplest: *Investing requires sacrifice*. Whether it's time or money, investing means setting it aside for future benefit. If you invest time in learning a skill, that same time can't be used to go fishing, watch a movie, or do some other fun activity. If you invest money in equipment to start a business, that money can't be used to buy a boat, a motorcycle, or to purchase some other fun toy. As we discussed in Chapter 7, getting from birth to death has a cost. What you spend today pays for today, but what you invest today pays for tomorrow.

The Learning Years

Mike would look back at this first year as an investment because his time was spent learning the business. He learned that there was a special type of paint used for signs, special brushes made specifically for lettering, a special type of plywood with a smooth coating made especially for signs, and that using these resulted in much higher quality signs. He spent hours practicing lettering techniques and styles, and learning how to lay out designs with balance so the lettering could be easily read. He learned that quality was key when it came to signs. They were to a business as clothes are to people—providing the look from which customers formed first impressions and often made decisions on whether to patronize an establishment. Imagine how you would feel about eating in a restaurant if its sign looked amateurishly made, was dirty, and the paint was peeling. It wouldn't present a very appetizing appearance, would it?

This learning investment began soon after he made the commitment to sell signs. He had made several calls on a real estate company that used many signs throughout the area, and was unsuccessful at convincing the company to buy his signs. This surprised him because, when he was learning how to price his work, he'd made anonymous calls to several other sign companies to get price quotes, and so he knew that the prices he was quoting were less than what the real estate company was currently paying. Finally, he pointedly asked the real estate broker why he kept getting his signs elsewhere when he could get them cheaper from him. The answer he got changed his entire outlook on business.

"Mike, I like you, but your work is a little rough for me," the broker said. "These signs are my image to the public, and I'm willing to pay a higher price for a more professional look."

That comment convinced Mike that he needed to invest time in learning the sign business and improving the quality of his work. As we mentioned in Chapter 6, with youthful naiveté, Mike paid a visit to one of the established sign shops in the area, where he met the owner, Dave Cheadle. When he explained that he was trying to get started in business, Dave welcomed him into his shop and spent hours helping and encouraging him. He showed Mike the right materials to use, explained how to lay the signs out for good balance, taught him the best color combinations to use for good readability, and even offered to let him make some signs in his shop so he could provide hands-on guidance. There was never a hint that he viewed Mike as a competitive threat to his business.

The time Mike spent learning and practicing the techniques Dave taught him was time he wasn't earning any income. It was time invested. The new brushes, paint, and other supplies he bought cost money, but it was money invested. The time that Dave spent helping a youngster get started was also time invested, but not an investment for which he ever expected to receive monetary compensation. As Mike would learn years later, Dave Cheadle was one of those rare individuals who placed helping others above helping himself. He must have subscribed to the idea that success stops when you do, because today, in his late 70s, Dave still goes to work each day at the sign shop where he taught Mike so much, more than 37 years ago.

Mike was different; his idea of success was spelled out in his written goal: *I will become a millionaire by age 30 and retire by age 50.* He was quickly learning that accomplishing that goal would be impossible without investing a tremendous amount of time, energy, and money. That's why he wasn't discouraged by the meager $3,200 he earned during his first year in business. He had made a substantial investment and was looking forward to the coming year; a year that would prove to pay big dividends and from which he would both earn and learn more on his journey to becoming a millionaire.

Key Points from This Chapter

- Bad things happen to everyone. It's your character that determines whether this will be a brief setback or a permanent disruption to your life.
- Don't use bad luck as an excuse to drop out of life. Take a brief look back to learn from what you did wrong, and then focus on the future.
- Investing in your future means using some of your time and your assets to make your future better even if it reduces what you can do today.
- Have the courage to ask other people to help you.
- Don't be discouraged if progress toward your goal is slow at first. The fact that you're making progress is more important in the beginning than the amount of progress you're making.

21

People Continue to Help Those Willing to Help Themselves

Mike's second year in business was a testament to the investment of time and energy made during his first year. By the end of it, his profits were slightly over $12,600, nearly four times as much as the previous year and the most he'd made in any year since he began working. And his profits would actually have been substantially greater had he not made a big blunder that he'd decided to pay for—which is an interesting story, and one that taught Mike a lot.

During his first year, Mike's jobs had consisted of small incidental signs that only brought in a few dollars each. But early in the second year, he landed his first big job. A local restaurant owner contracted with him to paint the word RESTAURANT on the wall of a building. The building was made of masonry block and was painted a light gray. The owner wanted the letters painted in red down the side of a windowless wall that faced a highway. The job would bring in several hundred dollars.

Mike was excited that he would finally have the opportunity to prove to the business community that he could do a large job as well as the small token jobs he had been doing. The letters on the building would be five feet tall and extend nearly 50 feet down the side of the building. Since he only had two ladders with a walk board between them to work from, he decided he would start in the middle of the wall and letter in both directions to get the word centered on the wall. He was about to learn the meaning of the old saying, "Measure twice, cut once."

Maybe because he was caught up in the enthusiasm of doing such a big job, or maybe he was already counting his money, but for some reason when he located the center point of the wall, he laid out the letter *T* on the left side of centerline and the letter *R* on the right side. He then continued to work to the right, adding the letters *ANT* and then moved back to the *T* and continued to the left, adding the letters *SER* in that sequence. When he finished the final letter *R*, he stepped back to admire his work, which looked great, except for the fact that neatly lettered down the side of the building was the word RESTRANT. His heart nearly stopped.

Before he could get up the courage to go inside and tell the restaurant owner what he had done, a customer pulled up in the parking lot and yelled, "Hey, you spelled 'Restaurant' wrong!" It was the last thing he needed to hear.

With his head down and butterflies in his stomach, Mike walked into the restaurant with the customer. When the restaurant owner greeted them, he must have sensed something was amiss because he looked at Mike and said, "What's wrong?"

"I've really screwed up," Mike said.

"What happened?" the owner asked.

"I wish I had an excuse," Mike began, "but the bottom line is, I just screwed up. I spelled 'Restaurant' wrong."

"You did what?"

"I spelled 'Restaurant' wrong," Mike repeated. "I left the *au* out of the middle."

The two of them walked out to look. Business people are not all greedy, self-centered, abusive individuals, as they're often portrayed. The generosity shown him by Dave Cheadle when he was trying to learn the business is a good example of this. If they've been in business any length of time and had any success, they've made some mistakes too.

The restaurant owner could have blown up and started screaming at Mike, but he just looked at the wall and laughed. "It looks like you're a better sign painter than you are speller," he said.

"I'm really sorry," Mike said. "Whatever it takes, I'll fix it."

At this point, Mike experienced another example of what he'd learned as a child: *that even as adults people continue to help those willing to help themselves.*

"Don't worry about it," the restaurant owner said. "I've got a couple of gallons of paint that were left over from when we painted the outside. You can use it to cover up the mistake and then letter it again."

Mike was so relieved that he immediately took the leftover building paint and quickly covered up his error where the lettering was dry enough to paint over. By the end of the day he had it completely covered. He waited until the next day, to give the paint time to dry, but when he returned to reletter the wall, he noticed that the old lettering was still visible. There wasn't enough leftover paint to put on a second coat, so he took the partial bucket that was left to the paint store, purchased two additional gallons, returned to the restaurant and applied a second coat over the lettering.

The following day it was obvious where he'd covered the old lettering; not because the lettering was still showing through, but because the fresh paint was nice and clean and the rest of the wall was weathered. Remembering the real estate broker's comment about signs representing his image to the public and his willingness to pay more for a professional job, Mike returned to the paint store, purchased additional paint, and repainted the entire side of the building.

When he finished relettering RESTAURANT on the building, he gave the owner an invoice for his work along with two fresh gallons of paint to replace what he'd used to correct his mistake. The owner was so impressed with the way Mike had handled the mistake that he gave him a letter of recommendation and told him to feel free to have anyone call him if he needed a personal reference.

By the time he finished the job, what was to have been a several hundred dollar profit turned into a loss, but the experience was invaluable. Sure, it was a disappointment to lose money on his first big job, but he had received a great deal of personal satisfaction from correcting his mistake, and the real benefits were yet to come.

Mike didn't know it at the time, but a local business group met once a month for breakfast at the restaurant. At their next meeting, the restaurant owner stood up and told the story about what had happened to the side of his building. One of the people attending that meeting later told Mike that the owner had given him the highest of praise for the way he'd handled the mistake and urged everyone in attendance to give him all of their sign work. This same businessman invited Mike to attend their next meeting as his guest.

When he showed up for the meeting, Mike was greeted with open arms. It seemed that everyone wanted to rib him about the spelling mistake, but it was all in fun. Once the meeting began, Mike was introduced and asked to say a few words about his new business. He was nervous when he got up in front of this group of businesspeople, and began by giving them a brief account of how he got started making signs for the plant. He followed by telling them about being laid off and his decision to go into business for himself. He also discussed his first year in business and explained how he had nearly starved to death trying to learn the business.

And once again learned that *people continue to help those willing to help themselves*. Before he left the meeting that morning, eight business owners had given him their cards and asked him to call on them about doing their sign work. This was the beginning of a dramatic increase in business that resulted in increasing his profits nearly fourfold his second year.

When he stopped to reflect on his success, he was excited and extremely enthusiastic, until he compared it with his written goals. His $12,600 profits were great, but it had taken nearly all of his time to produce the work. Just as he had when contemplating the future after being laid off from the plant, Mike took out his goal sheet, looked at it, and divided $12,600 into $1 million. Wow, he had really made an improvement; at this rate it would only take him a little over 79 years instead of 240 years to earn a million dollars. But even at that, becoming a millionaire meant having a net worth of a million dollars ... quite a difference.

Once again, focused on his goal sheet, Mike saw that he had earned nearly four times as much his second year as he did his first. He took out a calculator and did some multiplication. Four times $12,600 is $50,400. Four times $50,400 is $201,600. Four times $201,600 is $806,400. Four times $806,400 is $3,225,600. That's just four years of quadrupling profits. He still had six years before he would turn 30. Could he do it?

When he looked at the numbers, he knew that his goal was very optimistic, but he had faith in himself. He saw that he would have to spend his time doing more profitable jobs and at the same time find a way to invest part of his time in the creation of assets that would pay him into the future.

Although this is the last chapter in the section about the learning years, it doesn't mean that you should stop learning. As we transition to the next part, "The Earning Years," you will see that there are still lessons to learn, but these lessons merely enhance earnings; they are not a search for earnings, like Mike experienced when he was trying to "find himself." He had set a huge goal, established the course he would take to achieve this goal, and was ready to embark upon his earning years.

Key Points from This Chapter

- You're responsible for cleaning up your own messes. If you make a mistake, admit it, and fix it quickly, whatever it costs you.
- Treat people right and they will become your biggest supporters.
- If you are given a chance to stand up in front of a group and tell them what you do for a living, jump at it, even it scares you half to death.

PART IV

The
Earning Years

The earning years, as we define them, begin when individuals commit to career decisions and settle into consistent courses of action that determine the kind of future they will experience. Most of us attempt a number of jobs in our youth before we settle into a career. While Mike worked in textiles, selling encyclopedias, and in a defense-related research lab before making his commitment to the sign business, some people try five, 10, 15, or more jobs before settling into a career. Some enter the earning years early, some late, and, unfortunately, some never make it.

The Weekend Millionaire Mindset is a thought process through which the average working person can build wealth and ultimately become a millionaire. Career selections are not as important as the choices people make throughout their lives. Developing this mindset entails accepting personal responsibility, developing a pattern of investing, tracking where your money goes, developing a plan for success, keeping on track, repelling negative influences, and continuing to learn. In this part we will take you through a number of situations that will teach you how to make the kinds of decisions that will propel you to financial success.

The journey to financial independence is a slow and often difficult one, but one everyone can enjoy with the right mindset. Goal setting is so important to this journey that we devote an entire chapter to it in the next part; however, just a mention of it here may help you to better understand the part you are about to read.

One of the great tragedies we've observed throughout the years is the number of people who remain in their learning years most if not all of their lives because they have no goals. We watch them start down one career path, hit an obstacle, change careers, hit another obstacle, and change careers again and again and again. They never stick with anything long enough to realize success. Have you ever noticed that there are people who have become very wealthy in virtually any enterprise you can name? Have you also noticed that whatever the venture, there are usually many more people just surviving than becoming wealthy? Why? Could it be that the successful ones had goals and the unsuccessful ones just had wishes and dreams?

Mike's life changed when he set his goal to become a millionaire by age 30 and retire by age 50. As we take you through this part, you will learn that he never lost his focus on his goal. When he encountered obstacles, he found ways to go through them, over them, or around them. When faced with problems, he looked for solutions rather than excuses. One of the more important things he did was continue to learn, but probably the most important was to continually measure his performance. He didn't measure it against what others were doing, but against his own prior performance, which he then compared with his personal goals.

As we saw in the last part, if Mike had compared his first year performance with other people in the area who were in the sign business, he would have seen himself as a dismal failure. Although much improved, if he had compared his second year performance with others, he still would have looked like a failure. But because he compared the second year with the first, he was enthused and excited instead of being depressed. Without the goal to guide him, he might have quit before the end of his first year. Having his goal forced him to measure where he was against where he wanted to be, so he could determine if he was on track or needed to make adjustments.

It was during the examination of his first year's performance that he determined much of his time had been invested in improving himself so he could perform better in future years. Likewise, the examination of his second year's performance, compared with the first, revealed just how much that investment had paid off. The improvement showed him he was on track, but the distance he remained from his goal showed him that he still had much more to do.

Financial success is achieved one step at a time; it doesn't come overnight. One of the big fallacies people have is that wealthy people are just lucky. Sure, some were lucky enough to be born into wealth, but they're not the people for whom this book is written. Wealth doesn't just happen! Ask anyone who has created wealth on his or her own, first generation earners, and they will tell you it didn't happen overnight. They laid one small success on top of another until it became a big success. That's what the Weekend Millionaire Mindset is all about: developing the right frame of mind to "build" rather than to "attain" success. You can't arrive without taking the journey, and that's what this part is about.

The basic fundamentals of Mike's Weekend Millionaire Mindset were established during his formative years and learning years. In his earning years he perfected and polished these fundamentals as he laid one small success on top of another. As you will see, most of his success came not because he hit some lucky jackpot or had divine revelations come to him later in life, but from the consistent application of these fundamentals. In this part you will learn that building wealth and becoming a millionaire is something every working person can accomplish with patience, persistence, and a plan of action. Yes, setbacks can happen, but whether they remain setbacks or turn into ruin depends entirely on how you respond.

22

Accepting Personal Responsibility

Accepting personal responsibility means different things to different people. For some it merely means admitting mistakes when they make them. This has a depressing connotation, because with admitting mistakes there is usually an apology and acceptance of whatever punishment is meted out. In the end, the perpetrators feel absolved of further responsibility, and cleansed because they admitted their mistakes and paid the price for them.

Accepting personal responsibility for mistakes is one thing, but for wealth builders, it is quite different. When they set goals and commit to them, they accept responsibility for overcoming obstacles in order to complete the journey to achieving the goals. Mistakes are considered a part of that journey, not a reason to abandon it. A big part of developing the Weekend Millionaire Mindset involves understanding this concept. People who make mistakes, offer their apology, accept their punishment but lack the courage to try again, will never be wealth builders. That's one of the reasons why so many people change careers over and over. They just can't seem to face their peers after making a mistake or being reprimanded for shortcomings.

Accepting Personal Responsibility

Many people allow those around them to determine their destiny. They refuse to accept personal responsibility, are afraid to attempt new ventures without the approval of their friends or relatives, and, as our friend Zig Ziglar says, they become "SNIOPed"—Stymied by the Negative Influence of Other People.

Until you can accept personal responsibility for your actions, knowing that you will occasionally make mistakes, you will never understand that occasionally when the majority disagrees with you, it just means that all the fools are on the same side. If Christopher Columbus had failed to understand this concept, we might still be afraid to venture out to sea for fear of sailing off the edge. Having a Weekend Millionaire Mindset gives you confidence to make decisions and accept responsibility, knowing that some of them will be wrong. It opens your mind to allow you to learn from your errors, correct them, and avoid making similar ones in the future.

As Mike began his third year in business, an incident occurred that illustrates how accepting personal responsibility had a profound effect on the rest of his life. Bowling was a pastime that Mike enjoyed, and in time he became very proficient at it, bowling only the second perfect game in western North Carolina history and eventually becoming a member of the Professional Bowlers Association (PBA). But this story isn't about his bowling abilities, it's about an incident while he was bowling that demonstrated how far he had drifted away from the advice the psychiatrist had given him in high school. It's about how he accepted responsibility and by doing so changed his life for the better.

At the center where he bowled, there was a men's group called the Executive League, made up entirely of businessmen. It consisted of 10 four-man teams, and since Mike was in business for himself, he was invited to join one of the teams. Right from the start, he carried the highest average in the league and was recognized as a fiery competitor. His competitiveness and quick temper also made him the target of occasional unkind words from the other businessmen. One evening, he was on a long string of strikes, thinking of another possible perfect game. He rolled a ball perfectly into the one-three pocket, which should have produced another strike. Instead, it blasted all of the pins into the pit except for the eight pin, which didn't move.

"Damn it!" he yelled as he turned around and kicked the ball return.

The bowler on the lane next to him was a small mild-mannered man, Don Collins, who was in the mobile home business. When Mike kicked the ball return, it disrupted Don's approach and he rolled his ball into the gutter. When he came back to the ball return, Mike was still fuming over the eight pin as he waited for his ball to come back so he could roll again.

Don, who seemed to never get upset or raise his voice, turned to Mike and said, "Why don't you stop acting like an ignorant fool and just enjoy the game."

"Sorry," Mike replied sarcastically. "Did I make you mad?"

"No, you didn't make me mad," Don said calmly. "It takes someone smarter than me to make me mad."

Stung by Don's comment, for which he didn't have a comeback, Mike rolled his ball, made the spare, and sat down. Finally, what Don had said sunk in. "It takes someone smarter than me to make me mad" was a sentence that would stick with him for the rest of his life. Sure, he had been mad when he kicked the ball return; he was known throughout the league for his hot temper and short fuse. Mike had been making poor choices, allowing little things to upset him. That was his fault, not anyone else's, yet he was subjecting people around him to bad behavior because of his poor choices.

Don had made a better choice. Rather than engaging in a heated altercation, he clearly let Mike know that he wasn't going to allow the mocking behavior to intimidate him or cause him to react negatively. It was a staggering experience that Mike would not forget. It brought back memories of the advice the psychiatrist had given him years before, to think *positive, positive, positive* before responding, and if you can't come up with something positive, just don't say anything.

He sat quietly between frames as they concluded the evening's match, then went up to Don and apologized for his behavior. Don graciously accepted the apology, but never knew the profound impact of the incident. From that moment forward, Mike vowed to take personal responsibility for his actions and never again let anyone think they were smart enough to make him lose control of his emotions. Since that day, he has used that same line many times with hotheads who tried to engage him in heated discussions.

This was just one of many incidents that taught Mike the power of accepting personal responsibility in his life. The more he assumed responsibility for control of his actions, the more his business career flourished. He was also learning that accepting responsibility encompassed much more than just controlling his temper and making a few decisions. It also included accepting personal responsibility for developing the right mindset if he expected to reach his goals, which meant expunging any negative mental baggage he might still be carrying.

As his third year in business for himself was drawing to a close, Mike found himself struggling with some of this mental baggage. Although it was years in the past, the bad memories he harbored of his stepfather, Paul, and the estrangement from his natural father, weighed heavily on his mind. The animosity and hard feelings still lingered, and they were becoming burdens he needed to unload. He had proven he could make it on his own, so it no longer mattered what his father thought of his career choice. Plus the hatred he once held for Paul didn't seem to matter anymore. What mattered was the strained relationship with his family.

Deciding to take personal responsibility and mend fences, as soon as he completed his accounting for the third year of his business, he took his financial statements and went to visit his dad, who was still working as a bookkeeper. When Mike laid out his statements showing $3,200 profits his first year, Lee wasn't impressed. When he then laid down the statement for his second year showing that he had made $12,600, Lee looked up. That was more than he had made at his bookkeeping job. And when Mike laid down the statement for his third year showing profits of more than $55,000, Lee was shocked.

"That's not bad, boy," he said.

"Well, I just wanted you to know that I wasn't starving to death," Mike replied. He paused long enough for his dad to look at the statement again, and then he continued, "As you can see, the business is growing and I'm doing quite well, but that's not the real reason for my visit. I just wanted to come by and let you know that I have no hard feelings about the problems we had earlier. We just had different opinions, and I don't think either of us knew how to deal with them. I'd like to put those feelings behind us and discuss a business proposition with you.

"The business is doing so well that I'm going to need a bookkeeper before too long. I'd like for you to consider coming to work for me. I don't want an answer now, but I'd just like for you to be thinking about it. I'd also like to invite you to come by and visit the business so you can see what I'm doing."

"Well son, I don't know what to say," Lee responded.

"You don't have to say anything," Mike replied. "I just wanted to clear the air between us and ask you to think about it. You don't need to tell me anything until you feel comfortable about it."

That brief discussion reopened the relationship between them and removed one of Mike's burdens. One thing he noticed was that his dad had referred to him as "son" for the first time.

(Incidentally, Lee came to work for Mike two years later and worked for him until his death 10 years afterward, in 1986.)

After exceeding his goal of quadrupling his earnings over his second year, Mike decided he could afford to purchase a small sign crane for use in the business. He used this purchase as an excuse to attempt to heal the wounds with his stepfather. He had purchased a used truck in Asheville and made a deal to buy a used crane from the company in Kansas. That meant he would have to drive the truck to Kansas, a two-day trip, wait for the crane to be mounted, then drive it back. He called his stepfather Paul Kiser and asked if he would make the trip with him to keep him company. He knew they would be together at least six days, which would give them adequate time to hash out their differences. Paul accepted his offer and agreed to drive down from Bluefield to go with him.

They left Asheville on Saturday, heading west on Interstate 40 toward Tennessee. The plan was to make it make it to Sikeston, Missouri, the first day, then complete the drive to Ottawa, Kansas, on Sunday. Mike wanted to have the truck at the factory first thing Monday morning so they could start work on attaching the crane right away.

From the time Paul accepted his invitation, Mike knew the first day would be difficult, and it was. Their talk was strained and neither one of them could keep a conversation going. One would ask a question, the other would give a terse response, and there would then be silence until someone could think of another question to ask. The type of ongoing dialogue most people enjoy when traveling was nonexistent. They were both uncomfortable, and it showed.

Accepting Personal Responsibility

As the day wore on—and it did "wear" on—the atmosphere became increasingly tense. They stopped to stretch their legs and get lunch at a McDonald's in central Tennessee, went inside, ordered, and ate. Neither said a word. When they climbed back into the truck and headed west again, Mike didn't know how to begin to try to clear the air between them. Paul was probably just as uncomfortable, but he didn't make any effort to change things either.

They rode for nearly an hour with hardly a word spoken between them. Mike used this period of silence to contemplate the best way to open a dialogue about the subject he'd invited Paul along to discuss. Finally, he realized that it was he who had invited Paul, not the other way around. He would have to take personal responsibility for not only beginning, but also for bringing the conversation to a satisfactory conclusion if he expected to relieve himself of the burden he had been carrying.

"This is crazy," he finally said, breaking the silence.

"What?" Paul replied.

"The way we're acting. Here we are, two grown men riding together on a long trip, and not even speaking to each other."

"I thought that was the way you wanted it," Paul said.

At this point, Mike decided there wasn't a good or tactful way to broach the subject, so he decided to just jump in, speak his mind, and see what happened.

"The reason I invited you to come with me is because I want to talk about the feelings I've had toward you and why I left the way I did," he began. "I hated your guts growing up. I felt like you were totally unfair and even abusive at times. When I ran off at Grandma Sallie's, I vowed that I would never live with you again, nor would I ever have anything to do with you. I was so bitter, my insides were boiling with anger.

"But that was a long time ago, and I've since learned that a lot of my problems were self-initiated. I never let you know about it, but I went to a psychiatrist while I was in school in Abingdon. My anger was so intense that it caused problems for me there just as it had in Bluefield. I've never forgotten that visit to the psychiatrist or the advice he gave me. He helped me understand that my negative reactions usually made my problems worse. Once I started thinking positively and reacting accordingly, things actually did start getting better.

"I don't want to go back and rehash the past; I don't see that it would serve any purpose. I invited you to come on this trip so we could try to put the past behind us and let bygones be bygones. Now that I look back, I'm sure some of the things you did were caused by my behavior. I just want you to know that I accept full responsibility for all the problems we had and I apologize. Even if some of them were your fault, I forgive you. I just want to unburden myself with the guilt I've been carrying because of our strained relationship and the difficult position in which it has placed my mother."

"I don't know what to say," Paul replied.

"No reply is needed," Mike said. "I've gotten it off my chest, I've put the past behind me and sincerely apologized; that's all I can do. Now it's up to you whether or not you choose to accept my apology and put the past behind you."

Paul just sat there for a few moments, looking stunned. Then he shifted in his seat so he could face Mike and said, "You don't need to apologize. I was probably as much at fault as you were. I don't know when it started, but the older you got, the harder it was for me to deal with you. I know I did some things I probably shouldn't have done also, so I'll apologize as well."

"Apology accepted," Mike said.

"I'm glad we had this discussion," Paul continued. "I've also been troubled by the way we parted. In fact, I accepted the offer to go with you hoping we could resolve our differences. I never meant to be unreasonable or abusive; I just didn't know how to handle you, and the fact that you were my stepson made it even more difficult. It seemed like every time I had to get on you about your behavior, it caused me to question whether or not I was being fair."

"Well, that was all in the past, and like I said earlier, I've put the past behind me," Mike said.

"That's a good idea," Paul replied. "I'll try to do the same."

"Truce?" Mike said as he turned to Paul and stuck out his hand.

"Truce!" Paul said as he shook his hand.

For the next five days, the two of them had an ongoing conversation about the future. Mike talked about his business, his goals, what he had learned since leaving home, his newfound hobbies, and an endless variety of other topics. Paul spent a lot of time sharing the concerns he had for the rest of his family. He had suffered two massive heart attacks and was thankful that he'd lived long enough to take early retirement at age 62. He laughed about the trip being the first thing he had done since retiring. He talked about how he had learned to better control his temper, and he looked forward to retirement without the pressure he'd been under while working. The experience was a cleansing one for both of them.

(Note: Paul and Mike's mother eventually moved to Asheville, North Carolina, to be closer to Mike as they grew older. Paul and Mike maintained a good relationship until Paul's death in 1999.)

These three experiences proved to Mike that taking personal responsibility was much more than just admitting mistakes and accepting the consequences. When he decided to take full responsibility for his own happiness and stopped blaming others when things didn't go his way, he grew immeasurably. Once he finally understood that he controlled his destiny, not others, his confidence grew, his attitude improved, and his business relationships were enhanced. By learning to control his temper, repairing his relationship with his father and stepfather, and taking control of his actions, it released a surge of energy that had been suppressed for years. This energy propelled Mike into a period of strong earning years.

Key Points from This Chapter

- Accepting responsibility doesn't just mean apologizing for your mistakes and taking the punishment.
- It's not how many mistakes you make, but how quickly you learn to avoid making the same ones over again that leads to success.
- Just because everyone disagrees with you doesn't automatically mean that you are wrong.
- Don't let the negative influence of others ruin your life.
- When you lose your temper, it's because you weren't smart enough to keep control of your emotions.
- Have the courage to reach out to the people who have hurt you in the past and do whatever it takes to get rid of your animosities.

23

Knowing Where Your Money Goes

During his first few years in business, Mike saw an increasing stream of revenue flowing through his bank account, yet he always seemed to come to the end of the money before he got to the end of the month. He was not alone. Many people experience this whether they are in business or not. Many days, he would spend hours riding around trying to collect money for work he had completed just so he could pay his bills. This was not only an unpleasant, time-consuming experience for him, but often an inconvenience and an interruption for his good customers, the ones who paid within a few days after being billed.

What could he do? Shorter months were not an option. More income would solve the problem, but he was already working as hard as he could. It soon became clear that the problem was that he had very little cash reserves from which to operate.

Mike resolved to find out what was happening with his money. He had never viewed himself as a spendthrift, but for some reason no matter how much he made, it always seemed to slip away from him. He knew he needed

Knowing Where Your Money Goes

to start building some cash reserves, but couldn't figure out how he could do that when he was always out of money. Eventually he began writing down every penny he spent in a small spiral bound notebook that he carried in his shirt pocket. If he bought a soft drink, he wrote it down. If he bought a candy bar, he wrote it down. Everything! Groceries, gas, cigarettes (yes, unfortunately he smoked at the time), clothes, bowling, even a piece of bubble gum; he wrote it all down. He continued this exercise for an entire month before he sat down to analyze his spending.

His analysis was simple: He just categorized each outlay as necessary or unnecessary. Loan payments, utilities, food, and similar expenditures fell into the necessary category. Unnecessary meant it was something he wanted enough to purchase, but something he could do without. Cigarettes, candy, soft drinks, records, a new pocketknife, and a new bowling ball were among the items that showed up on the unnecessary list. What shocked him most when he totaled the list was the discovery that in just one month, he had spent over $600 on unnecessary items.

This exercise accomplished three things. First, it identified a pool of money from which Mike could start building cash reserves or investing. Second, it left him paying much greater attention to his spending habits. But the third and the most important thing was that it showed him that you have to *know where your money goes* if you expect to achieve financial success.

When we have taught this concept, a few people acknowledge that they waste a little money, but most assume a defensive posture and deny that any of their spending might be frivolous. The tighter their finances, the more adamant they are that they don't waste money. Invariably they blame their problems on others; prices are too high, they don't make enough to cover expenses, or they've just had a run of bad luck. They remind us of functioning alcoholics who continue to deny they have a problem.

Everyone wastes money; some people just waste more than others. Until you're willing to face the fact that you do waste money, it will be very difficult to develop a Weekend Millionaire Mindset. Don't get us wrong—we're not advocating that you live an austere life with no frivolous spending at all and no fun, in order to achieve financial success. That's the image we have of misers, and it's the last thing we want you to become. But once you *know where your money goes* you have options.

The Earning Years

After identifying the exact amount of your unnecessary spending, you can begin making life-changing decisions. You get to decide what portion of this money you want to redirect into building cash reserves or other investments. We don't suggest that anyone attempt to redirect all of their discretionary money. For most, redirecting a third to half of it will produce life-changing results if invested wisely.

In Mike's case, once he saw the amount of his unnecessary spending, he came up with a novel idea to redirect part of it. He decided that he would pay for all purchases with bills, and any change he received he would bring home and put in a jar. You may think that's a silly idea, but after the first month, his loose change totaled more than $50. The second month, it was once again over $50, and his experiment of paying with bills and saving the change was becoming a habit; one that has stuck with him all his life and that he continues today.

After several months of saving change and watching it accumulate from a few nickels, dimes, and quarters to several hundred dollars, it dawned on Mike that he hadn't missed the money. He couldn't think of anything he'd sacrificed, yet had accumulated more than he had ever been able to save before. It wasn't the amount he had that made the difference; it was the way he saved.

By only paying with bills, he noticed that he would often bypass frivolous expenditures when it meant breaking a large bill to make small purchases, like a candy bar or a soft drink. By religiously refusing to spend change for these small items, it reinforced his decisions not to break the large bills to get them. Unknowingly, he was training himself to be more responsible with his discretionary spending, and the results were showing. Each month he seemed to have a little extra money, in addition to the change he was saving.

This small exercise in thriftiness that quickly turned into a habit was the first of many similar experiments during his learning years that would become part of Mike's Weekend Millionaire Mindset. It helped him discover the power of the three Ds of success. He had the Desire to curb his unnecessary spending. He had the Discipline to pay for each purchase, no matter how small, with a bill. And, he had the Dedication to continue doing so until it became a habit. The results have been outstanding; he has saved over

$50,000 throughout his career by adopting just this one small, almost insignificant habit. Few people accumulate as much cash in a lifetime of conscious saving.

We have dedicated this entire chapter to discussing the importance of *knowing where your money goes* because we believe that it is essential to building wealth. Many people think wealth comes from what you earn. We believe that wealth is not accumulated by what you earn; it is accumulated by what you invest. If you make a million dollars a year and spend a million dollars a year on consumable items like food, trips, recreation, and entertainment, are you any better off at the end of the year than someone who makes $50,000 a year and spends $50,000? At the end of the year, both people have to earn more to live the following year. By knowing where your money goes, you are able to redirect portions of it into investments that can pay you for the rest of your life. That's one of the benefits that come with developing a Weekend Millionaire Mindset.

Now, hold that thought as we move to the next chapter, where we will discuss developing a pattern of investing.

Key Points from This Chapter

- You cannot operate efficiently without cash reserves.
- Start by analyzing every penny you spend.
- Divide all of your expenditures into those that are necessary and those that are unnecessary.
- Turn unnecessary expenses into cash reserves or working capital.
- Paying only with bills and saving the coins is a painless way to start saving. (If you have to break a big bill to buy a small item, make it a red flag. Do you really need it?)
- Knowing where your money goes is essential to building wealth.
- Keep working the three Ds: Discipline, Dedication, and Desire.

24

Developing a Pattern of Investing

As we mentioned in the previous chapter, the habit Mike developed of paying for purchases with bills and saving the loose change led him to be more responsible with his discretionary spending. This gave him his first investment capital. He was early into his earning years, and the temptations of youth were strong. He had the same desires that most young people have to spend these funds rather than invest them, but he found himself pouring every penny he could back into his business.

As we mentioned in Chapter 6, Mike began building highway signs to rent rather than sell. Each new billboard was another investment that would provide him with a growing income stream, but each one also cost hundreds of dollars to construct. Unlike the ease with which he saved loose change and watched it grow, it was difficult to find such large sums of money. For years he endured a continuing struggle with banks. When he tried to borrow money to invest in new signs, the bankers he encountered didn't understood his business, didn't know how to collateralize a loan with signs built on leased property and rented to clients for whom they didn't have financial information.

Mike tried everything to get more financing. He wrote proposals, prepared projections, called on every bank in town; he even went to the local university and took a course titled "The Economics of Money and Banking." He was obsessed with finding the money to continue investing in building more signs to rent. One day he was talking with one of his good customers, a fine gentleman named George Duke who had moved to North Carolina from Florida and purchased a local campground. He had done extensive sign work for the campground for over a year and developed a close friendship with George. During their discussion, Mike expressed his frustration over not being able to obtain bank financing when he had plenty of clients ready and willing to rent signs.

"How much are you trying to borrow?" George asked.

"About $30,000," Mike replied.

"And how long do you need it for?"

"I could easily pay it back in three years," Mike said.

"Well, banks can be difficult to do business with at times," George responded. "I know, I was in the building business in Florida and I had to deal with them all the time. Tell you what; I've seen how hard you work—you do a good job and you've always been fair with me—so I'd like to help you if I can. Why don't you check with your bank and see if they will let you have the money if I cosign the note with you."

"You'd actually do that?" Mike exclaimed.

"I'd be happy to; just check with the bank and see if that will work."

This was the break Mike needed. The bank made the loan, and he was quickly able to construct several new signs that produced substantially more income than the required loan payments.

We should mention here that George was extraordinarily generous and trusting in cosigning for the loan. Very few people would have done that, because there's a real danger that they would not only lose the money, but also ruin their credit rating, which is far more serious. Had he not known Mike and been comfortable that Mike would repay the loan, he might have been better off giving him the $30,000 with a promise to pay it back.

The Earning Years

Mike was learning the power of investing. His business kept growing and soon he had to hire his first employee, a talented sign painter, Joe Letterman (yes, that is his real name), who produced the signs that Mike sold.

Now, in his fourth year of business and still on track to achieve his goal of becoming a millionaire by age 30, Mike found himself in a situation where business growth was easily consuming all his profits plus any additional money he could borrow. Unfortunately, another event occurred that led him to think that maybe he should consider investing at least a little money into something other than his company. The passage of the Highway Beautification Act, also known as the Lady Bird Johnson act, caused concern because it regulated billboards and limited where new ones could be built.

In the summer of 1973, shortly after the new regulations went into effect, Mike visited his mother and his stepfather in Bluefield. Since he had repaired his relationship with Paul, he felt comfortable talking with him about his business concerns. Paul, who had been in the life insurance business, suggested that he take out a whole life policy insuring his life. He explained that this type of policy would not only provide insurance, but would act as a forced savings plan as well. He showed Mike how he had been able to borrow against his own life insurance to purchase his cars, and was able to do so at a very favorable rate. He described how these policies began building cash value after a couple of years and could even provide a retirement income years into the future.

Although he was retired, Paul was still able to write insurance, so Mike decided to purchase a $100,000 policy through him and have the $106.87 premium deducted directly from his bank account. He recalled how he had been able to save over $50 per month, without even noticing it, just by saving his loose change. Now that his business was doing better, he was sure he wouldn't miss the insurance premium, and it would give him another way of saving a little money outside of the business. It might also give his bankers a bit of security, knowing that if something happened to him, they would get paid. When he finished completing the application, he left for the return trip to Asheville.

As he drove, he thought about the insurance. He was proud of himself for making the commitment to invest over $100 per month into the insurance, but the more he thought about it, the more he wished he had doubled the amount. This thought kept running through his mind for a month, especially after he saw how thrilled his bankers were to learn that he now had life insurance. He knew he would be borrowing much more money, so he decided to buy another $100,000 policy. This time he talked to the agent where he carried his business insurance and found that he could get a comparable policy to the one he had already purchased for just $101.90 per month. These policies were issued in September and October 1973.

By the following spring, business was booming, he had been able to secure two more bank loans to invest in new sign construction, and he had hardly missed the premiums that were deducted monthly from his account. In May he was once again visiting his mother and Paul. He told Paul about buying the second $100,000 policy. They also talked about the two new loans he had gotten from his banks. Eventually, he got around to telling Paul that he wanted to purchase another $250,000 policy.

"I know it's not the best investment as far as getting a high return," Mike said, "but having the premium deducted directly from my account becomes a habit. I don't miss it. It reminds me of the loose change I still save everyday. If I don't have it, I don't spend it."

"Well, I think you're making a smart move," Paul replied. "If you keep the insurance, you'll be surprised at what it will be worth as you get older, plus it will give you security and peace of mind."

The $250,000 policy was issued in June 1974, and little did either of them realize the impact this insurance would have in just two short years. We won't go into the details here, but two years later, a pledge of this insurance policy enabled Mike to purchase another company with no money down and full owner financing—a purchase that was so favorable, it enabled him to reach his goal of becoming a millionaire, not by the age of 30, but by the time he was 28.

Most people might assume that the big loans Mike made to secure financing for his billboard investments were the reason he reached his goal two years ahead of schedule. But if you ask him, he'll tell you that he learned more from saving loose change than from all the difficult meetings he had with bankers. Sure the bank loans accounted for the growth of his business, but the effects of patiently accomplishing a little each day, every day, was far more responsible for the development of his Weekend Millionaire Mindset than any of his bigger successes. In fact, it was this mindset that made the bigger successes possible.

Throughout his career, Mike has never forgotten what he learned from saving loose change; that setting aside a little each day and, consistently, day after day can add up to quite a sum over a long period of time. This is the message that investment counselors try to drum into clients when they talk about investing in IRA and 401(k) accounts or other retirement plans. Most people have a hard time grasping the concept when they can't touch or feel their investments. For Mike, watching the ever increasing volume of coins grow provided visible reinforcement and encouraged him to continue.

Mike has applied this concept throughout life. When it was announced that effective January 1, 1990, U.S. Savings bonds would earn interest tax free if used for education, he began purchasing a $100 bond each week for his two sons, who would not enter college until more than a decade later. Just as with the loose change and the insurance premiums, the money he put into the bonds went practically unnoticed. This too became a habit, and he didn't miss a week buying the bonds. As with the loose change, he watched the stack of bonds continue to grow year after year. When his son Jason entered Florida State University in the fall of 2000, the cost of his entire four-year college education was in hand. Furthermore, Mike continued purchasing the bonds even after his youngest son, Matt, entered Furman University in 2002 and didn't stop until 2004, when it was determined that he had all the savings he would need to cover their education.

Roger recalls when he first came to America and was flat broke. He had a job at a Montgomery Ward store that paid $93 a week before deductions. But every Friday, when he got paid, he walked across the town square in Napa, California, and bought a $25 U.S. Savings bond at the Bank of America, which cost him $18.75. It doesn't sound like much, does it? But when he needed money to buy a new car and later to buy his first home, it was there.

Go back to Chapter 4 and review the chart in Figure 6 where we show how you can drive a Chevrolet or a Cadillac for the same amount of earned income. The Cadillac owner and the Chevrolet owner paid the same amount for their cars. The only difference was that the Cadillac owner saved for his car and paid cash. The Chevrolet owner borrowed the money to buy his car and paid interest for the use of the bank's money. The notable difference is that the Cadillac was five years newer than the Chevrolet! The way Mike saved to pay for his son's college education is a perfect example of this concept of saving to spend rather than borrowing to spend. Most people wait until the money is needed and then go in debt to help their children. This negatively impacts their standard of living long after the children graduate, while they pay off the debt. On the other hand, Mike could improve his standard of living because he was able to stop buying the bonds two years before his youngest son graduated, with the knowledge that his education was already paid for. This is another example of the positive effects of the Weekend Millionaire Mindset.

If you have read this far, you already know that the Weekend Millionaire Mindset is rooted in patience and persistence. Throughout his earning years, Mike lived on a salary from his billboard business, but it was what he did with his salary and his spare time that ultimately brought him success. Saving loose change, paying premiums on cash-building life insurance, and buying U.S. Savings bonds are typical of the things many working people do to save money, but they rarely bring financial success because most of them lack the stick-to-itiveness to make these actions become habits. Even if they do, it's still difficult to save your way to financial success.

In the late 1970s the billboard business was becoming more volatile, and the uncertainty of its future caused Mike some major concerns. His bankers were becoming increasingly nervous each time a new ordinance was passed, and his accountant and lawyer expressed doubts about the future of the industry and recommended that he begin diversifying his investments. At the time, the loose change he had saved and the cash value of his life insurance accounted for less than 1 percent of his assets. Everything else he owned was invested in his company, which was still consuming all his profits plus what he could borrow to keep it growing.

Mike had a discussion with then his CPA, John Kledis, about investment options that might be available to him. He told John that he didn't have any extra money to invest and he certainly couldn't take any out of his billboard business. It's hard to diversify when you don't have any money. John said that investing in real estate was similar to investing in signs, except that every city and county around wasn't trying to pass regulations to do away with houses. He went on to explain that real estate could often be purchased with very little or no money down by simply assuming someone else's loan or getting the seller to finance the purchase. This conversation would become the forerunner of what we know today as the Weekend Millionaire investing concept.

Mike didn't have any extra money, but he did have a little spare time. He began using some of it to look at houses that were for sale, and he started making offers that he could affford if one was accepted. It took him nearly a year to buy his first investment house, but when he did, he only had to come up with a few dollars to close the deal. The spare time he invested in looking at houses soon became like the loose change and the insurance premiums—a habit. Although the results were anything but spectacular, he came to enjoy the time he spent inspecting properties and making offers. Over time, he was able to purchase a second house, and then a third.

He set up a separate bank account to handle the rental income and expenses. He obtained amortization schedules on each mortgage loan, and every month when he made the payment, he'd circle the principal and interest amounts, the loan balance, and write down the date and check number with which he made the payment. Each month, he noticed that a little more went to principal and a little less to interest. Monitoring the declining loan balances and increasing rents soon became a game, much like playing the board game Monopoly.

When we said earlier that what he learned from saving loose change taught Mike more than what he learned from high-powered meetings with his bankers, we were talking about the value of patience and persistence. Watching the loan balances decline each month was similar to watching the loose change fill up in the jar, only this time other people were making the deposits; namely, his tenants.

He soon acquired a fourth and a fifth house; then a sixth and seventh. Each month as he recorded the income and expenses, he watched his debt go down and the value of his assets go up as rents increased. This truly was like the Monopoly games Mike remembered playing as a child. He recalled the times he would seem flat broke during a game, when everyone else had loads of cash and all he had were properties. But this also brought to mind the number of those games he ultimately won as the people who failed to invest began landing on his properties and had to pay rent. He saw no reason why he couldn't do the same thing in real life, and that's what he eventually did. By 1997 his real estate was so profitable that he sold the sign business and retired, just as he'd planned. He learned that investing in real estate was like playing Monopoly for keeps.

Since we're on the subject, if you're interested, you can learn how to build wealth investing in real estate by reading our book *The Weekend Millionaire's Secrets of Investing in Real Estate: How to Become Wealthy in Your Spare Time* (McGraw-Hill 2003).

This chapter is designed to teach you the value of *developing a pattern of investing*. It's not nearly as important how much you invest as it is how consistently and over what duration you invest. As we said before, "A mouse can eat an elephant if you give it long enough." It's the habits you acquire when you develop a pattern of investing that ultimately brings financial success. It's amazing what ordinary people can accomplish when these principles are applied.

Key Points from This Chapter

- Saving a little bit regularly is the key to building investment funds. Even if it's only the change from your pockets or purse.
- Persistence is the key to success; don't quit just because one bank or 10 banks turn you down.
- Develop the habit of regularly saving, whether it's to purchase life insurance, savings bonds, or other investments; do it consistently.
- Anticipate large expenditures such as college tuition or replacing automobiles and start saving the money now, so you don't have to go into debt later. You're going to have to make the payments one way or another, so why not make them before the purchase rather than after?
- The effect of saving is greatly multiplied when you invest in rental properties, because your tenants pay down the mortgages for you.
- Saving and investing are essential to building wealth; the sooner you develop these habits, the quicker you will achieve financial independence.

25

Developing a Personal Budget, Tracking Your Money

We've covered many different topics and events that contribute to the enhancement of a Weekend Millionaire Mindset, but until you start tracking where your money goes, you'll find it difficult to stay on course to becoming financially independent. You've probably heard the saying, "The road to Hell is paved with good intentions." What you may not have heard is, "The road to financial ruin is paved with 'I'm gonnas' and 'I wish I had-das.'" If you're serious about building wealth, you have to make a lifelong commitment to understanding where your money goes.

The key to wealth building is not the amount of money you make, but being aware what you can buy and when you can buy it. We've all seen people who make huge salaries and file for bankruptcy because they spent more than they made. But the most interesting phenomenon we've discovered is that *most ordinary people pay enough in interest over the course of their lifetime to become millionaires*. Why? We think the reason is simple. They don't have a plan, but they do have an "I want it now" mentality, and this leads them to buy things before they can afford them. As a result, they finance the purchases and pay exorbitant amounts of their hard-earned income in finance charges.

The sad part is that these purchases are not all big, expensive items. More often than not they're small things like going to a movie, eating out in a restaurant, buying a new dress, or any of the thousand other things they charge on their credit cards. Instead of asking, "Can I afford this?" they ask, "Can I make the payments?" Again, we urge you to go back and reread Chapter 6, "Debt: Constructive or Destructive." In this chapter we're going to teach you how to avoid destructive debt, which is debt to purchase things that don't produce income and that go down in value the longer you own them.

In Chapter 23 we discussed an exercise in which Mike wrote down every expenditure he made for a full month in order to determine where he was spending his money. This is a valuable exercise for you to try. Before you can establish a plan to achieve financial independence, you have to be honest about what you are currently doing with your money. You can't just "wing it" and expect positive results. This exercise is important because it may reveal that you are already living above your means. If this is the case, if you're spending more than you make, then no matter how well intentioned you are, you can't build wealth. The first thing you need to know is that budgeting is flexible. Preparing a budget merely establishes what you plan to do with your money. It becomes the benchmark against which you compare what you actually did with what you planned to do. If worked properly and consistently, a budget can become a tool that helps you make the kind of financial decisions that lift you from the Lifestyle of Ordinary to the Lifestyle of Success.

We believe that the biggest reason ordinary people have a problem with financial planning is because they try to make it too complicated. Have you ever met with a financial planner and walked away from the meeting wondering what he or she said? Could it be that if they simplified things, you wouldn't need them?

First, we want you to understand that financial planning is different from debt counseling and investment counseling. Debt counseling helps you get out of debt if you're already in the hole. Investment counseling helps you decide where and how to invest your money once your financial house is in order. And finally, financial planning is what you use to put your financial house in order.

The system we're going to teach you is a simple way to evaluate your personal finances to determine the course of action you'll need to take to achieve financial independence. Some of you will see that you have adequate income; you just need to manage it better. Some of you may find that you have to reduce your standard of living temporarily, or that you must earn more, if that's easier to do than giving up things to which you've grown accustomed. But no matter what your situation, we're going to teach you how to make it better and how to establish a course of action that will take you to financial independence. We call this "flexible budgeting" because it can be adjusted each month.

The first thing you need for this exercise is a columnar pad. The best type of pad for this use is an accountant's three-column pad that can be purchased at any office supply store. Most of the columnar pads come pre-punched, to fit in a three-ring binder, which we recommend you use. You'll need several sheets, on which the columns should be labeled as shown in Figure 13.

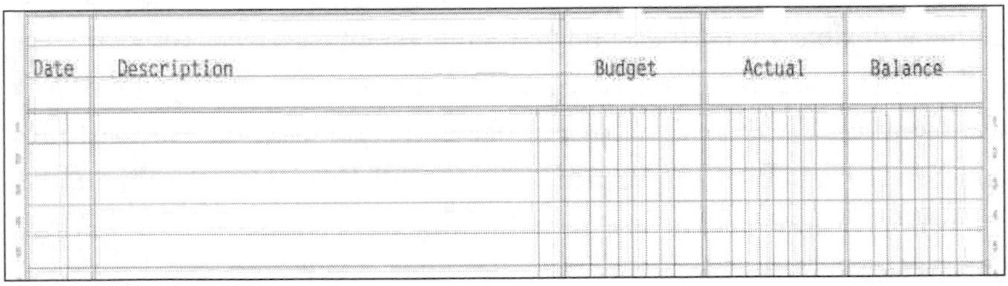

Date	Description	Budget	Actual	Balance

Figure 13

It will take a little time to set up this system for the first time, but it is well worth the effort. Start by making out a sheet for everything that you pay on a regular basis, including the things you pay quarterly, semiannually, or annually. Put the name of the account on the top of the sheet and label the columns as shown in Figure 13. You will eventually need to set up some other sheets, but for now let's just make ones for the things you have to pay. Here's a partial list to help you get started: Electric, Water, Gas/Heating Oil,

Developing a Personal Budget, Tracking Your Money

Phone, Cell Phone, Cable TV, Trash Collection, Groceries, Clothing, Newspaper, Credit Card (one sheet for each credit card), Other Credit Accounts (one for each account), House Payment/Rent, Car Payment (one sheet for each car loan), Gasoline, Homeowners/Renters Insurance, Car Insurance, Hospitalization Insurance, Life Insurance, Property Taxes, etc. Don't forget to set up a "Contingency Account" for unforeseen expenses such as car, home repairs, accidents, etc. Whatever you put into this contingency account is money you won't have to come up with when unexpected expenses arise.

Each person's situation is different. You may need accounts that are not listed above, or there may be ones on it that don't apply to you. This is just the first step toward putting your financial house in order, so at this time only make sheets for recurring payments. We'll discuss other sheets you might want a little later.

For our illustrations, we're going to assume we are starting at the beginning of a calendar year, so the first entry on all our examples will be for January; however, it doesn't matter which month you begin. Once you've completed a sheet for each of your recurring payments, let's select one with which to get started. Since nearly everyone has an electric bill, let's use the first one from our above list, Electric.

Now, we want you to do a little research. Check your back records and try to determine what your average electric bill has been over the past year. If you don't have records, make your best educated guess. Then enter this amount on the first line as the "budget" for the month from which you will be starting. Of course, if you've been paying bills on your computer, you'll quickly be able to pull up a list of your paid bills. Your sheet will look like this:

Electric Company Name				
Date	Description	Budget	Actual	Balance
Jan. 1	January	$235.00		$235.00

As you can see from the example above, we selected $235.00 as the budgeted amount for electricity for the month of January. Your entry will be the amount you determined to be your average monthly electric cost. Now, complete a sheet like this for each one of your accounts. For items that you pay quarterly, semiannually, or annually, enter the amount you would need to set aside each month between now and the next due date in order to have the money on hand to pay the bill when it comes due.

When you've completed all of your sheets, add up the total budgeted amounts from all of them. This total will be the minimum amount you'll need to earn for the month to be solvent. We say the minimum amount because we have not yet allowed for any discretionary spending. If you cannot earn this amount during the month, you need to stop right here and reevaluate your spending. Unless you adjust your standard of living to fit your income, you're heading for financial disaster.

You will need to plan on depositing the total amount of your budgeted expenses into a bank account and earmark this money to pay your monthly bills. This is known as "funding your budget." When the actual bills come in, you pay them and note the date and amount you pay on the next line below your first entry. Your sheets should then look like this:

Electric Company				
Date	**Description**	**Budget**	**Actual**	**Balance**
Jan. 1	January	$235.00		$235.00
Jan. 14	January Payment		$231.25	$ 3.75

Again using our Electric Company sheet as an example, you can see that the actual amount was less than what we budgeted. When we subtracted the actual from the budgeted amount, it left $3.75 remaining in the account. We will leave this amount in the account and budget an additional $235.00 for the month of February. After doing that, our sheet now looks like this:

Electric Company				
Date	**Description**	**Budget**	**Actual**	**Balance**
Jan. 1	January	$235.00		$235.00
Jan. 14	January Payment		$231.25	$ 3.75
Feb. 1	February	$235.00		$238.75

Developing a Personal Budget, Tracking Your Money

As you can see, our electric account now has $238.75 budgeted for February. "But," you say, "what if my electric bill is more than what I budget?" Good question! Let's continue with the assumption that this is exactly what happens in February. After paying the bill, your sheet will look like this:

Electric Company				
Date	**Description**	**Budget**	**Actual**	**Balance**
Jan. 1	January	$235.00		$235.00
Jan. 14	January Payment		$231.25	$ 3.75
Feb. 1	February	$235.00		$238.75
Feb. 14	February Payment		$247.65	$ −8.90

As you can see, our account is now in the hole $8.90. When this happens to you, what you are going to do is budget another $235.00 for the upcoming month plus the shortage from the prior month. When we do this, our sheet looks as follows:

Electric Company				
Date	**Description**	**Budget**	**Actual**	**Balance**
Jan. 1	January	$235.00		$235.00
Jan. 14	January Payment		$231.25	$ 3.75
Feb. 1	February	$235.00		$238.75
Feb. 14	February Payment		$247.65	$ −8.90
Mar. 1	March	$243.90		$235.00

As you can see, we needed to put more into the electric account than we did in the previous months just to get the balance back to our regular monthly budgeted amount. Such flexible budgeting allows you to correct shortages immediately rather than having them accumulate unknowingly until they cause problems. We want you to leave any overages in the accounts to help compensate for future shortages that may arise. If you consistently run short each month, you will need to adjust your budgeted amount upward. Likewise, if you budget more than you need for several months, you can lower the amount you put in the account. You will do this for each of your accounts each month. When you total the amount you will need to meet your regular expenses, you'll find that it fluctuates up and down a little each month.

For those accounts of which you pay quarterly, semiannually or annually, your sheets will look a little different. The following is an example of what your sheet for Auto Insurance may look like if you pay the premium semiannually in June and December.

Auto Insurance Premium due $435.00 in June and December				
Date	Description	Budget	Actual	Balance
Jan. 1	January Budget	$72.50		$ 72.50
Feb. 1	February Budget	$72.50		$145.00
Mar. 1	March Budget	$72.50		$217.50
Apr. 1	April Budget	$72.50		$290.00
May 1	May Budget	$72.50		$362.50
June 1	June Budget	$72.50		$435.50
June 10	Semiannual Payment		$435.00	$ −0
July 1	July Budget	$72.50		$ 72.50

As you can see from the above example, one-sixth of the semiannual premium was budgeted each month. This amount was placed into the bank account to cover the premium when it came due. When you plan this way, you are not put in a bind when these larger, less frequent expenses come due. With this system, you always know how much of the money in your bank account is needed to cover these larger expenses. By adding up the amounts in the balance column of all your sheets, at any give time you can determine how much money should be in your bank account to meet your upcoming obligations. This is important, because even if your intentions are good, without a system like this it is very easy to spend the money and then come up short when the large bills come due.

Developing a Personal Budget, Tracking Your Money

Your sheets for items like clothing or other irregularly occurring accounts will look similar to the previous example. You will budget an amount for clothing each month, but you may not purchase anything for several months. When you do get ready to buy, you can refer to your budget sheet and know exactly how much you can spend without going into debt. The same holds true for car payments. If you are making a car payment and it is in your budget, continue to budget the payment even after you pay off the loan. By doing so, you will end up financing less, or possibly none at all, when you trade cars. Your car account will give you a better indication of when you are ready to trade than your emotions will.

Let's now take things a step further. Up to this point we have only dealt with mandatory expenses, and you're probably thinking, "What about discretionary spending; things like dining out, recreation, etc.? What about savings?" The reason we left these items until last is because we wanted you to determine if you had any extra money before discussing them. If, when budgeting for mandatory expenses, you found that you had no extra money; you only have three alternatives. You can earn more, spend less, or go into debt. Of these options, going into debt is the one that is sure to cause future difficulties and result in one of the other two options being forced upon you.

If you're like most ordinary working people, you will find that you have some discretionary funds. The amount will vary depending on your income and the standard of living you have chosen, but most responsible people have some extra money after paying their bills. What you do with these funds is what determines if or when you achieve financial independence.

Many people view life as a drudgery and complain that they are simply working day after day just to survive. The pressure this places on them mentally often results in binge spending, which invariably puts them deeper in the hole and subjects them to an even more depressing life of hard work and toil. It's a vicious cycle that becomes as difficult to break as a drug or alcohol habit.

If you're already caught in this cycle, we're going to show you how to break out of it. If you aren't, we're going to explain how to avoid it. Everyone needs to have some pleasure in life. Things like dining out, vacations, recreational activities, and hobbies are as important to a healthy mindset as anything else. You've heard it said that there's more to life than just making money. We totally agree. There's also nothing more stabilizing in life than having a solid control over your finances and watching the security of your growing nest egg. With our simple flexible budgeting system you will be able to achieve all of these things and more.

Once you have established your budget for mandatory expenses and adjusted your standard of living, if necessary, to ensure that you have some discretionary funds, here's what you do next. Set up a sheet for long-term savings. This can be an amount budgeted for your IRA, 401(k), or other retirement account. It is money that you don't plan to touch until you're ready to retire. Then you set up additional sheets for other savings that you'll use for shorter term expenditures like Dining Out, Vacations, Recreation, or any other activity that brings you pleasure. Set up a savings sheet for Christmas and another for Miscellaneous Gifts like birthdays and anniversaries. The key is to avoid getting caught with unplanned expenses.

These sheets will allow you to secure your future while planning for activities you can afford without going into debt. We recommend that you establish a budget for your retirement account first. Be as generous as possible when you set your budgeted amount because the more you budget, the quicker you will achieve financial independence, but don't try to budget so much that you can't have a little fun in life too. If you do leave fun out of it, you'll constantly be tempted to dip into your retirement account to fill your emotional needs for merriment.

Once you've established your budget for retirement, look at the money you have remaining and allocate it to discretionary spending. You may want to spread it over several discretionary accounts. For our example, we'll use the Dining Out account to demonstrate how this works. Set up a sheet titled "Dining Out," just as you did for the mandatory expense accounts. Select an amount based on your remaining funds that you would like to spend on dining each month. Your sheet will look similar to the one on the next page.

As you can see from our example, we budgeted $100.00 per month to dine out. Each time we ate out, we recorded the expenditure on the Dining Out sheet and deducted the amount we spent from what was in the account. Since we planned on spending a budgeted amount of $100.00 per month, by keeping our sheet current, whenever we get the urge to go out for dinner, we can refer to the sheet and make an informed decision as to whether we can afford it, and if so, how much we can spend without having to charge it.

Dining Out				
Date	**Description**	**Budget**	**Actual**	**Balance**
Jan. 1	January Budget	$100.00		$100.00
Jan. 8	Dinner @ ?		$42.50	$ 57.50
Jan. 22	Dinner @ ?		$32.65	$ 24.85
Jan. 26	Lunch @ ?		$12.50	$ 12.35
Feb. 1	February Budget	$100.00		$112.35
Feb. 14	Dinner @ ?		$58.85	$ 53.50
Feb. 22	Dinner @ ?		$28.25	$ 25.25
Mar. 1	March Budget	$100.00		$125.25
Mar. 6	Lunch @ ?		$13.50	$111.75
Mar. 12	Lunch @ ?		$16.35	$ 95.40
Mar. 20	Dinner @ ?		$56.45	$ 38.95

By using this method to budget discretionary spending, you will not only be able to see if you have the money for an expenditure, but in the event that you don't, you'll be able to determine how soon you will have it based on the amount you are budgeting. If you've been budgeting to buy a new piece of furniture, a boat, or some other large ticket item and you want to get it sooner than the projected budget will allow, you can reevaluate your other discretionary spending accounts and make adjustments. You may decide to eat out less, skip a vacation or other recreational activity, and transfer the money you would spend on these items to the account for the big item so you can get it sooner.

The bottom line is, this simple budgeting system allows you to take total control of your finances, enables you to know when and how much you can spend, and prevents you from making hasty and often expensive mistakes. Sure, it requires a little time and effort to maintain, but the value you receive will far and away offset any inconvenience.

Now for one last tip before moving on to the next chapter: We recommend that you set up a cover sheet to bring forward the totals from your individual account sheets. On the first of each month, total the budgeted amounts from each sheet and bring this total forward to the cover sheet. On the last day of each month, do the same with the actual expenditures you paid out during the month. This will allow you to see where you stand at a glance. You can use multiple sheets of the three-column paper you use for the individual sheets, or you can get a pad of 13-column sheets and have an entire year on a single page. Your cover sheet should look like this:

Budget Reconciliation Sheet				
Description	January	February	March	April
Beginning Bank Balance	$ 500	$1,150	$1,380	$ 850
Budgeted Amount (memo)	$3,500	$3,650	$3,600	$3,550
Amount Deposited	$3,500	$3,650	$3,600	$3,550
Actual Expenditures	$2,850	$3,420	$4,130	$2,975
Ending Bank Balance	$1,150	$1,380	$ 850	$1,425

This cover sheet gives you a quick snapshot of how you did each month and shows you how much money you should have in the bank account from which you pay your bills. Let's take a minute and analyze the information in the above example. You can see that we started with a Beginning Bank Balance in January of $500. Our budget for the month was $3,500. We funded our budget by depositing this amount into the bank account. Although we budgeted and funded $3,500 for the month, we only spent $2,850. The difference was money representing a month's share of our quarterly, semiannual, and annual payments. Since we didn't have to pay out these amounts in January, our bank balance grew from $500 to $1,150.

We carried forward the Ending Bank Balance from January and posted it as the Beginning Bank Balance for February. When we totaled our sheets for February, we found that our flexible budgeting system increased our budget by $150, to $3,650. Once again, in February we didn't spend the full amount, so our bank balance grew to $1,380.

Just as we did the previous month, we carried the Ending Bank Balance for February forward to the Beginning Bank Balance for March. Once again our budgeted amount changed. This time it dropped $50 to $3,600. We again funded the budget by depositing this amount into our bank account, but this month Actual Expenditures were $4,130, which is $530 more than we budgeted. This could have been due to one or more of our larger infrequent payments coming due, but it did not create a problem. The only effect it had was reducing our bank balance from $1,380 at the beginning of the month to $850 at the end of the month. We had already planned for the extra $530, and our budget caused us to reserve the funds to pay it, so it didn't cause a cash flow problem.

We have a couple more thoughts before leaving this subject. First, some people prefer to keep a bit of cash out each month to use as "mad money." And others prefer to track this as well. If you want to track it, set up a Cash Account sheet just as you did for other expenditures. Budget yourself an amount of miscellaneous cash to spend as you please. Post this budgeted amount to the sheet and include it in what you deposit into your bank account. When you withdraw part or all of it, write yourself a check and deduct it from the sheet. Just as with your other expenditures, you can look at the sheet and know how much, if any, "mad money" you have at any time.

Second, the amounts we use in our examples are only for illustration purposes. Your numbers will be different, but whether your monthly budget is $2,000 or $20,000, the system works the same. It allows you to maintain control of your finances.

Finally, we want to remind you again that keeping up with this system will take a little time, but the security and confidence you'll gain by getting control of your finances makes it well worth the effort.

Key Points from This Chapter

- Make a lifelong commitment to understanding where your money goes.

- Most people spend enough money on finance charges to become millionaires over a lifetime.
- The important thing is not what you buy, but when you buy it.
- Planning for savings provides the seed money you will need to acquire constructive debt on purchases like investment properties.
- Planning for purchases in advance helps you avoid accumulating mounds of destructive consumer debt.
- Prepare a flexible budget that will accommodate every item for which you spend money.
- Set up an account for long-term savings.

26

Repel Negative Influences, Focus on the Positive

Throughout this book, we have driven home the importance of being positive, of surrounding yourself with positive people and staying focused on your goals. We've discussed the way people respond when you're trying to climb the ladder of success; how some will give you a boost up while others will try to drag you down. So far we've dealt primarily with how individuals can positively or negatively influence your success. In this chapter, we want to take it a step further and show you how corporations, as impersonal as they can seem, can often do the same thing.

In the late 1990s Mike undertook a large multi-million-dollar construction project in which numerous vendors and subcontractors were involved. The project spanned a four and a half year period. As with any large project, occasionally problems arise, and this project was no different. Two vendors, Lutron Electronics Incorporated and Philips Products, provided materials that were not satisfactory. The contrasting way these companies handled the problems provides a wonderful example of what makes some corporations a joy to do business with and why others should be avoided whenever possible. Poor customer service can make your blood boil and negatively impact your performance if you allow it to do so.

We'll discuss Lutron Electronics first, a company that makes the Maestro line of incandescent/halogen dimmer switches. These switches offer consumers a wide array of features in a flat-faced decorative switch. They allow you to set a wide range of lighting levels that you can return to with the touch of a button. They also allow you to adjust levels up or down with the simple touch of another button. They're attractive and offer additional options beyond simply being a dimmer switch.

Mike installed dozens of these switches throughout his construction project. But before the project was even completed, he noticed that some of the switches were malfunctioning. It appeared that a spring inside the switch was breaking or coming loose, preventing the on/off button from working properly. He called the electric supply house where he'd purchased the switches and described the problem. They advised him that they would have the Lutron sales representative call within the next few days on his next scheduled visit to their store.

True to their word, the following week Mike received a call from the Lutron sales representative. The sales rep asked if he could come by and inspect the bad switches, and when he arrived, only had to look at two of the switches before telling Mike that they were indeed not working right and that Lutron would cover the cost of replacing them. Then he inspected the other broken switches and apologized for the problem.

What happened next is what makes this such a wonderful story to tell. Before the bad switches could be replaced, two additional ones broke. Mike called the Lutron sales rep, who had left a business card with his office and cell phone numbers. When he told him that two more of the switches had failed, the sales rep said he'd call his company and would call Mike back afterward. The following day, he phoned to say that his company didn't know why the switches were failing, but they wanted to make it right; that in case there may have been a defective production run, the company wanted to replace all of the switches in the project with new ones. What's more, the company would not only provide new switches, but would cover the cost of the labor to replace them.

Repel Negative Influences, Focus on the Positive

Within days the new switches arrived at the electric supply house where the original ones were purchased, and Lutron contacted the electrical company that had originally installed them and contracted with them to replace the switches. What impressed Mike most was the fact that they replaced switches that were functioning perfectly, rather than risk more of them failing. The positive effect of their customer service was immeasurable, and you can bet that Mike will continue to use Lutron Electronics products on future projects.

In contrast, Philips Products supplied dozens of windows for the project through their Malta Windows division. All of the windows were satisfactory with the exception of just five, which arrived in a separate shipment and were eventually installed in five dormers. Shortly after their installation and a driving rainstorm, Mike noticed leakage coming into the building. He didn't think much of it at the time because the roof shingles and exterior siding had not been completed. Although the leakage was unusual, he wasn't concerned.

Over the next several weeks, however, additional leakage was noticed each time windblown rain pelted the face of the windows. Eventually, the exterior siding and roofing was completed and Mike assumed it would solve the problem. Wrong! The first driving rain that occurred, water continued to pour into the building and run down the walls below the windows.

Just as he had done with the dimmer switches, Mike called the vendor from whom he had purchased the windows. They sent a service person to inspect the installation, and he said the water was coming into the building because the roofer had not properly installed the flashing around the base of the dormers. In response, Mike called the roofer and told him what the window company's serviceman had told him.

The roofer immediately came to the project and tore off the shingles around one of the dormers to reveal properly installed copper flashing. This involved considerable work and the reinstallation of several shingles, but the roofer did not charge for the trip. He wanted to be sure his work was not the problem.

Mike once again called the window vendor and reported what the roofer had found. Once again the company sent people to look at the problem. On this trip, the service people connected a water hose and pulled it up on the roof in order to spray water on the face of the windows. When they did, it poured into the inside of the building. This time they told Mike that the windows were not properly installed and that the water must be coming in around the nailing flange.

The windows had been installed exactly the same way as dozens more had been, but Mike called the building contractor and told him what the window service people had said. Just as the roofer had done, the building contractor, a man with over 40 years experience, immediately came to the project to inspect his work. He took off all the trim around one of the windows, which revealed that it had been properly installed. Mike could readily see that it would be virtually impossible for water to come in around the nailing flange.

The next time a blowing rain occurred, water again poured into the now finished interior of the building. Mike called the vendor once again to report the problem. This time he was informed that they no longer sold the windows and provided him a phone number and name to contact at Philips Products, the window manufacturer. When he called and explained the problem to the Philips representative, he was told he would have to complete their warranty claim forms and provide proper documentation before anything could be done.

The forms, which consisted of several pages, were sent to Mike. He completed them and returned them with all of the requested documentation, including copies of the invoices showing where he had purchased the windows and what he had paid. Finally, Philips agreed to send its division service manager from the home office in Elkhart, Indiana, to look at the problem. Meanwhile, water was continuing to pour into the finished room and run down the face of expensive woodwork.

Once an appointment was set for the division service manager to visit the project, Mike also arranged for the roofer and building contractor to be present, to avoid any more buck passing. With everyone present, numerous tests were conducted on the windows, most of which involved spraying them with high pressure water from a hose. Eventually the trim from one of the windows was completely removed along with the shingles and copper flashing so the Philips representative could see what the contractor and roofer had previously inspected.

Repel Negative Influences, Focus on the Positive

He then began pointing out ways the windows could be reinstalled to prevent leakage. Mike stopped him and suggested another test. This time plastic sheeting was duct-taped around the outer frame of a window so that only its face was exposed and no sprayed water could get over, under, or around the plastic. When this test was conducted, water still leaked through into the inside of the building.

At this point Mike advised the Philips division manager that he was tired of excuses and delays. He said the potential damage to the interior was so great that he wanted the windows replaced. In the presence of the other subcontractors, the Philips representative told Mike to get the windows replaced and send him copies of the bills.

It took some extensive searching, but Mike eventually found a window manufactured by a different company that matched the profile of the Philips windows. It took six weeks from the time he placed the order for the new windows to arrive and another two weeks for them to be installed. This resulted in eight additional weeks of mopping up water each time a blowing rain occurred. When the Philips windows were removed, the flaw was obvious. The windows had moisture trails showing where water had entered around the sashes and flowed out from the bottom and into the building.

The new windows were installed exactly as the Philips windows had been. Even though he had already paid the bills, Mike waited several months to confirm that they were the problem, not the installation or the roofing. Had the problem persisted with the new windows, he would gladly have apologized to Philips, but after numerous hard-blowing rains, there was no further leaking. He sent the bills to the Philips division service manager, as he had been instructed. He waited patiently for his reimbursement, and after several weeks with no reply, called the division manager to see when he could expect a check. To his surprise, the division manager told him he had not received the bills. This time Mike sent the documents Certified Mail, Return Receipt Requested.

An additional two weeks passed after the letter was received before Mike got a letter from the division manager denying that he had agreed there was a problem, denying that he had agreed to pay for replacing the windows, and advising that he was forwarding the correspondence to the company's legal department.

Mike's initial reaction was to just turn the matter over to his attorney and sue the company. He even went so far as to send his files to the attorney with instructions to begin the legal process. Then he realized that he was allowing the company to negatively impact his life by occupying so much of his time with an issue that was insignificantly small in relation to the overall size of the project. Eventually he visited Philips Web site at www.philipsproducts.com and gained a better understanding of their methods. On the Web site page titled "Our Company," Mike found an interesting explanation for their behavior. The text on the page described the weakening economy and rising interest rates of the 1980s, followed by the sentence: "Our organization reacted to this change by pursuing every approach to increase profitability, and throughout the '80s, Philips found ways to cut costs and save creatively...."

Mike realized that the company's creative cost-cutting measures must have been to blame others and avoid taking responsibility with unsatisfied customers. As any large company would know, the cost of litigation deters most people, thereby allowing it to escape financial responsibility. This tactic may be good for the bottom line in the short run, but can you imagine what it must be like to work for a company that backs up its products this way? Imagine being a salesperson and trying to earn a living representing a company this shortsighted?

Philips is one of the country's leading manufacturers of replacement vinyl windows, something Mike uses large quantities of in the maintenance of his investment properties, but do you think he will ever purchase another one of their products? In his case, the company may have won the battle, but it definitely lost the war. Although it cost him several thousand dollars to replace the windows, he did just what the company wanted and decided that it wasn't worth his time to keep arguing with them. What he would spend in time and legal fees he could easily replace by focusing on more productive endeavors

These contrasting examples demonstrate the positive and negative influence corporations can have on your time and energy. It's clear why Mike would want to sing the praises of Lutron Electronics but avoid any future dealings with Phillips Products. Corporations are no different than individuals. Some give you a boost up and hope you will remember them on your climb to the top, while others will attempt to hold you back or drag you down to their level. As we discussed in Chapter 14, it's how you respond to these negative people or corporations that determine how well you will perform on your journey to financial independence.

In neither of our illustrations was the amount of money involved enough to make a noticeable difference in either Mike's lifestyle or the corporation's bottom lines. But the long-term effects of these differing behavior patterns can be significant. The lesson to be learned from these experiences is that Weekend Millionaires *repel negative influences and focus on the positives*. They don't get bogged down in minor skirmishes over insignificant matters. Sure, it means walking away from some situations and cutting your losses, but maintaining control over your emotions when adversity strikes will always serve you better.

Key Points from This Chapter

- Corporations, like individuals, have good and bad character and varying ethical standards.
- Give individuals and companies the opportunity to remedy problems before choosing not to do business with them.
- Praise and support the companies that do the right thing.
- Avoid getting dragged down emotionally by individuals or companies whose products or services are inferior.
- Learn to repel negative influences and focus on the positives.

27

The Application of Audio Learning

The vast majority of people who win large lottery prizes end up broke or nearly so within a few years of receiving their millions. Why? Could it be that the same reason most ordinary working people fail to achieve financial independence is the same reason so many lottery winners end up broke after becoming instant millionaires? We think so; and we think we know what that reason is and how to deal with it.

What do you think would happen if you took a professional truck driver used to making numerous trips across the country in a semitruck but who had never flown in an airplane and suddenly put him or her in the cockpit of the simplest single engine airplane and said, "Can you fly this from New York to Los Angeles?" Not only would the truck driver not be able to fly across the country, but he or she might not even know how to start the engine. The truck driver, who may be well into his or her earning years and eminently qualified to drive a truck, would probably be baffled by the simplest of airplanes.

Although piloting a large commercial airplane pays several times as much as driving a truck, without the corresponding increase in knowledge required to fly a plane, even a truck driver who could get one started would stand a better than average chance of crashing and being killed before completing the first flight. Winning the lottery is much like putting a truck driver in the cockpit of an airplane. Without knowing how to handle money, a lottery winner stands a better than average chance of crashing and burning financially. Just as the lottery winner may lose the newfound wealth, the ordinary working person will never attain wealth without first acquiring a corresponding increase in knowledge. That's where the application of audio learning can make such a difference to an aspiring Weekend Millionaire.

In Chapter 18 we discussed the advice Dr. Godfrey gave Mike when he was working at the defense plant. To reiterate:

If you will read an hour a day about something you know nothing about, within five years you will be amazed at the impact it will have on your life.

This advice was given to Mike in the late 1960s and he followed it religiously. He readily attributes his ability to start and to build a business to this valuable guidance, which he still follows today. But another event occurred years later, in the early 1980s, that expanded upon this advice and carried him to even greater success.

By this time, Mike had purchased a few single-family houses as investment properties. One day he received a call from his property manager asking if he would like to go to Charlotte, North Carolina, to hear Zig Ziglar speak to a Realtor's group of which he was a member. Mike had never heard of Zig Ziglar, so he initially declined the offer, but when his property manager told him that Ziglar was the country's leading motivational speaker and someone he would surely learn from, he decided to go. That was Mike's first such experience, and one he will never forget.

Zig Ziglar awed the audience, including Mike, with his total command of the stage and his inspiring motivational message. His enthusiasm was contagious, and when he closed the program with an invitation to purchase his audiocassette programs, Mike was at the head of the line to buy. This was his first experience with audio learning, but far from his last.

The Earning Years

On the return trip from Charlotte, Mike and his property manager listened to several of the tapes, and on one of them Ziglar stressed that you needed to listen to each tape at least 16 times to grasp its full content. The message was so positive and so uplifting that Mike vowed to do just that.

His commute to and from his office was about 30 minutes each way, and he began listening to the tapes every day. When he came to the last tape in the series, he put a mark on the album cover and started over. Each time he completed all the tapes, he added another mark to the cover and once again went back to tape one. He was determined to listen 16 times, as Ziglar had recommended. It wasn't long before he realized why listening repeatedly over and over was so important. Each time he went through the program, he heard something he'd missed in his previous listening. Sometimes he heard things but didn't fully understand them until after he had an experience where they applied.

It wasn't until a few years later that Mike began to fully grasp the power of audio learning. One of the tapes he had gotten from Zig Ziglar was a music tape titled *Born to Win*, which was the title of its lead song. Mike thought the collection of positive motivational songs would be good listening for his young children. His wife began playing the tape in the car as she transported them to and from play school.

A few months later they decided to go to dinner with a young couple and their three daughters who had recently moved to town. The new friends and their children met at Mike's house prior to dinner for a visit and to allow the children to play. When they loaded up to go to dinner, the two men went in one car with Mike's older son, Jason, and the couple's two oldest daughters. The women took the two younger children with them in a second car.

As they were driving to the restaurant, Mike was talking with the other father, and the children were in the backseat talking. Jason, who was about four at the time, was younger than the girls, who were seven and nine. Being new to town, the girls told Jason where they were born.

The oldest said, "I was born in Gainesville, Florida."

Then the younger girl chimed in, "Me too, I was born in Gainesville too."

The older girl turned to Jason and asked, "Where were you born?"

"I was born to win," Jason loudly proclaimed.

When Mike and his friend finally stopped laughing, he told the story about how his boys had been listening to Zig Ziglar's *Born to Win* tape. That's when Mike realized the subliminal effects that repeated listening to audiotapes could have on even young children. He also realized how most ordinary people waste hours riding around in their cars listening to radio programs that teach them nothing when instead they could have been listening to a tape like *Born to Win*. What a waste of time.

Following his experience with Zig Ziglar's audio program, Mike began to seek out other audio programs from which he could expand his knowledge and came upon the Nightingale-Conant Corporation, the country's largest producer of self-help programs. It was through them that he eventually met and became close friends with Roger Dawson. One of the first tape programs he purchased was Roger's *Secrets of Power Negotiating*. Mike only had to listen to this program once for him to realize that the people in his industry could greatly benefit from hearing Roger speak.

In his role as president of the North Carolina Outdoor Advertising Association, Mike contacted Nightingale-Conant and arranged to book Roger to speak at their next state conference. This led to another speaking engagement with the Outdoor Advertising Association of America, and a budding friendship between Mike and Roger that would grow and endure for more than 20 years and culminate in the two men combining their talents to produce the Weekend Millionaire series of books and audio programs.

Mike also purchased Carleton Sheets's *No Money Down* real estate investing program, a purchase that would lead to another long-term friendship and greatly enhance his growing real estate portfolio. In fact, both of us have continued to read and listen and learn throughout our entire earning years. If you visit our respective homes and offices, you will find extensive libraries of books and audio and video programs that reflect our mutual desire to learn and improve our performances. We even borrow from each other when we spot a book or program we haven't seen before.

Now, here's a little secret we want to share with everyone who reads this book. There are books and audio and video learning programs on virtually any subject imaginable. Unlike formal education, which can often be boring and dull, especially when you can't see its purpose, these tools allow you to acquire skills as you need them, when you need them, so you can apply them immediately.

The Earning Years

When Mike failed at his first management job, he read numerous books on management, and later purchased several audio programs on the subject to avoid repeating his mistakes. When he struggled with obtaining bank financing, he studied books and tape programs on economics, banking, and finance to gain a better understanding of things from a banker's perspective. He studied programs on psychology, motivation, creative thinking, ambition, peak performance, and self-esteem. As his real estate investing career took off, he not only studied Carleton Sheets's *No Money Down* program, but every other real estate investing program he could find, plus programs on negotiating, sales, and other subjects that could enhance his abilities as an investor. When he reached a point where he felt overwhelmed with work, he studied time-management programs to learn how to get things done more efficiently.

Roger, the country's most sought after speaker on negotiating skills, also continued to expand his knowledge in this area of expertise the same way Mike did, by reading and listening and learning continually throughout his life. Together we can assure you that acquiring a Weekend Millionaire Mindset is not an accomplishment, it's a lifelong journey that evolves and grows and gets better with each learning experience.

When Mike was in the outdoor advertising business, he encouraged his employees to continue expanding their knowledge and skills just as he was doing. He offered them an opportunity to use payroll deductions to build their own self-improvement libraries. Employees could sign up for as large or as small a payroll deduction as they wanted, but whatever they chose, Mike agreed to match it provided the money was spent on self-improvement materials. He also passed on any discounts his company received when it ordered books or tapes for the employees.

He was constantly bewildered by the number of employees who complained about their finances but refused to do anything to improve them, until one day he overheard a conversation in which several of his least productive employees were chiding another about wasting money on the audio program he had in his car. What keeps more people from achieving success than any other single thing is the negative influence of other people. Sure, books and audio programs cost money to buy and they require time to study, but if you get just one idea from each one that you can put to use, it's well worth the cost. It's like going to a gem mine: Until you learn to look for the gems, all you see are mounds of dirt.

We'll leave you with this thought: Imagine what could happen if everyone suddenly decided to use the time they spend riding in a car or the few minutes just before going to sleep or just after waking in the morning to improve their knowledge and skills. Would we have more financially secure people? Absolutely! Would we have more emotionally secure people? You bet we would! Would we see a growing number of people developing Weekend Millionaire Mindsets? We think so, because we know that your mind is like a muscle: When you use it, it expands and gets stronger; when you don't, it withers and fades away.

Key Points from This Chapter

- Whether you inherit wealth, hit the lottery, or simply want to build financial independence, you have to learn money management skills if you expect to be successful.
- Use otherwise unproductive time like driving to and from work to learn by listening to audio programs.
- Spaced repetition is a powerful tool, and listening to audiotapes over and over implants messages in your subconscious mind that become part of you.
- Feed your mind regularly, just as you do your body; because it's like a muscle that needs to be nourished and exercised every day.

28

Don't Let Frustrations Deter You

Throughout this book we have described how experiences from our formative years, our learning years, and our earning years have helped us develop a Weekend Millionaire Mindset. We have described events that shaped our outlook on life, our approach to problem solving, and our quest for knowledge. In the final two chapters of this part, we will conclude by discussing two problems that prevent many ordinary people from developing a Weekend Millionaire Mindset.

Unwillingness to practice and succumbing to frustrations can sink even the best of us. Many people know what to do, but refuse to practice doing it long enough to master it. They become frustrated when everything doesn't go perfectly the first time, and they lack the determination to keep at it long enough to get it right. They let small failures and insignificant shortcomings keep them from doing great things. Let us give you some examples.

We host scheduled chats on our Web site, www.weekendmillionaire.com, in which we answer questions about real estate investing, financing, negotiating, and other real estate–related inquiries. (These chats are free, by the way, and if you would like to join us, just log on to the Web site and register as a "new user." When you do, you will receive e-mail notices about the dates and times of the chats.) In our best selling book *The Weekend Millionaire's Secrets to Investing in Real Estate*, we urge new investors to disregard asking prices and instead to make offers that will work for them. Invariably, in nearly every chat, someone questions this advice. They will say something like, "That doesn't work where I live. I've made four offers and all I've done is insult people. I don't want to keep doing that." These people are allowing other people's reactions to their offers to put doubts in their minds. Until they come to the realization that unless the numbers work, a purchase will not be a good one anyway, they will continue to be frustrated and have doubts. No one has ever been ruined financially by a purchase they did not make.

Mike once made over 50 consecutive offers that were rejected before finally having one accepted, but of the 10 that followed, six were accepted. Establishing your own personal guidelines and then sticking with them is the best way to ensure success. Succumbing to frustration when success doesn't come quickly is the best way to ensure failure.

Mike has had many opportunities to let frustration get in the way of success, but throughout his life he resisted that temptation. Possibly it began as early as his experience with buying his first bicycle in War, West Virginia, or any one of the other frustrations he worked through during his early years. Wherever it started, Mike attributes much of his success to his ability to cope with frustrations without allowing them to deter him from his goals.

Frustrations come into play all across life's spectrum; they aren't just limited to major events. Learning to deal with frustrations, even small ones, can make life more fun as well as make you more enjoyable to be around. A couple of days before this chapter was written, an incident occurred that demonstrates this well.

The day after New Year's day 2005, Mike took his sons, Jason and Matt, bowling, together with their girlfriends and two of his young nieces. Although he had bowled professionally when he was in his 20s, Mike hadn't bowled in years and had never taken up the game with his sons. They got two lanes at the bowling center; put the girls on one lane and the guys on the other. They arranged for the girls lane to have bumpers put up to keep their balls from going in the gutters, but the guys, being the macho men that they were, didn't use the bumpers.

The first game, Jason had trouble keeping his ball on the lane and ended up with the lowest score of everyone. With each ball he rolled, he was becoming more frustrated. By the latter part of the second game he was stomping and huffing to the point that it was annoying everyone. Finally, Mike called him over, told him to sit down and cool off, that it was only a game.

"Yeah, I know," Jason said. "But it is so frustrating I can't enjoy it."

"Would you like some coaching?" Mike asked.

"It won't do any good," he huffed. "I'm just no good at bowling."

"Well, will you at least try something to see if it works?"

He huffed and puffed some more and finally said, "What?"

"Come on," Mike said when Jason's next turn came. "I'm going up on the lane with you and I want you to try something just once or twice and see what happens."

Mike then took him to the approach, lined him up near the center of the lane and pointed to the arrows painted several feet down the lane. "I want you to start here," he said, and pointed out a spot on the approach. "Then I want you to take your time, walk straight toward the second arrow from the right gutter and roll the ball directly over it. Forget about the pins way down at the end of the lane, just try to roll the ball to the arrow and let's see what happens."

Jason stood on the spot his dad had pointed out and slowly approached the foul line. He rolled the ball and it went right over the second arrow. The ball went down the lane and hit the head pin dead center. All of the pins went down except the six pin. When he turned around and started back from the foul line, he had a big grin on his face. "How'd I do that?" he said.

Mike then went back up on the approach with him, pointed out a spot about four boards to the left of where he had started when he rolled the first ball, and said, "I want you to stand right here and once again roll the ball over the second arrow from the right gutter."

"But won't that make the ball go more to the left?" Jason asked.

"Just try it and see what happens."

Don't Let Frustrations Deter You

Once again Jason approached the foul line slowly and rolled the ball directly over the second arrow. This time the ball went toward the right side of the lane and solidly hit the six pin. It was the first spare Jason had made in nearly two games. Again when he came off the lane, he had a big grin on his face.

Mike sat him down and explained to him that the dots and arrows on the approach and out on the lane were like sights on a rifle. If he could find the right spot on the approach to start and roll the ball consistently over the same spot on the lane, the ball would go to the same spot down at the pins every time. Then by adjusting where he started on the lane (the back site) and continuing to hit the same spot on the lane (the front site), he could make just about any spare.

"If you will just trust me and try to do what I tell you each time you roll a ball, I think you'll begin to figure out what I'm talking about," Mike said.

Throughout the remainder of the second game and all through the third game, Jason did exactly what his dad told him. Sure, he was like the rest of us and missed his target a few times, but by the end of the third game he'd gone from being the worst bowler of the group to having the second highest score and a totally different attitude. His frustrations were calmed by learning more about the game and understanding how to use the markings to improve his score. And he was no longer stomping and huffing; by learning about and concentrating on the things that would improve his score, not on the score itself, he conquered his frustrations.

The way Jason liberated himself from his bowling frustrations is the same way anyone would deal with bigger frustrations: You learn more and then practice what you learn.

Mike had an even greater frustration during his early years as a pilot. After earning his private pilot certificate years earlier, he had finally completed the required classroom and flight training, passed the FAA written exam, and was within a couple of hours of the minimum 200 hours of flight time needed to take the flight test to get his instrument rating. He was planning an extended vacation later in the month and wanted to add the rating to his license before he left home.

In July 1978 his flight instructor signed his logbook authorizing him to take the flight test he would need to pass to obtain the rating and arranged for him to fly to Morristown, Tennessee, to take his check ride with FAA examiner Evelyn Bryan Johnson. The flight to Morristown gave him the additional time he needed to make up the 200 hours.

From the minute he first saw her, Mike could tell that Ms. Johnson, who looked to be in her 60s, was an all business, tough as nails examiner. After giving him a route to fly and the procedures to expect, she had him file an IFR flight plan. Another hour or so of questioning on the ground passed before she announced that she was ready to fly.

They got in Mike's single engine Piper Arrow, cranked the engine, taxied out to the end of the runway, and took off. For the next two hours she put Mike through a series of maneuvers and approaches, which he flew perfectly, although he was required to wear a hood that restricted his vision to the instrument panel and prevented him from seeing outside the cockpit. She even took the controls and put the airplane in several unusual attitudes and then had him make the corrections to bring the plane back to normal flight. Finally, she had him make an unexpected flight to Knoxville, 27 miles away, covered up part of the instruments to simulate their failure, and instructed him to fly back to Morristown using only partial instruments and then make an approach to the airport. (Mike had never heard of an FAA check pilot requiring such a procedure, and still hasn't.) When he thought he had arrived at the missed approach point at Morristown, she told him to lift the hood and look outside. He was several hundred feet to the left of the runway.

She told him to go ahead and land the airplane, but didn't say anything else. They landed, taxied in to the ramp, and shut down the plane's engine. Finally she said, "You didn't pass."

Mike was devastated. He was counting on having the instrument rating before he left on his trip. "What did I do wrong?" he asked.

"You need to go back and do some more primary [no gyro] work," she said, and noted as much in his logbook.

Mike knew this was nonsense. He had perfectly flown the route and approaches for which she'd asked him to file a flight plan. It was not until after the test flight was over that she had suddenly told him go to Knoxville and make a 27-mile partial panel approach, and even at that, he'd still arrived within a few hundred feet of the airport and at a safe altitude to make corrections before landing. He was furious and frustrated.

Don't Let Frustrations Deter You

When he returned to Asheville and talked with his instructor, he couldn't believe that she had failed him. "We can go fly some partial panel approaches, but I don't know how much good it will do," his instructor said.

"The problem is, I'm leaving on a trip to go out West and then to the Bahamas, and I don't have time to go back for another check ride," Mike said.

"Well, if I were you, I'd go ahead with your trip and just be careful," his instructor replied. "Without your instrument rating, you won't be legal to fly in bad weather, but it's usually good this time of year."

And that's just what Mike did. He flew from Asheville to Kansas City, Missouri; Medicine Bow, Wyoming; Salt Lake City; Las Vegas, Nevada; Alamosa, Colorado; Ashland, Kansas; Fort Smith, Arkansas; Mobile, Alabama; Bartow and West Palm Beach, Florida; then on to Bimini, Freeport, and Nassau in the Bahamas, before returning to Savannah, Georgia, and then back to Asheville. It was an extended sightseeing and pleasure trip that added nearly 100 hours to his flight time. He won't say whether he fudged a bit when it came to getting through some weather fronts he encountered, but the trip went well, and when he returned he was ready to go retake the instrument flight test.

Once again he flew to Morristown to take on Ms. Evelyn Bryan Johnson. This time all she did was have him take off, fly one time around the airport, make a single approach, and land. As they taxied in, he looked over to her and asked, "What did I do wrong this time?"

"Nothing," she replied. "You passed."

"Well, why didn't I have to do all that stuff you had me do before?" he asked.

"Didn't need to," she said. "You did fine before, I just don't give instrument ratings to people with minimum time. I know that doesn't seem fair, but that's the way I do it. From the looks of your logbook, it didn't keep you from flying all over the country. Did you enjoy your trip?"

Mike had to admit that he was a much better pilot than he had been when he took his first check ride. Although he'd been frustrated with his failure on the first attempt, it made him hone his skills to the point where he would have been comfortable flying that same 27-mile partial panel approach again.

Roger experienced a similar frustration when he first learned to scuba dive. He was spending a week at Club Med in Playa Blanca, Mexico. He signed up for a five-day scuba-diving course. One of his frustrations was that the instructor taught the entire course in French, and in spite of taking five years of French in high school, he had trouble understanding everything.

On the third day of instruction the instructor gave him a heavier weight belt than he needed, and he had some difficulty staying up in the water. It didn't seem serious to him, but made him work harder. At the end of the session the instructor failed him without any explanation that Roger could understand. He was furious because he felt perfectly capable of finishing the course. He was sure that the instructor was being unfair, and his initial reaction was to forget the entire idea of scuba diving altogether. Then he decided that he wasn't going to let this incident affect his desire to learn scuba diving, so he swallowed his pride and the next day signed up for the course again and started the entire process over. If he hadn't done that, he would have missed out on all the joy and excitement of scuba-diving trips that he later took from Tahiti to the Virgin Islands.

It's an important part of the Weekend Millionaire Mindset: Losers get frustrated and quit when they think they've been treated unfairly; winners swallow their pride and get back in the game.

We could write a whole book on dealing with frustrations, but we think you get the point from these few stories. If you let frustrations deter you, you will never develop a Weekend Millionaire Mindset. When frustrations arise, deal with them by learning more and practicing what you learn. You will find that your frustrations, no matter how great, will slowly subside and eventually go away if you take this approach.

Now let's move on to the last chapter in this part and talk about practicing what you learn.

Key Points from This Chapter

- Don't give up just because things are tough. Giving up never gets you anywhere. Successful people are the ones who battle on and find a way to get it done.
- You're never too old or too smart that a little coaching won't help.

Don't Let Frustrations Deter You

- Just as learning how the marks on a bowling lane help guide you to a strike, the more you learn about a difficult task, the easier it becomes.
- Don't let stinging and unfair rejections stop you from continuing to try; choosing to quit before you master a task leaves you feeling dejected and apprehensive about trying other new things.

29

Practice, the Key to Power Performance

We're flabbergasted at the number of people who want to play the game but don't want to practice. Athletes in every sport love to play the game but hate to go to practice. Football players hate to hit tackling dummies, but will gladly give it their best shot in a game. Basketball players hate to run sprints in the gym, but will gladly give it their best shot in a game. Baseball players hate to chase fly balls for hours during practice, but will gladly give it their best shot during a game. Tennis players hate to spend time hitting balls thrown to them by a machine, but gladly give it their best shot during a match. The problem is that their best shot is seldom good enough unless they practice.

This same phenomenon holds true not just for athletics, but for almost any endeavor. People who seek perfection and practice the hardest are the ones who usually rise to the top, whether it's in sports, business, entertainment, or any other enterprise. So why are people so reluctant to practice? Could it be because practice tends to highlight weaknesses rather than strengths? When you practice, you are looking for ways to improve, which means you, or your coach, or your advisor, are looking for weaknesses upon which you can improve. When you perfect one weakness, it usually means you immediately move on to another and another. In the beginning, little emphasis is placed on what you do well. It's not until you're already accomplished that the emphasis begins to shift from strengthening weaknesses to enhancing strengths.

The reluctance to practice derails many good intentions. Hardly anyone likes to do things they aren't good at doing, so they avoid their weaknesses and focus on their strengths. Unfortunately, a balanced and successful life is much like a chain: It's no stronger than its weakest link. Unless you are willing to practice and improve upon your weaknesses, you will always be vulnerable to disappointments and failures. If you're trying to achieve financial independence and your weakness is earning money, you won't make it by becoming the biggest tightwad in town. Likewise, if you're great at earning money but your weakness is that you're a spendthrift, you won't get there by focusing on additional earnings. It takes strengthening your weaknesses to build a stronger future, and that requires practice.

Practice is important in every area of life. If you want to be a better athlete, you have to practice; if you want to be a better teacher, you have to practice; if you want to be a better speaker, you have to practice. Whenever you want to get better at doing anything, you have to practice. Practice will not only improve whatever you're doing, it may even save your life, as Mike learned a few years ago.

As we mentioned in the previous chapter, Mike is a licensed pilot. When he travels, he pilots his own airplane to the destination. In January 1989 he had flown his twin-engine Beechcraft King Air to a maintenance facility in Greer, South Carolina, for some minor repairs. He had other business in the area, so he didn't return to the airport until the next day after eight o'clock in the evening. He had spoken with the maintenance shop foreman earlier in the day and was told that his plane was ready and would be waiting for him on the ramp at the private terminal.

When he arrived at the airport, it was dark and weather conditions were deteriorating. Conditions at Asheville and Greer were similar. There was no severe weather in the forecast; the ceilings at both airports were 400-foot overcast with one-mile visibility, light rain, and fog. Mike had flown many flights in this kind of weather, so he felt comfortable filing an instrument flight plan for the short 36-mile trip back to Asheville.

He boarded the plane and started the engines. While they were warming up, he called ground control to obtain his clearance. He was cleared as filed, to fly the runway heading until reaching 2,000 feet, then to make a climbing right turn to the north, continue climbing to 5,000 feet, and proceed direct to Asheville. The field elevation at Greer is just less than 1,000 feet, but at Asheville, which is in the mountains of Western North Carolina, it is more than 2,100 feet. Five thousand feet is the minimum altitude for an aircraft approaching Asheville from the south when flying on instruments.

Mike taxied out to the runway and was cleared for takeoff. Everything was normal throughout the takeoff roll, climb, and turn toward Asheville. Almost immediately after takeoff he entered the clouds and was still in them upon reaching 5,000 feet. Light rain was pelting the windshield, but the ride was smooth and nothing was showing on the weather radar. He expected a normal flight that would take less than 15 minutes.

Shortly after reaching 5,000 feet, and just as he was approaching the edge of the mountains, Greer Departure radioed, giving him a new radio frequency and advising him to contact Asheville Approach. Mike acknowledged the change and put the handheld microphone back on its hook while he switched radio frequencies. Before he could pick up the microphone again, the plane suddenly pitched up violently and started a rapid roll to the right. It was as though a big gorilla had grabbed it and was throwing it around.

Mike forgot about the radio and grabbed the yolk with both hands, trying to regain control of the plane. Within seconds the plane had rolled until the wings were perpendicular to the artificial horizon on the instrument panel; altitude was passing 6,000 feet and climbing at a rate of more than 8,000 feet per minute. Mike had the controls all the way to the stops in the opposite direction, but the plane was continuing to roll, when just as suddenly as it began, the plane shuddered and then the roll stopped as if it had hit something hard. The stop was so sudden, it slammed Mike's head against the metal post framing the side window of the cockpit hard enough to open a gash beside and above his left eye.

Practice, the Key to Power Performance

Almost instantly the plane shook violently, began to rapidly roll in the opposite direction and started a rapid descent. Mike didn't even notice that blood was pouring down the side of his face. His only thought was to get the wings level and regain control of the plane. Although the instruments were blurred, he could see that the airplane was descending over 5,000 feet per minute even with its nose in a climb attitude. He pushed the throttles forward and started to lift the nose a little more trying to arrest the descent, but the plane was continuing to roll left in spite of the fact that he now had the controls locked as far as they would go to the right.

Within seconds his altitude had fallen below 5,000 feet and the wings had rolled to the left until once again they were beyond perpendicular with the artificial horizon. Mike was just on the verge of moving the controls to roll the plane a full 360 degrees in an attempt to get it back upright when just as it had before, it abruptly stopped the roll. This time the change was so sudden that it tore loose the nylon netting holding his overnight bag in place in the luggage area at the rear of the cabin. A small handheld recorder he had laid in one of the seats was thrown into the cockpit.

Fortunately, the roll to the left stopped and, as he was leveling the wings, the plane began another rapid ascent. The roll had stopped, but now with the engines running at full power from when he'd pushed the throttles forward, airspeed was rapidly increasing, even though the plane's nose was above the horizon and it was climbing at a rate of over 10,000 feet per minute.

Mike reached over and pulled the throttles back to idle, but the airspeed kept increasing. Since the plane was climbing, he kept the wings level and pulled back on the controls to lift the nose and try to slow down the airspeed. Throughout the ordeal, he kept recalling what he had practiced over and over in training: Keep the wings level and control the airspeed. When he saw the needle on the airspeed indicator go well past the red line, with the power pulled all the way back and the nose up, he yelled out, "My God, this is easier said than done."

No sooner had the words escaped his mouth than the plane suddenly stopped climbing and started back down again. The overnight bag that had torn loose in the baggage area now came floating through the cabin door and hit the instrument panel. Mike shoved it toward the empty copilot's seat

225

and looked back at the airspeed indicator. Now the needle was rapidly falling and the airspeed was approaching stall speed. When a plane's momentum doesn't support the angle of climb, it won't fly anymore. It flutters like a dead bird and falls to the ground. He pushed the nose forward and reapplied full power. This descent was not as intense as the previous one had been, and Mike was aware that he was getting out of the turbulence when he heard the voice of a controller from the Asheville airport coming from the speaker above his head.

Apparently, information transmitted by reporting instruments on the plane had allowed the controller to see on his radar screen that the aircraft was experiencing sudden and rapid altitude changes. That could only mean problems. Evidently he had been trying to contact Mike, with no response, because when he came on the air he calmly said, "November 28 Mike Sierra, Asheville Approach. If you copy you are cleared for the ILS approach to runway 16 and cleared to land, you need not acknowledge."

That was good to know, because by that time Mike was beginning to regain control of the plane, but he had no idea where his microphone was. It had jumped off its hook, and apparently its weight flying around in the cockpit had pulled the plug loose that connected it to the transmitter. Gradually Mike flew out of the turbulent air and quickly set the instruments to make the approach to the airport. His route was taking him across the initial approach fix, and when he passed it, he began a descent down the glide path to the airport. He was beginning to recover his composure from the violent experience when he noticed his face stinging just above the eye. He reached up to touch it and felt the blood running down his cheek and dripping off his chin onto his pants. That was the least of his worries at the moment; he still had to get the airplane safely on the ground with less than desirable weather conditions.

As he continued down the approach, he was totally focused on keeping the glide path and runway centerline in the crosshairs of his instruments. Finally, just a little over 300 feet from the ground, he exited the base of the clouds and saw the runway stretching out directly in front of him. The wheels touched and the plane rolled down the runway until speed slowed enough for him to turn it off the runway. As soon as he hit the taxiway, he stopped the plane, located the microphone, plugged it back in and called Asheville Ground Control. The first thing they said was, "What happened out there?"

"You don't even want to know." Mike said. Then, to break the tension he was feeling, he added, "I think Ms. Evelyn Bryan Johnson just gave me another instrument competency check ride."

Although it was said in jest at a very stressful time, Mike's comment reflected his newfound respect for the lady who didn't want him flying under instrument conditions until he had more experience. He would hate to think what the outcome would have been had this experience happened earlier in his flying career. Now, thousands of flying hours later, the experience reinforced his belief in practice. Had he not continued to receive recurrent training and practiced emergency procedures, Mike would probably not be around to talk about the experience today. Practice had truly saved his life.

Mike felt lucky to have survived the ordeal. Then he remembered what he had often told others: "Luck is really just preparation meeting opportunity."

There are many additional sidebars to this story that would make for interesting reading, but the lesson from the experience is that *practice is the key to power performance*. Whether it's practicing flying skills, buying skills, speaking skills, writing skills, or any of the other skills we have developed, we'd never be where we are today if we hadn't been willing to practice. No matter what you do, practice will make you better. No matter what your goals, practice will enable you to reach them faster and enjoy them more when you get there. Just never doubt that *practice, practice, practice is the key to power performance*.

Key Points from This Chapter

- Don't wait until you're in a crisis situation to start practicing.
- Practice embeds the practiced performance in your subconscious mind, thereby making it second nature when reaction time dictates immediate action.
- If you can't make a speech, write a letter, negotiate a deal, or fly an airplane when you aren't under pressure, you'll never be able to do it when the pressure is on.

- "Luck" is the word we use to describe the coming together of preparation and opportunity.
- You build a better life by strengthening your weaknesses than by focusing only on your strengths.

PART V

The Skills You'll Need

Your journey to a Weekend Millionaire Mindset and the financial independence that follows depends on two things: your motivation and your skills. As the old song goes, "you can't have one without the other."

Motivation is strengthened by the three Ds of success that we've talked about: Discipline, Dedication, and Desire. Do you have enough creative discontent in your life to really want to make major changes? Discontent is the crucible in which desire is created. Have you developed the discipline to keep plowing on when the going gets tough? Do you have the dedication to see it through?

Some motivational speakers would tell you that enthusiasm is *all* you need. We respectfully disagree. We think that developing the skills to be financially independent is equally important. Without skills, you're like the Roadrunner in the old cartoons: You're a bundle of energy and you stir up a lot of dust, but when it all settles, you're still right where you started.

We recall the time when David Chou, who was promoting Roger's Taiwanese seminars at the time, was visiting him at his home in Southern California. They planned to play golf together at Hacienda Golf Club, where Roger is a member. Before the match, David called and said, "One of my motivational speakers is traveling with me. Would it be okay if he joins us?"

"Is he a good player?" Roger asked. "Hacienda is a tough course."

"I've never played with him, but he says he's really good."

That turned out to be a bit of an overstatement. The motivational speaker was enthusiastic and tried hard, but he had difficulty getting the club head to connect with the ball, which is a fairly important skill in golf. David and Roger let him tee up the ball in the fairway and he was still having trouble. After a few holes he gave up and went back to the practice range to take a lesson. "I thought you told me he was a good player?" Roger said to David.

David replied, "Well, you know how these motivational speakers are. They think they can do anything!"

So you need skills, not just motivation. If you're highly motivated and don't have the skills, you'll expend a lot of energy but it won't get you where you want to go. If you have the skills and don't have the motivation, you will tend to analyze situations to the point where you'll become paralyzed and take no action.

In this part we're going to teach you the skills you need to succeed. We'll begin by discussing how to get motivated and stay motivated. There's a lot more to it than rah-rah. Then we'll go into the science of goal setting. There's a lot more to it than putting a picture of a Ferrari on your mirror. Then we'll move on to the importance of integrity and how it affects everyone around you. In Chapter 33 we'll discuss the magic of consistency and how it's been the key ingredient for success for most leaders in history, and then how to change your world by changing the way you think. In the Chapters 35 and 36, you'll learn two essential skills: decision making and time management. Finally, we'll teach you how to stop thinking like a consumer and start thinking like an investor.

So keep reading and we'll teach you what we've learned about these vital skills.

30

How to Stay Motivated

In this chapter we're going to teach you how to get motivated and stay motivated. Your ability to stay motivated has very little to do with what happens to you. It has everything to do with how you react to what happens to you.

Let's say you studied our previous book, *The Weekend Millionaire's Secrets to Investing in Real Estate*. You find a house for sale and make an offer to buy it. The sellers think your offer is ridiculously low and won't even consider giving you a counteroffer.

The reaction of an optimistic, motivated person to this disappointment would be with the three I's: that the event is Impermanent, Impersonal, and Isolated. By *Impermanent* we mean that they don't draw the conclusion that because this seller said no now, he or she will always say no. Also, the market will not always stay the same. It could be a seller's market now and a buyer's market a month from now. By *Impersonal* we mean that the buyer doesn't feel it was his or her fault the seller said no. By *Isolated* we mean they don't come to the conclusion that because this seller said no, all sellers will say no.

Contrast that with the pessimistic, unmotivated person. Instead of responding to this bad event with the three I's, he or she responds with the three Ps. That it was Permanent—this seller will always say no and it will always be a seller's market. That the event was Personal, a direct rejection of the buyer. That this event was Pervasive, and all sellers will say no to low offers.

If you will take to heart what we've taught you here, you will find that you can train yourself to be optimistic even when disappointing things happen to you. Just remember the three I's when bad things happen to you. This bad event is Impermanent, Impersonal, and Isolated.

What about when good things happen to you? That's when you react with the three Ps. Good events are Permanent, Personal, and Pervasive, Good things will continue to happen, they happen to you because you're good, and that good things are happening all over.

If you'd like to learn more about properly interpreting the events in your life, we highly recommend Dr. Martin Seligman's great book *Learned Optimism* (Knopf, 1991). Dr. Seligman is a professor at the University of Pennsylvania. His writing style is entertaining, and we know you'll enjoy reading the book.

So, your ability to stay motivated depends upon the three Ps and the three I's. Let's go through it one more time. The first P stands for Permanence, and the first I stands for the opposite, Impermanence. Permanence refers to whether you consider an event a permanent condition or only a temporary occurrence. Therefore it refers to time. The optimist sees good things as always happening again in similar circumstances, and sees bad things as a onetime fluke. The pessimist sees good things as a onetime fluke and bad things as always recurring.

The second P stands for Personal, and the second I stands for Impersonal. The optimist sees good events as being to their credit, and bad things as being someone else's fault. The pessimist sees good things as someone else's doing and bad things as their fault.

The third P stands for Pervasive, and the third I stands for Isolated. The optimist sees good things as an indication of good things happening all over, and sees bad things as an isolated event. The pessimist sees good things as an isolated event and bad things as an indication that bad things are happening everywhere.

How to Stay Motivated

Let's take a look at these responses in Figure 14.

	Good Events	Bad Events
Optimistic Thinking	Permanent	Impermanent
	Personal	Impersonal
	Pervasive	Isolated
Pessimistic Thinking	Impermanent	Permanent
	Impersonal	Personal
	Isolated	Pervasive

Figure 14

What we've given you is a quick run-through of what Dr. Seligman's research revealed, and we can understand if you find it a bit confusing. A full reading of his book will bring it all into focus.

But for our abbreviated version, it's not that complicated. Just be an optimist, whether good or bad things happen to you. Good things are Permanent, Personal, and Pervasive. Meaning that good things will continue to happen, they're happening because you caused them to happen, and they're happening all over. Bad things, on the other hand, are Impermanent, Impersonal, and Isolated. Meaning the bad things aren't going to keep happening, they weren't your fault, and they are not happening all over.

Optimistic people see good events as Permanent, Personal, and Pervasive. They see bad events as Impermanent, Impersonal, and Isolated. Pessimistic people have it backward: They see good events as Impermanent, Impersonal, and Isolated, and they see bad events as Permanent, Personal, and Pervasive. That's why you don't see very many pessimistic people enjoying success.

We realize this may seem like an oversimplification, but the ability to stay motivated is one of the key characteristics of success. When good things happen, people with a Weekend Millionaire Mindset think P! P! P!, and when something bad happens they think I! I! I! This ability to stay motivated is another key characteristic of the Weekend Millionaire Mindset.

Key Points from This Chapter

- You can train yourself to be optimistic.
- You condition your thinking so that you react well when good or bad things happen.
- Good things are Permanent, Personal, and Pervasive.
- Bad things are Impermanent, Impersonal, and Isolated.

31

Goal Setting

There is no question that you can accelerate your journey to financial independence by mastering the art of goal setting. Having a clear set of written goals encourages you to stay on track, motivates you to attain your next step, and can actually create opportunities for you.

Your goal is to develop enough passive income so you can quit working if you choose to and not have to modify your lifestyle. How do you go about that?

The first thing you should do is write your goal down on a piece of paper and start carrying it around with you. Oh! How many times have you heard that? That you should write down your objectives and carry them with you all the time? So why don't you quit giving it lip service and start doing it? Your subconscious mind is so much more aware of objectives when you have them written down.

When comedian Jim Carrey was a struggling Canadian comic, he wrote himself a check for $10 million. On the memo line he wrote, "For services rendered." His goal was to get paid $10 million for starring in a movie. He carried that check with him for the next 10 years through thick and thin, through ups and downs, until he was able to take it out of his pocket and lay it next to his contract for starring in *Ace Ventura*, a role that catapulted him into the $20 million per movie bracket. Does he still have the check? No. At his father's funeral he slipped it into his father's pocket to thank him for the inspiration he had provided.

Suze Orman, best-selling author and Wall Street guru, was a $400 dollar a month waitress when she wrote out her goal: "I am young, powerful, and successful, producing at least $10,000 a month." Every morning before she went to work at her new job at Merrill Lynch, she would write out her goal over and over.

One evening when Roger's son Dwight was a teenager, Roger took him out to dinner and talked about the future. Sometimes parents have to play little games to catch the attention of teenagers, because the youngster's minds are full of so many other things. He said, "Dwight, I'm going to do something for you only 3 percent of the people in this world can do." With that he pulled his list of objectives from his pocket and showed them to him. Study after study has shown only 3 percent of people carry their objectives with them, despite having been told to do so time after time after time. Only 10 percent of the people in this country can even tell you what they'd like to be doing five years from now.

Isn't it amazing that you could walk up to 100 people on any city street and say something such as, "Pardon me, but here we are, travelers together on Planet Earth spinning through the heavens; would you mind telling me exactly what you're doing here?"

Ninety percent of them would have to answer, "Well, I don't know. I haven't really given it that much thought." Ninety percent of the people in the world have no more direction in their life than that.

How to Plan Your Objectives

Your objective is a perfect future where your passive or unearned income is enough to maintain your lifestyle without working. You should have this as a written objective, but how do you go about writing it down?

Goal Setting

There's quite an art to writing objectives. An objective doesn't need to be all-encompassing or profound, but it does need to have a precise format. First, it must include an action verb: any verb with a "to" in front of it—to do, to have, to become, to attain. A well-written objective also needs a time frame. "To generate $500 a month in passive income from investments within one year." That's a well-written objective because it has a verb and a time frame. Remember that without a time frame, it's not an objective, it's just wishful thinking ... a daydream.

Write down your objective here:

My objective is to:

_____

I will accomplish this by:

_____

Having learned how to format your objective, we now want you to create a form on which you'll write your objectives, so you can carry them with you always. It should look like this:

My Goal

My one-year goal is:

My five-year goal is:

Skills and knowledge I'll need:

I'm willing to give up:

What I'll do this month:

It's an excellent format for the goals that you'll carry around with you in your pocket. As you can see, it includes a one-year objective as a part of a much longer range five-year objective; detailed information to help you accomplish your objective, and an immediate activity objective.

Take the time to photocopy it and make 21 copies. Our purpose is to get you in the habit of looking at your objectives every day. If we can get you to do it for 21 consecutive days, it will become a lifetime habit.

Pavlov, the man who discovered that you could make a dog salivate by ringing a dinner bell, said that it takes 21 days for anyone to develop a new habit. You'll notice that if you move the wastepaper basket to the other side of your desk, you'll throw paper on the floor for about 21 days until you break your old habit and start a new one. If you move to a new home, it takes about 21 days before it starts feeling like home. If you start a new job, it takes about 21 days for it to feel as if it's what you do for a living rather than a new job.

So if you get into the habit of looking at your objectives every day for the next 21 days, you will have created a new habit, and what a difference it will make in your life.

How to Complete the Goals Sheet

So on the first of the 21 days, use one of the sheets to write out your objectives. Here are some things to consider as you fill it in.

Your One-Year Objective.   It may be that it will take you five years to accomplish your objective; however, you need guideposts along the way. You need some intermediate stops on which you can set your sights and pause to revel in your accomplishment. Be sure that your one-year objective is consistent with your five-year objective. Don't give yourself an objective to own that Mercedes 600 in one year and an objective of having $100,000 cash in the bank in five years. Unless in some way you must have the Mercedes to earn the $100,000, the two objectives are conflicting. Better to set a one-year objective of having $10,000, $15,000, or $20,000 in the bank.

Your Five-Year Objective.   Of course, this would be an extension of your one-year objective. You may even want to write this goal first and then make sure your one-year goal is a step on the road to achieving it. Stretch yourself, but make the objective believable. If you don't believe that you can achieve it now, even though it excites you and while your right-brain creative mind is in control, you'll never be able to maintain a positive attitude when your left brain starts to present all the obstacles to you.

Skills and Qualifications You'll Need.   Skills you'll need may include:

- Public speaking skills
- Writing skills
- Persuasion skills
- Selling skills
- Computer skills

Qualifications you'll need may include:

- College courses
- Professional designations
- State licenses
- Published articles or books
- Citizenship
- Residency in a city or state

What You're Willing to Give Up.   The measure of your desire is what you're willing to give up to accomplish your objective. This is a good gauge of your desire. You might be willing to give up:

- Expensive vacations
- Your bowling league, so you can attend class
- That new car you were thinking about buying this year
- Dining out for lunch instead of packing a lunch
- The long distance trip to visit friends that you'd planned

What You'll Do This Month.   Getting started is half the battle. Haven't you found that to be true? Perhaps you've dreaded the thought of doing your income tax return and have been putting it off for weeks. However, once you start, you realize that it's not half as much work as you expected.

Writing a book like this takes a tremendous amount of time. We typed over 600,000 keystrokes before we finished it. It took us at least six months of constant effort to get it done. It was a daunting challenge. How did we do it? We got started! We promised ourselves that at 7:00 A.M. the next day we would be sitting in front of our computers with a hot cup of coffee. We called up a new page on our word processing program, set the margins and the type style. Then we typed a title for the chapter we were going to start that day. Then we switched to an outlining program and started dropping in all our thoughts on the topic, and began to rearrange them into a coherent outline. Soon it was evening and we had a fairly good outline for the chapter and were ready for the rewrite work later. Simply getting started was so valuable. Once you commit to getting started, you've taken the biggest step to getting there.

This part of your goal pad may include:

- Sign up for a college course
- Get a part-time job to gain experience
- Buy and read three books on the topic
- Make contact with three people who can give you guidance

On the second day, take out a new piece of paper—throw away the old piece—and rewrite your objectives. It will take you only a few seconds, and the results are amazing.

You'll find that during the first week you will reformulate your objectives. Things that may have seemed important on the first day may not seem important anymore, because your subconscious mind has been playing with these ideas. Now you're beginning to formulate a plan that you're enthusiastic about, and you're getting excited.

By the middle of the second week you'll probably do something unconsciously that's a step toward your objective. You might find yourself reading a college catalog, for instance, and as you glance at the courses, you realize these are some of the skills you'll need to be successful in your new venture. You didn't consciously pick it up for that reason, but your subconscious mind is pushing you in the right direction.

As you near the end of the three-week period, you'll find you've made substantial progress toward making your objectives happen.

Lifetime Objectives

Notice that we didn't give you a place to write anything longer than a five-year objective. Lifetime objectives are great. As we told you, Mike's objective of becoming a millionaire by age 30 and retiring by age 50 was a powerful driving force for many decades. Lifetime goals are not to be taken lightly. They are the goals to which you're going to commit your entire life.

For this exercise, we suggest that you think in smaller time frames as you begin developing your goal-setting abilities. Start with where you want to be five years from now. Just be sure that your one-year and five-year goals are consistent with your lifetime goals once you have them established. When you set your lifetime goals, be sure to put them in writing and carry them with you.

Why We Don't Accomplish Our Objectives

Now let's examine the four reasons we don't accomplish our objectives. They are:

1. They're unrealistic.
2. They're dictated by others.
3. They're too vague.
4. We lack the motivation.

Let's take a close look at each one of these.

Unrealistic Objectives

Many people go through life setting unrealistic objectives and never accomplishing any of them. It's an interesting phenomenon: People who set unrealistic objectives often have a negative self-image. Subconsciously, they think of themselves as losers. However, they like to go through the motions of setting objectives, so when they fail they can say to themselves, "Poor me, I'm such a failure, I keep trying but I never seem to make it." In this way, they feed their self-image as a loser. When someone visits a weight-loss doctor and says, "I want to lose 50 pounds," the doctor usually tells him: "Let's set an objective of 10 pounds first, and see how it goes." A good doctor pushes the patient back to reality because he or she realizes it's essential that objectives are realistic.

Objectives Dictated by Others

Be sure that you set objectives only for those things you truly want. Set objectives that are important to you regardless of what the rest of the world thinks. Your son might give his right arm for a Porsche, but you're perfectly happy driving your pickup.

Unfortunately, we live in a world where advertising messages constantly bombard us, telling us what we should want out of life. Too often they overwhelm us and we never stop to determine what we really want. You wouldn't let someone else sit down and write out your objectives for you, would you? Then why should you let yourself be controlled by subliminal advertising messages or other people's comments about what you should be doing?

They're Too Vague

The third reason we fail to accomplish our objectives is that they're too vague. Be specific. For example, if one of your objectives is to acquire an apartment building, don't word it vaguely. Even saying you want a 16-unit apartment building is too vague. Feed your subconscious as many details as possible; you should be able to feel the objective in all its reality: "I want to own a 16-unit apartment building within 10 miles of my home. It will have at least 12 two-bedroom apartments. It will have a swimming pool with a security fence, and the tenants will all pay their own utilities."

The more clearly you see the objective, the closer you'll be to accomplishing it. An objective like, "I want to have a comfortable cash reserve in the bank within a year," is not as powerful as, "I want $12,500 in the bank as a cash reserve by next April fifteenth."

We Lack the Motivation

Lack of motivation is the fourth reason so many objectives fall by the wayside. Motivation always follows desire, doesn't it? Do you have enough desire? Do you have enough reasons to pursue your objective?

There's a story about Socrates that tells of a young man who approached him and asked, "How do I become as wise as you? How can I get the knowledge?" Socrates walked with the young man to the beach, and when they reached the ocean, he pushed the man under the water and held him there with his hand. The young man pulled himself out, gurgling for breath, and Socrates pushed him under again. Again the young man surfaced, and Socrates pushed him under a third time. Finally, when the young man's lungs were nearly bursting and he was on the verge of passing out, Socrates freed him and the man lay there, gulping for air. Socrates stood over him and said, "Young man, when you want knowledge as much as you just wanted air, you'll get it."

There's an old proverb that says, "When a student is ready, a teacher will appear." Understand that when the desire to fulfill a mental picture is strong enough, the opportunity will appear. Be sure your objectives excite you so much that they give you a driving desire to accomplish them. When you've trained yourself to review your objectives daily and you've started to build a mental picture in such detail and with such clarity that it demands to become real, you'll have arrived on the road to financial independence.

Setting realistic, specific, and motivating objectives is the only way any of us can begin to define the direction of our lives. Believe this with every fiber of your being, and apply it on a daily basis throughout your life. Know that only with sharply defined, imaginative, and stimulating objectives will you be able to achieve your goals.

Before you go on to the next chapter, define and write down your five-year and one-year objectives. Commit to thinking about them for a few minutes every day for the next 21 days. Then start to act as though it's impossible to fail.

Key Points from This Chapter

- Write down your goals and carry them with you.
- The goal must have an action verb and a time frame. For example: "To generate $500 a month in passive income from investments within one year from now."
- Create a goals form and use it to rewrite your goals every day for the next 21 days.
- Be sure your one- and five-year objectives aren't in conflict with your lifetime goals.
- Set realistic goals that are meaningful to you.
- Be specific, and set motivating goals.

32

Integrity

In 1959 the Walt Disney Company starting looking for an East Coast location in order to develop a second Disneyland. At that time, only 2 percent of Disneyland's visitors came from the East, but 75 percent of the population lived east of the Mississippi River. For years they secretly bought up land under dummy corporations.

On the morning of October 20, 1965, company representatives shook hands with the owner of the final parcel of land they needed to put the entire project together. But that afternoon, before the rancher signed the final papers, they were shocked to learn that the *Orlando Sentinel* had broken the story about the Disney World development. They feared that the land the rancher had been willing to sell for hundreds of dollars an acre would now be worth millions. To their amazement and delight, there was no conflict in the rancher's mind. He had shaken hands on the deal that morning and had no intention of reneging.

Wouldn't it be a great world if everyone had that rancher's high sense of integrity? We could once again live in a world where we didn't have to lock our cars and put alarms on our houses and never need to shred our paper-work again.

Waiting for that to happen would get us accused of shameless wishful thinking. Instead we want you to adopt a high level of personal integrity because we think it's the best way to get rich and stay rich. Our late friend and mentor Earl Nightingale once wrote, "If honesty did not exist, it would have to be invented, as it is the surest way of getting rich."

We agree with this because every really successful person we have ever met had a very high level of personal integrity. Sure, we've met people who have made a lot of money using standards that were less than perfect, some even unethical, but ultimately they always fell from grace.

Roger can point to so many people who were talented, hardworking, and dedicated to their profession, but they weren't quite forthright. They weren't crooks, but if they saw an opportunity to cut a corner they would do it.

When he was 10 years old, Roger helped a friend pick up a load of hay from a farmer. His friend paid the farmer and was told to help himself to 32 bales of hay from the hay stored in the barn. By the time they'd counted out 32 bales, the farmer had left. Roger's friend then deliberately threw four more bales onto the truck. When Roger protested, his friend said, "Every-body does it."

How many times have you heard that? Over the years, Roger watched his friend's progress. He always worked hard and had many successes, but they didn't last. He had a very rich business partner and they were doing well until the partner was caught in a scam and had to leave the country overnight. This caused his friend's business to collapse. His baby son died. His wife left him. His next business failed. To Roger, the reason for all these setbacks was very clear. He was not a crook. He didn't belong in jail, but he was not quite aboveboard.

Mike had a similar experience while still in the outdoor advertising business. A young man who worked for his company as an account execu-tive reminded him a lot of Roger's friend. The youngster was a real go-get-ter and top producer, but an incident occurred that caused Mike to keep a close watch on his activities.

After several months of very high expense reports, Mike decided to ver-ify the mileage being turned in by the young man. He checked the odometer reading on his car against what he'd put on his expense report he found a wide discrepancy in mileage. When Mike confronted the young man about it, he told Mike that he would soon have to turn in the leased car, and he'd had someone he knew in a speedometer shop roll the odometer back so he wouldn't have to pay for going over his allotted miles.

Mike rejected his claim for mileage on the expense report and had a lengthy discussion with the young man about honesty and integrity. He explained that rolling back the miles on the odometer was no different than stealing from the leasing company. The young man was very apologetic and remorseful and vowed never to do anything like that again, but it left lingering doubts in Mike's mind.

A few weeks following this incident, our good friend Zig Ziglar was in Asheville, North Carolina, conducting a large public seminar. On his way out of town, he stopped by Mike's office, which was near the airport, for a visit. While he was there, Mike thought Zig, who is a highly principled man, could be a positive influence on his young account executive, so he called him to his office and introduced the man to him.

The young man was excited to have the opportunity to talk with this man who is so well known in the area of motivation, personal growth, and development.

"Mr. Ziglar," Mike recalls the young executive saying, "if you could give me one bit of advice, knowing that I am just getting into the business world, what would it be?"

Ziglar leaned forward, placed a hand on his shoulder and said, "Young man, always, always maintain a high degree of personal integrity and you will do just fine."

Sadly, within a month of this encounter, Mike discovered that the young account executive had signed a client's name to an advertising contract in an attempt to win a sales contest. Needless to say, the young man did not remain with Mike's company, nor did he fare any better in future endeavors during the following years.

So when people tell you "everybody does it," alarm bells should go off in your head. You're down at the Cineplex and your friends want to sneak into another movie. "But everybody does it," they tell you. Maybe so, but you're not everybody. In the simplest of terms, what goes around comes around. According to some Eastern religions, if your behavior is less than exemplary, it negatively affects your dharma (who you are), and that in turn ruins your karma (how the universe treats you).

Maintaining integrity is not easy at times. Temptations can arise that make sacrificing integrity financially attractive. Mike had such a temptation once when he sold an airplane he'd owned for a while. After several weeks of discussing it with a prospective buyer, they agreed upon a price and shook hands to cement the deal. As often happens, Mike's integrity was tested the very next day when he received a call from another prospective buyer who had just learned that he was selling the plane. This buyer offered him $100,000 more for the plane than what Mike had agreed to sell it for the previous day. This buyer even offered cash, whereas the first buyer's purchase was contingent upon getting financing. No contracts had been signed, so it would have been easy for Mike to back out of the first deal and pocket the extra $100,000, except for one thing: He had integrity. In his mind, the handshake was just as valid as a written contract; therefore, he completed the transaction with the original buyer. Was it painful? Of course it was! Was it worth it? "Without question," Mike says. "Sure I lost $100,000, but I maintained my integrity and I didn't lose my self-respect."

The best advice we can give you to help you develop your own high standards of integrity is to study the lives of people you admire. By doing so you will learn that their most endearing characteristic is their integrity and reliability. They could be counted upon in difficult times. Mike's and Roger's offices and libraries are filled with books about great people.

Study the lives and stories of people like George Washington, Abraham Lincoln, Winston Churchill, Florence Nightingale, Susan B. Anthony, Ronald Reagan, and Margaret Thatcher. Study the people whose strength of character helped them change our world. How would you have behaved if you were facing the difficulties that they faced?

Napoleon Hill was a well-known writer who virtually kick-started the entire human potential movement in this country when he wrote the classic book *Think and Grow Rich*. He was also a big believer in mastermind groups. His advice was to gather together a group of friends who share your ambition and your level of integrity. Meet with them once a week and share your challenges and successes with them. The synergy of the group, he said, will produce far more than the sum of the individual's combined efforts.

Napoleon Hill also created an imaginary board of personal advisors made up of great figures of history. He chose people like Napoleon, Lincoln, Jesus, and Alexander the Great. Whenever he had to make a decision, he would relax deeply and then imagine that the members of his advisory council were sitting at a large table in front of him. He would visualize himself asking them what he should do to deal effectively with a particular situation. In time, he would sense the answers, observations, and insights that these great advisors might give, and it would help him see more clearly and act more effectively.

You can do the same thing. Select people whom you admire for their qualities of courage, tenacity, honesty, or wisdom. Ask yourself, "What would Franklin Delano Roosevelt do in my situation?" or, "What would Winston Churchill do if he were here at this time?" By doing this, you'll find that you receive guidance that enables you to resist temptation and maintain the high degree of personal integrity that Zig Ziglar was talking about when he gave his advice to Mike's young account executive. Maybe if that young man and Roger's friend had done this, they wouldn't have fallen victim to the temptations that plagued their careers.

Key Points from This Chapter

- Develop your own sense of personal integrity and live by it even when it costs you.
- Encourage others to live by the same high standards.
- If honesty did not exist, it would have to be invented, as it is the surest way of getting rich.
- Live your life straight up. Don't be tempted to stray because "everybody does it."
- What goes around comes around. You can only cheat the system temporarily.
- Study the lives of those whom you admire.
- Develop a mastermind group of friends who have similar objectives and motivation. Meet with them regularly.
- Develop an imaginary mastermind group of people you respect and admire. When tempted, ask them what they would do.

33

Consistency

In this chapter we'll discuss what may be the most powerful Weekend Millionaire Mindset trait of all: consistency. People are drawn to you if you act consistently, and they are repelled if you act inconsistently. It's a concept that takes only seconds to learn, but it may take a lifetime to fully appreciate its power.

Why do we admire this characteristic so much? Our need for consistency comes from the tremendous need we have to develop a predictable world in which to exist. You realize, of course, that your most basic and intense need is survival. This is the key reason why humans, above all other species, have survived and prospered on earth. When our backs are against the wall, we will adapt, change, or do almost anything to assure our survival.

Our next strongest instinct is the need for security in our lives. Security is the assurance that we can continue to survive.

Think of being on vacation on a beautiful island off the coast of Thailand. A giant tsunami wave rolls in and destroys everything in sight. You're glad to survive but it looks as though you are alone on the island. Your first concern would be to figure out if you could survive on the island. Is there enough food and fresh water? Once you establish that you can survive on a short-term basis, your next concern would be to assure the continuance of your survival. You might develop a system to store rainwater, so you wouldn't run out of drinking water. You might build a compound in which you could store supplies of food, protecting it from the elements and any rodents or animals that might be there.

The same basic need for survival and security, which would be obvious to us on a deserted island, still drives us in our city lives. We surround ourselves with an environment that is consistent and predictable. Instead of foraging for food on a day-to-day basis to assure our survival, we store it in huge freezers. Instead of daily looking for ways to make money, we prefer to associate ourselves with an endeavor that consistently offers us predictable rewards.

In our minds, we equate consistency with our two most basic needs: survival and security. If there is consistency in our world, we feel secure. When faced with inconsistent people and circumstances, we feel insecure. In our relationships, we admire people who act in consistent patterns of behavior. We are much more likely to be persuaded by someone we view as consistent.

We revere people who behave consistently. We despise and fear people who are erratic. We understand that exhibiting consistency in behavior is an incredibly potent force, because it conditions the other person to trust you.

In our minds a high degree of consistency is synonymous with intellectual and personal strength. We'll overlook almost anything if a person is reliable. Winston Churchill was a bellicose, belligerent person. His desire to impose total control on the British Empire beyond the end of World War II was hopelessly archaic, and could have led to anarchy. However, we loved and respected him for his strength of convictions.

Similarly, we came to love Harry Truman, and forgave him for his salty language and outbursts of temper.

John F. Kennedy spoke in grand terms of the "New Frontier," of the mantle of power passing to a new generation born in this century. He projected a consistent set of standards. He did it well. His brother Robert did it brilliantly. Do you remember his slogan? "Some men look at things the way they are and say, 'Why?' I dream of things that never were and say, 'Why not?'" That's good stuff.

Consistency

One of the most beloved Presidents of the last century, Ronald Reagan, was brilliant at projecting the power of consistency. You never had a question in your mind about where he stood on an issue.

Conversely, to illustrate how suspicious we are of inconsistent behavior, let's look at this scenario. Let's say you're on a camping trip. Perhaps you've backpacked into a remote area of the Grand Teton National Park. You appear to be the only person for miles around, until a man comes into the clearing and starts to set up his tent. The stranger may make you a little nervous. Could this be the serial killer you read about in the Jackson Hole newspaper? Will he steal from you, or threaten you in some way? You watch him closely and you don't trust him until he's established a consistent pattern of nonthreatening behavior.

We like and admire consistent behavior in other people. They like and admire it in us. If we're willing to take a stand for our principles, especially if it appears we're risking financial loss, it builds trust in the other person, and they love us for it.

Suppose a heart surgeon told you that you needed triple bypass heart surgery, and you said, "I think I can get by with a double bypass."

If he said, "Okay, let's try a double and see how it works out," how would you feel about him then? Would you let him near you with a knife? We don't think so!

Many people had misgivings about George W. Bush's decision to invade Iraq without the support of our allies. But he never wavered in his decision and was reelected by a clear majority. Meanwhile, John Kerry couldn't shake the perception that he wavered on his beliefs; could that have been what cost him the election?

People want to follow; they want to be led, but they want it to be by someone they see as consistent in behavior. Realize that this power can be used for evil also. Dictators like Adolph Hitler and Saddam Hussein projected consistency. In our world, consistency must be tempered with integrity; otherwise it can turn into a negative.

There's also a tremendous personal benefit to developing consistent behavior. It frees up your energy for more important things. Do you sometimes feel that you lack energy, even when you're healthy and rested?

The Skills You'll Need

Roy Disney, the financial genius behind Walt Disney Enterprises, used to say that "decision making is easy when values are clear." Very early, the Disney brothers established a clear-cut doctrine. Part of it was the policy to only produce movies suitable for all of the family to watch. Over the years, outsiders presented Walt Disney with many projects that would have made him another fortune, and during times of financial crisis, it would have meant an infusion of desperately needed capital. However, he never wasted any energy considering these projects, agonizing over whether to take them on, because the projects would have violated his preestablished values.

If we all had a value blueprint with which to work, a life plan against which we applied our decision making, we could free up vast stores of energy for the really important things.

Let's take the simple act of driving the car to the store. It's only a mile away—should we bother to put on the seat belt? If our value blueprint says that we always drive with a seat belt, there's no wasted energy making a decision. We slip it on almost without realizing it.

On the way to the store, the traffic signal turns yellow. A surge of adrenaline occurs. Should we go for it, or hit the brakes? If our value blueprint is that we always stop for yellow lights, we stop calmly, without wasted energy.

A car is standing in a driveway, waiting for an opening to pull into traffic. Should we wave it ahead of us or let it wait? With a value blueprint in place, there's no hesitation.

Now please understand that we're not telling you how to drive, although we do care about your safety. If your blueprint tells you to gun it for yellow lights, or never wear a seat belt, and never let a jerk pull in front of you, that—we suppose—is your business. The point that we're making here is that if you don't have a value blueprint by which you run your days, you're operating an inefficient, energy-wasting life.

Let's say that part of your personal value blueprint is that you won't take anything that isn't yours. Does that seem like a lofty goal? We hope not. Moses carried it down from Mount Sinai on stone tablets. Thou shalt not steal. For clarification, let's also say that we've decided that stealing means taking something that's not ours.

Fair enough, no problem, that shouldn't be hard to live with: Simply don't take anything that's not ours. But what about on the golf course? There's not another golfer in sight, and there, nestled in the rough, is a brand new Top Flight XL? Another golfer obviously abandoned it. Surely it's okay to take that, isn't it? No! If your value blueprint says that you won't take anything that's not yours, you leave it where it is. Let someone else pick it up, but not you. Roger's golfing buddy Alex Durbin told him, "I learned never to pick up a golf ball that wasn't mine soon after I joined this club. I saw a ball lying there. There wasn't anyone else in sight, so I put it in my pocket, convinced that another golfer had abandoned it long ago. A few minutes later another golfer came roaring up to me and screamed, 'Did you pick up my ball? You just cost me a $200 bet!' I've never picked up another golf ball since that day."

Suppose you're walking along a resort beach and there, half buried in the sand, you see a gold Rolex watch. Clearly it was lost at sea and drifted in with the tide. It would be okay to take it, wouldn't it? No! If you do pick it up, turn it in to Lost and Found, wherever that may be; otherwise leave it there and let someone else take it, but not you.

Okay, now let's try a tougher one. What if you were walking down Wall Street and found a pouch full of negotiable bearer certificates worth over $37 million. Then couldn't you … ? No! That's exactly what 44-year-old assistant cashier Jim Priceman found, and returned it to the owners, the A.G. Becker Company. He got a $250 reward from them. Two hundred fifty dollars for returning $37 million! Oh, well, nobody said it was going to be easy!

Key Points from This Chapter

- People are drawn to you if you act consistently, and they're repelled if you act inconsistently.
- Our need for consistency comes from our tremendous need to develop a predictable world in which to exist.
- In our minds, we equate consistency with our two most basic needs: survival and security.
- We only trust strangers when they've established a consistent pattern of nonthreatening behavior.
- Make a decision and then stick with it, because projecting that you're consistent in your behavior is the most powerful persuasion factor you have going for you.

The Skills You'll Need

- People want to follow; they want to be led, but by someone they see as consistent in their behavior.
- Develop a personal value blueprint—it frees up your energy for more important things.

34

Changing Your World by Changing the Way You Think

Napoleon Hill's *Think and Grow Rich* is probably the great-granddaddy of all self-help books. Hill was a newspaper editor and later a speechwriter for President Franklin Delano Roosevelt. It was Hill who wrote the famous sentence: "Let me assert my firm belief that the only thing we have to fear is fear itself."

The book came about because industrialist Andrew Carnegie hired Hill to write about his success principles. Carnegie had come to the United States penniless from Scotland and worked as a telegraph operator for the Pennsylvania Railroad for 12 years. He became the richest man in the world because he saw the potential of steel beams for railway-bridge construction, rather than wood trestles. This simple insight led to his starting the Carnegie Steel Company, which he sold to U.S. Steel for $250 million in 1901.

It's fascinating that we human beings tend to forget the difficulties of accomplishment once we've reached our objective. Once we've done something, we tend to look at others and think, "Why are you having so much trouble? It's not that hard." We do that regardless of the difficulty we may have had when we first tried it. Carnegie felt that way about making money.

Roger felt that way about climbing Mount Rainier the first time. It was an incredible challenge for him, and he was in agony afterward. For a week following the climb, his legs were so stiff that he couldn't lift his feet up onto sidewalk curbs and would have to reach down and pick his legs up by his knees.

Just as mothers quickly forget the pain of childbirth when they first hold their baby, so we soon put behind us the pain of attacking and conquering life's objectives. Only two weeks later, when people would say to Roger, "How tough was it? Do you think I could do it?" He would cheerfully respond, "Go for it, anyone can do it. It's not that hard."

During Andrew Carnegie's rise to power, we're sure he faced incredible difficulties, but after his success he couldn't understand the poverty that he saw all around him. It astounded him that so many people were having trouble surviving in a country that had given him a fortune.

He wanted to endow the world with his secrets of success. A high school dropout, he lacked the education to write a book, so he hired Napoleon Hill to write it for him.

Hill says in the preface:

In every chapter of this book, mention has been made of the money-making secret which has made fortunes for hundreds of exceedingly wealthy men whom I have carefully analyzed over a long period of years.

The secret was brought to my attention by Andrew Carnegie, more than half a century ago. The canny lovable old Scotsman carelessly tossed it into my mind, when I was but a boy. Then he sat back in his chair, with a merry twinkle in his eyes, and watched carefully to see if I had brains enough to understand the full significance of what he had said to me.

When he saw that I had grasped the idea, he asked if I would be willing to spend 20 years or more preparing myself to take it to the world, to men and women who, without the secret, might go through life as failures. I said I would, and with Mr. Carnegie's cooperation, I have kept my promise.

Changing Your World by Changing the Way You Think

Hill followed Carnegie around for many years, watching everything the billionaire did. From this experience, he wrote *Think and Grow Rich*. If you haven't already done so, we urge you to read it or to listen to Earl Nightingale's brilliant audio condensation. It amazes us that everyone doesn't read and covet this book, which is available at Amazon.com for around $8 new and $3 used. The book will make an incredible difference in your perspective. As Earl Nightingale says, "The hand that puts this book down after finishing it is a different hand." The book fascinates us because Hill never spells out Carnegie's success secret.

In the preface, he assures you that by reading it, you'll learn the secret of accumulating wealth. "The secret to which I refer has been mentioned no fewer than a 100 times throughout this book. It has not been directly named … if you are ready to put it to use, you will recognize this secret at least once in every chapter." So you can't turn to a page and find the secret carefully outlined in a little box. Nevertheless, you'll understand the secret as soon as you've finished the book because you will have planted it in your subconscious mind. This was consistent with Andrew Carnegie's feelings that you have to make people work for their own success. As he said, "There is no use whatever trying to help people who do not help themselves. You cannot push anyone up a ladder unless he is willing to climb himself." Although it may be cheating, we're going to tell you the message that's buried in that book.

In his day, Carnegie had an opportunity to rub shoulders with hundreds of self-made millionaires. As he got to know them, he realized that there was a common denominator among all of them. What they all shared was that even in the earliest days of their careers, these millionaires knew what they wanted and what it would feel like to be successful. They experienced their success long before they achieved it.

They could create a visual image of their success. They could experience the feeling of stepping into their Cadillac and sinking into the fine leather seats. They knew what it would be like to wear the world's finest clothes and have dozens of employees at their disposal. They knew how it would feel to walk into the boardroom of a corporation they owned and have everyone present rise in respect. They knew what it would be like to enter a ballroom filled with people who would turn and be awed by their approach.

Hill called this ability to experience the future "imagizing." These high achievers were able to imagine—to create in their mind—the feel of success. When Carnegie first looked at a wooden trestle railway bridge and visualized how steel beams could replace all that wood, he didn't see himself as a steel salesman. He saw himself owning a great steel mill.

Napoleon Hill taught us that to become successful we must first change our subconscious thoughts. To develop a Weekend Millionaire Mindset, you must first "imagize"—project onto your subconscious mind—the experience of having great success.

Can you visualize and hold in your mind the image of yourself as a Weekend Millionaire? Can you experience your success before you achieve it? Can you "imagize" the day when petty fears and worries no longer influence you, and when every day is an exciting adventure?

Harry Belafonte used to wash dishes in a restaurant in Harlem. What a tragedy if a limiting self-image had stopped him from sharing his true talent with the world. What if you had that kind of talent within you and never explored it?

At the height of her career, Barbra Streisand risked everything to produce and direct the movie *Yentl*. "Why on earth would she do such a thing?" her friends asked. "It had nothing to do with the desire for fame and fortune," she said. "I had all that. I did it because one night I dreamed that I had died, and God revealed my true potential to me. He told me about all the things I could have done but didn't because I was afraid. That was when I decided that I had to create *Yentl* even if it cost me everything I had."

For a really chilling story of a positive self-image lost and regained, listen to best-selling author Og Mandino tell the story of hitting rock bottom one day in Cleveland. Thirty-five years old, he'd lost his family, his home, his job, and his self-respect. He stood in front of a pawnshop window in the rain, with his last $30 in his pocket, looking at a handgun for sale, thinking of ending his life. He could never say why, but he was drawn instead to a library down the street. There, a self-help book by W. Clement Stone captured his interest. The book was *Success Through a Positive Mental Attitude*, and reading it saved Mandino's life. He put his life back together, eventually went to work for Mr. Stone at his insurance company, and later became the editor of his magazine, *Success Unlimited*. He went on to write

Changing Your World by Changing the Way You Think

The Greatest Salesman in the World and eventually sold over 15 million self-help books.

So "imagizing" your success is the way to start changing your self-image. Learning to mentally experience success will help you to achieve it.

The next step is to change your self-talk from negative fears to positive expectations. Eliminate "I can't do this" and "It'll never work" and "Other people are just lucky." Replace them with "I can do this" and "No problem, I'll make it work" and "I'm the lucky one." Soon you'll find your image of yourself changing—you'll see yourself as a different person, and then gradually you'll become a different person.

Mike plays a little game with this positive thinking approach. Each time he drives into the parking lot of a restaurant or large store, he says to himself, "There is someone getting ready to pull out of the parking space closest to the door because they know I'm coming and it belongs to me." Amazingly, over 90 percent of the time that's just what happens. Recently he visited the local Sam's Club just two days before Christmas. The parking lot was filled to capacity. He noticed people turning off the highway and immediately heading to the far corners of the lot where a few parking spaces remained. "Hum!" he jokingly said to himself. "I guess they're going there so I can have my space at the front." He drove directly to the front of the store just in time to see a car pulling out of the space closest to the front door. Positive thinking really does work!

Did positive thinking make the parking space magically appear? Of course not! That would be metaphysical madness! The parking space was always there, but only a positive thinker goes to look for it. As Mei Li sings in Rodgers and Hammerstein's *Flower Drum Song*: "A hundred million miracles are happening every day, and those who say they don't agree are those who do not hear or see."

Many people besides Andrew Carnegie have promoted the idea that if we are to change our lives we must first change our self-image. The best-selling talking record of all time is Earl Nightingale's *The Strangest Secret*. Earl was a successful radio personality on WGN in Chicago with his own daily commentary show. He did so well that he was able to achieve financial independence and retire at the age of 35. One of his investments was a life insurance company, and he got in the habit of attending their sales meetings and giving the salespeople a motivation talk. When he was leaving for a vacation, his sales manager begged him to record a message for him to play to the salespeople when he was away. It's said that in one sitting he recorded the message that was to sell over a million copies and win a gold record.

Unlike Napoleon Hill, who preferred to bury the secret of success in his book, Earl Nightingale revealed it in the first two paragraphs:

Why do men with goals succeed in life ... and men without them fail? Well, let me tell you something, which, if you really understand it, will alter your life immediately. You'll suddenly find that you seem to attract good luck. The things you want just seem to fall in line. And from now on you won't have the problems, the worries, the gnawing lump of anxiety that perhaps you've experienced before. Doubt ... fear ... well, they'll be things of the past.

Here's the key to success and the key to failure: We become what we think about. Let me tell you that again. We become what we think about.

His theory that we become what we think about has changed the lives of millions. If a person thinks all day long about becoming rich, he or she will become rich one way or another. If a person is single and thinks all the time about being married, it won't be long before he or she will marry. Conversely, if a person with a negative self-image thinks constantly of nothing but becoming poorer, that will probably happen too. In other words, a self-image is self-fulfilling.

Every self-image psychologist agrees that before you can change your life dramatically, you must first change your self-image. You must train your mind to "imagize" the person you can become. Self-image psychology explains why the lives of people with a Weekend Millionaire Mindset seem charmed. It seems they can do no wrong. Success washes over them in gigantic tidal waves. Good things happen to them much faster and in larger quantities than seems possible. Napoleon Hill put this beautifully in the first chapter of *Think and Grow Rich* when he said:

We believe you are entitled to receive this important suggestion. When riches begin to come, they come so quickly and in such great abundance that one wonders where they have been hiding during all those lean years.

This is an astonishing statement, especially considering the popular belief that success comes only to those who work long and hard.

People with a Weekend Millionaire Mindset know you can learn to change your whole life by changing the way you think about yourself. They learn to experience success—to taste it and smell it—long before they actually achieve it. Every step of the long journey to accomplishment, they carry an image of what they want to be. They change their own mental image of themselves, and in doing so make the rest of their lives a stage on which they act out a fascinating and fulfilling script. So concentrate on what you really want to be, change your self-talk, and become a Weekend Millionaire.

From this moment on you must stop thinking of yourself as someone who *could* become a Weekend Millionaire. Think of yourself as already being a Weekend Millionaire. We don't care how little money you have in the bank, and we don't care how much in debt you may be. We don't care how down and out you feel. When you begin to think of yourself as a Weekend Millionaire, accumulating wealth and influence become only the details that you'll put together later.

Key Points from This Chapter

- Read and reread Napoleon Hill's book *Think and Grow Rich*.
- Everything seems to be harder the first time you do it.
- The common denominator of all successful people is that long before they were successful, they could "imagize," or imagine, themselves as being successful.
- Listen to Earl Nightingale's recording of *The Strangest Secret*, available from Nightingale.com. Learn how to "become what you think about."

35

Smart Decision Making

An important part of the Weekend Millionaire Mindset is the ability to make smart decisions. We are where we are today because of the choices we've made in the past. Think again about the story of Mike's upbringing and look at how the decisions he made affected everything that was to follow. The decision to run away from his abusive stepfather! The decision to find the father he had never known! The decision to leave home and sell encyclopedias! All of these substantially affected the person he is today.

Not only have the decisions you've made brought you to where you are today, but your future will be comprised of the decisions you make from this point forward. Decisions are the building blocks of your past and your future.

Most of us don't know how to make decisions. If we feel good that day and the money is flowing, we tend to do it. If we don't feel good or money is tight, we don't do it. That's no way to build a life! In this chapter we're going to give you a brief look at what we've learned about decision making.

The Key Is to Gather Information

The first thought you should have when asked to make a decision is this: "Do I have enough information to make an 'informed' decision?" If the answer to that question is no, we advise you not to go ahead. Having said this, we must admit that it's not the right thing to do every time. Once in a while you'll miss a great opportunity because you don't close your eyes and take a big chance. Roger recalls the time when one of his real estate agents came into his office and said, "You're not going to believe this, but there's a building site in San Dimas where they are preselling condominiums before they've even started construction!"

"Why on earth would they do that?" Roger asked. "It doesn't make sense. This is such a hot real estate market that they'll go up in value at least 20 percent before they've got them finished!"

He drove over to the construction site, and sure enough, there was a sales trailer on a bare construction site. He found the salesman eating a sandwich at his desk. "You got condos for sale?" he asked.

"Yup, they're $55,000 each. You want one?" the salesman said through a mouthful of ham and cheese. That was the extent of his sales pitch!

Roger thought, "I'm not ready for this. I don't see how I could go wrong, but for $55,000, I'd like to get romanced a little." So he drove around the block and thought about it. He would have to write a check for a $1,000 deposit. There was no sign of any construction yet, so it would take at least a year before they would want the balance. The condos would have gone up in value at least $10,000 by then. How could he lose? He drove back and told the salesman, "I'll take one."

It took them 18 months to finish the project; Roger resold the condo for a $20,000 profit, and the only time he was ever in it was for the final construction walk-through. So sometimes you do well when you close your eyes and take a chance, but it's not the right way to play the game. If you don't have enough information to make an informed decision, we suggest that you don't go ahead.

Categorize the Problem or Opportunity

The next step is to categorize, which is the cornerstone of good decision making. Problems and opportunities fall into one of these four groups, and each one requires a different response:

1. It's a "do we or don't we" decision. Do we buy the building or the stock in the company, or don't we? Do we go on vacation or don't we? Do we buy the SUV or don't we? When you're faced with a "do we or don't we" decision, your first thought should be: "What happens if I do nothing? Will the building or the stock go up in value or down? Will it still be available next month or won't it?"

   The decision to invade the Branch Davidian compound in Waco, Texas, was a "do we or don't we" decision. Attorney General Janet Reno should have thought, "What happens if we do nothing?" It would have been clear that there was no compelling reason to invade. The right decision would have been to cordon off the area and do nothing. By the time the FBI was faced with the Montana Freemen rebellion three years later, they had learned this lesson. They did nothing, and 81 days later the rebels surrendered without a shot being fired.

2. I understand the problem but I don't know what to do about it. There is no apparent solution. That's when a good dose of creative thinking comes into play. You need to create solutions that are not apparent and that require some thinking out of the box.

3. Is this a dichotomy? Is there a right and a wrong answer, but you don't know which one to pick? You solve dichotomies by develop a rating system. Let's say that you're being sued and you don't know whether to settle or to defend yourself in court.

   The simplest rating system is: How do you feel about each choice on a scale on one to 10? Sometimes that simple method brings the answer into focus for you. You immediately think that the last thing you want to do is spend the next year paying attorneys to take depositions.

   A more complicated rating system is to break down each element of the decision and give it a rating. Add them up and go with the one that gets the highest score. So you solve dichotomies with some kind of rating system. But a word of caution here: You often feel that you are faced with a dichotomy when, with a little creative thinking, you could come up with potential solutions. Perhaps you're better off to act like you'll go to court and then settle.

4. The fourth category of decision is when several choices are available to you and you don't know which one to pick. This requires a more involved form of indexing all of the potential choices. Perhaps you weigh each of the elements involved in all of those choices and bring that into play.

Even more involved are decision trees. Decision trees not only rate each of your choices, they consider the possibility of varying responses from the other side when you make a proposal to them. Let's say that you have 10 job offers and you don't know which one to accept. A decision tree would take into account all of the proposals that you might make to those employers and how they might respond to those proposals. To go to that much trouble would require a very involved and critical decision, but just knowing how these decisions are made can be very helpful.

Prepare to Make the Decision

Before you make the decision, consider these points:

1. Does it require a complex decision? Let's say you're on the late night flight home from a business trip. In the airport bookstore, you are looking for a no-brainer paperback, in case you can't get to sleep on the plane. The more you look, the harder the choice gets. Hey, come on! This situation doesn't justify a major decision. You establish parameters, pick something, and move on. Perhaps you don't want to pay for a hardcover, don't like romances or war stories, and you're too tired to read a business book. Anything else is okay, so you should pick the first book that falls within those parameters and move on.

2. Is there a policy in place? If you have a policy in place, you follow the policy unless you have a compelling reason to change the policy. Don't break the policy, change it. Mike has two policies when he buys real estate. He won't buy unless he can control the investment—no partners—and he won't buy unless he can structure the financing so he

can at least break even. With those two policies firmly in place, he can exclude 80 percent of the deals that are brought to him without having to spend a lot of time deciding.

3. Is the problem unique? This trips up a lot of people. They've got a sick relative to deal with or a complicated legal problem to solve. They get so wrapped up in trying to solve the problem that they think it's unique. There are virtually no unique problems unless you're a rocket scientist or a microbiologist. Every problem we'll ever face has been solved by thousands of people before us. We just don't know who they are or how to ask them. That's when you find an expert. They face this problem several times a month and know what to do.

4. Is it a money problem or a people problem? There really are only two different kinds of problems. You'll never find a problem or opportunity that can't be separated this way: money problems or people problems. Or they involve both money and people.

5. You hear this kind of thing all the time: "My 20-year-old son is driving me insane. I love him, but I can't stand him living at the house anymore. He's driving me crazy with his late night carousing. I've tried laying down ground rules, but nothing seems to work. I ought to throw him out of the house and let him make his own way in the world. It would probably do him a world of good. But I hate to break the ties completely. He's my own son, and I might never see him again." This mother is confusing a people problem with a money problem. If you asked her how the son would feel if she gave him $800 a month to rent his own apartment, she'd say: "Well, that would solve everything, but we don't have the $800 a month to give him." That may be so, but when you point this out to her, she'll see for the first time that it isn't a people problem she's facing, it's a money problem.

Key Points from This Chapter

- You are where you are today because of the decisions you've made in the past.
- Your future will consist of the decisions you make from today forward.
- Decisions are the building blocks of your life.

Smart Decision Making

- First consider: Do you have enough information to make an informed decision?
- Do we or don't we make a decision: Consider what happens if you do nothing.
- When there is no apparent solution, use creative thinking.
- Use a rating system when there appears to be a dichotomy.
- Use weighted rating systems or decision trees when there appear to be many choices available.
- Use parameters when a complex decision is required.
- Follow established policies to make decisions regarding day-to-day occurrences.
- When a problem seems unique, consult an expert.
- Identify whether problems are money problems or people problems.

To further develop your decision-making skills, invest in Roger Dawson's six-hour audio program *Confident Decision Making*. It's available at www.weekendmillionaire.com, where you can also listen to excerpts from the program.

36

Time Management

As we pointed out in Chapter 7, the one thing we all have in common is time. Young, old, rich, or poor, everyone has 24 hours in a day and seven days in a week. What you do with your time determines how quickly, if ever, you reach financial independence.

It's critical for four important reasons:

1. Time management enables you to get more done in less time. Doing so allows you to free up those four hours a week you need to devote to wealth building that we mention in our book *The Weekend Millionaire's Secrets to Investing in Real Estate*. People who don't understand time management will approach their week with dread. They'll spend the entire week scurrying around doing busy work and complaining about how they don't have time for anything else. A good manager of time can get more done in an hour than many people can all day.

   Your willingness to work long hours may be noble, but we don't want you to spend all of your spare time working. If you're like most people, after eight hours on your job you're tired and just want to get home and rest. That's fine, but with good time management, you can schedule time to rest plus all those little things around the house that need to be done and still set aside a few hours on the weekend to devote to building wealth.

2. Time management takes the pressure and stress out of working, thereby making it more fun. When you plan ahead to spend four hours a week on wealth building, you'll not only look forward to accomplishing your other objectives for the week, but will feel even better knowing that part of what you're doing is contributing to your goal of financial independence.

3. Time management enables you to plan time for recreation and family life, to enrich your experience of life. You may think that a good manager of time is someone who is capable of taking on monumental amounts of work but still gets everything done. Our perspective of someone who manages time well conjures up a vision of a parent fishing with their children on a Saturday afternoon because he or she finished all their wealth-building tasks on Saturday morning.

4. Good time management gives you an incredible reputation for reliability. If you say you'll call your financial advisor for an update at 9:45 Saturday morning, he or she can count on it. They'll be sitting by the phone with the information you need. If you say you'll mail someone information, then the person can expect it. If you tell someone you'll take care of it, then the person doesn't have to waste time following up on you to see if you remembered to do it. People with whom you do business will admire you so much for this that they will be drawn to you. The people you hire to do work for you will soon learn that if they committed to complete a project for you, they should do it on time or you will be right behind them, following up.

Eight Rules for Good Time Management

1. Concentrate on One Thing at a Time

Good managers of time know that the key element to getting control of their lives is to constantly be breaking projects down into pieces small enough that they can concentrate on one thing at a time.

The Skills You'll Need

Roger once went on a 10-day speaking tour that would take him from his home in La Habra Heights, California, to speaking engagements in Orlando, San Antonio, back to Orlando, on to Huntsville and New York, and then finally to Atlanta, before returning to California.

On that trip, he gave six talks to five different industries, all of which he had to learn about so he could customize the talk to their particular needs. The talks ranged in length from a 30-minute keynote to an all-day seminar. His office had shipped home-study courses to each location to sell at the event, and he had to coordinate handouts and workbooks. Here's the point: If he had left on this trip and worried about all the things that had to fall into place for the trip to go well, it would have blown his mind. Instead of being the adventure it was, it would have been one big frustrating hassle.

Roger has learned to handle schedules such as this by concentrating on one day at a time. He makes a plan for the entire trip and double-checks it before he leaves. Once he leaves on a trip like the one detailed above, however, he worries only about getting from San Antonio to Orlando and giving the best talk he's ever given. The next day he'll worry only about getting from Orlando to Huntsville and doing the best job there. And so on. Learn to break your long-term tasks in daily bites. By taking each day as a separate unit, you can handle the most incredibly complicated schedules.

Let us pose this question: If, when you were born, someone had magically appeared in front of you and told you all the things you'd have to face throughout life—all the problems, trials, and tribulations that a lifetime would bring you—you'd probably have crawled back into the womb, wouldn't you? You would have looked up at the doctor who was hanging you by your ankles, and said, "Get me out of here!" However, taking one day at a time, you can handle just about anything.

Learning how to concentrate on one thing at a time may take a great deal of personal discipline. A good time-management system encourages you to concentrate on each task separately. It breaks down all of your responsibilities into pint-size pieces, so you can concentrate on "one thing at a time." You trust your system to bring the right thing to your attention at the right time.

2. Use a Daily Planning System Customized to Complement the Way You Work

Don't attempt to change the way you work to fit a prepackaged time management system. We're quite sure that you've had the experience of getting so frustrated by being disorganized that you went out and bought an expensive time management system. You probably spent hours learning how to use it and days setting it up. Then you discovered that it was more trouble than it was worth. It simply didn't complement the way you work or the type of work you do. If possible, find a computer-based time management system that has the flexibility to be adapted to your needs.

3. Prioritize Your Work

Before you do anything, it is essential that you prioritize your tasks. It's the only way that you'll force yourself to do the most important things first. If you don't prioritize your duties, you'll find yourself looking down your list and gravitating to one of two categories:

1. *The most enjoyable things.* "I have to call my real estate agent and see what came on the market this week," you might think, because you enjoy talking to your real estate agent. It's not a threatening situation to you. So you follow that phone call up with another call to a friend, and after that you read your e-mails. You'll never get to the more important things.
2. *Those things that take the least time.* You say, "It'll only take me a minute to read my e-mails, so I'll do that first." Then you'll spend the first 15 minutes of your day reading spam, which is probably the least important thing you need to do—with the possible exception of sitting there, not being able to decide whether to read the spam or not.

You may have heard the story of Ivy Lee and Bethlehem Steel, but if not, it bears repeating. Charles Schwab was the president of the company and a very successful business manager. He was the first man ever to earn a salary of more than $1 million a year, and that was back in the 1930s when a million dollars was a great deal of money. (Incidentally, he died penniless, after spending the last few years of his life on borrowed money. He never developed a true Weekend Millionaire Mindset.)

Ivy Lee was a management consultant who wanted a contract with the company. Schwab rebuffed him, saying that they already knew more about producing and selling steel than Lee would ever know. Then he gave Lee a challenge that would go down in business folklore. Schwab told Lee that the only thing he lacked was the time to implement all the ideas he had and that if Lee would show him a way to get more things done with his time, he would pay him any fee within reason.

According to management expert Donald Schoeller, Lee replied, "Write down the most important tasks you have to do tomorrow and number them in order of importance. When you arrive in the morning, begin at once on number one and stay on it till it's completed. Recheck your priorities; then begin with number two. If any task takes all day, never mind. Stick with it as long as it's the most important one. If you don't finish them all, you probably couldn't do so with any other method, and without some system you'd probably not even decide which one was most important. Make this a habit every working day. When it works for you, give it to your men. Try it as long as you like. Then send me your check for what you think it's worth."

What he was saying is so unbelievably simple that you may find it hard to grasp its importance. Charles Schwab loved it. He sent Ivy Lee a check for $25,000, calling the advice the most profitable lesson he'd ever learned. He credited this system with turning Bethlehem Steel around and making it, in its day, the biggest independent steel producer in the world. Business experts later chided Schwab for his extravagance in sending Lee so much more than he expected, but Schwab insisted that it was the best investment he'd made all year, saying that it was only when he'd adopted this system that he found all of his people doing the most important things first.

4. Give Yourself Deadlines by Scheduling Blocks of Time

If you're up against a deadline, you can get an incredible amount of work done. Haven't you noticed that? If you have to leave for the airport in an hour and won't be back for a week, you can skim through a large pile of work that might take you all day if you had all day. C. Northcote Parkinson's Law says: "Work expands so as to fill the amount of time available for its completion." So a key to getting more done is to force yourself to work against a deadline. If you have a stack of mail to answer, allocate an hour to it, and when the hour is over set it aside for another day. Don't let meetings be open-ended. If you've scheduled a meeting with your property manager or stockbroker, tell them how long you've allocated for the meeting and that they'll have to work hard and stay on track to get everything done in that time.

We disagree with Ivy Lee that you should stick with one task all day if you have to. If you take that approach, you find other issues piling up so much that it may take you several days to climb out of the hole you've dug for yourself. Better to say, "I'm going to take the hour after lunch to get caught up on my other work, but at exactly 2:00 P.M., I'm going to return to this task." Forcing yourself to work against deadlines like this dramatically increases your effectiveness.

5. Get Comfortable with Voice Mail

Instead of cursing that you can't reach the person, take advantage of a system that allows you to leave a detailed message in a short amount of time. Roger recently got a call from a friend who left a message asking him to return the call. He returned the call but got a message machine. For two weeks they played phone tag until they finally got to talk to each other. All the friend wanted to do was schedule a golf game. Look how much time and effort it would have saved if the friend had left a message saying, "Let's play golf. I'm free any time on these three days ... " Roger's return message would be, "See you at the course at eight on Thursday."

6. Read Paper Once

Break the habit of reading a sheet of paper more than once. Here's what typically happens: The morning's mail includes a letter from someone with whom you do business, and they're asking you for some action. You say, "Okay, I'll need to take care of that later on today," and you put it into your pending basket. Then later in the day you'll go through your pending basket and see the letter again and say, "Oh, how urgent was that?" So you read the letter again, and maybe then you'll schedule it for some positive action. However, very often you'll find yourself reading the same letter three or four times.

Here's a system to break that bad habit. Every time you read a piece of paper, tear off a corner. It will amaze you how often you'll tear off all four corners before you get around to taking action on that particular item.

Instead of wasting time by rereading letters like that, get into the habit of quickly reviewing what you need to do and making a decision about when and how you're going to do it. Then make a quick notation on your computer time management system, ending the message with a *P* for "projects file." Drop the project into a projects file or an in basket. When the project comes up for completion, you'll know that it's in your projects file because of the *P*. Then move on, so you don't read the paper a second time. You'll free up a tremendous amount of time.

7. Don't Ask for Time to Think Things Over

You either have enough information to make a decision or you don't. As we told you in the chapter on decision making, a basic fundamental of good decision making is that you first determine if you have enough information to make a decision. If you don't have enough information, don't ask for more time—ask for more information, and be as specific as possible about what information you want. If you do have enough information, stop procrastinating and make the decision. If the decision involves doing something you don't want to do, using "Let me think it over" as a way to avoid saying no wastes not only your time, but the time of everyone else involved as well.

8. Develop a Daily Planning System That Works for You

First, find a computer program that works for you, and from then on list anything that you need to do on your computer time management program. No more little notes tucked away in pockets. No more writing down phone messages on odd scraps of paper. You must *believe in the system, trust the system, and always use the system*. If your answering machine gives you six messages that require action, immediately transfer them to your daily plan. If you wrote a lot of notes as you listened to the message, put the slip of paper into your projects file. Don't forget to cross-reference it to your daily plan by writing down "Call Fred. *P.*" *P* means that there's more information in your projects file (see section below).

Your computer program enables you to mark the date when this needs to be done. Don't list more than you think you can reasonably get done in one day. If you find yourself looking at the list and groaning at the thought of all the work you have to do, you're attempting too much for that day.

Move some of the projects to future days. Don't overload yourself. It's essential that you feel comfortable that you can get everything done, because during the day other things will come up and you need to have enough cushion in your plan to be able to take care of them.

Some of the things you've been planning may not be for tomorrow, even if you would have time to do them then. They are things better taken care of at a future date; for example, a reminder to follow up on something on which you're working, or to call someone when he or she returns from vacation. In that case, simply list these for the day they're to be done.

Your Projects File.   Anytime you have something that relates to an upcoming project, write *P* by the task on your list. This, as we said above, *P* stands for "projects." Somewhere in your work area you should find a place to keep all of these *P*s—a file drawer or a specific basket, or anything handy. We use an in box. When you work your way down to this project, you'll see the *P* and know exactly where to find the extra information. Once a week, go through your projects file to be sure that nothing is in there that isn't on your daily plan.

Prioritizing Your Commitments

The next thing to do is prioritize the commitments you have. We find that three levels are enough.

1. "Highest" projects are those you must accomplish that day, although they may not all be the most important commitments. For example, making a deposit to your checking account may be a "Highest," while calling a real estate agent about a new listing that came on the market may be a "High," simply because you must make the deposit today. The call could wait until tomorrow.
2. "High" are those projects you'd like to get done that day.
3. "Normal" are those projects it would be good to get done, but they aren't essential.

Be sparing with your "Highests." Fifteen "highest" priorities are probably the maximum load you can carry, and we hope you'll have far fewer. Only the truly critical things get a "highest." You must do them or else.

These are the projects that if you don't have them done by 5:00 P.M., you'll have to cancel dinner with your spouse.

When you're prioritizing, don't give something a high priority just because it has been sitting on your desk for ages. Always prioritize with these two things in mind:

1. How much closer it will bring you to your long-term objectives.
2. What is the consequence of its not getting done today?

Having prioritized "Highest," "High," and "Normal," now go back and number them for importance. "Highest—1," for example, would be the most important thing to do that day. "Highest—2" is the second most important, and so on. Again, think strictly about moving yourself closer to your objective, instead of how many people are bugging you to get it done.

1. Prioritize the "Highs" only when you've completed all the "Highests."
2. Prioritize the "Normals" only when you've completed all the "Highests" and the "Highs."

At this point you may be thinking, "I'm much too busy to go through that prioritizing process. It would take me at least 15 minutes a day." Perhaps it will, but remember that if you want to spend four hours a week on wealth building, it takes less than a 10 percent improvement in the efficient use of your other time to free up these four hours. Doesn't that make the 15 minutes you spend prioritizing a good investment?

Once you've prioritized your list, begin with "Highest—1." Don't begin your day by rereading the list. You've already done that. Just begin your day with the most important task and work on it until it's completed. When you've done that, then automatically, without reading the list, move on to task "Highest—2." From there move to "Highest—3," and so on. That's another point on which we disagree with management consultant Ivy Lee. Remember that he told Charles Schwab at Bethlehem Steel to "begin at once on number one and stay on it till it's completed. Recheck your priorities; then begin with number two." We find that rechecking your priorities slows you down because it distracts you. Certainly reorder your priorities if you need to, because your system must be flexible and you shouldn't become a slave to it. However, we think you'll get much more done if you move right on to the next task without rechecking your priorities.

There may be a project that you're unable to complete. Perhaps you have to set it aside for a while and get more information. In that case, you should renumber it or reassign it to another day for completion. Don't jump around on your list. Consider and deal with each item in order. Don't worry if you have 15 "Highests" on your list and you get only five of them accomplished that day. At least you'll have done the five most important things on your schedule.

Be careful, as you prioritize, that you don't assign tasks a low priority just because they're things you'd rather not do. If you have an unpleasant job to do, such as calling a partner to tell him that his project fell through or that you've been unable to perform the way he wanted, then get that job off your desk the first thing in the morning.

This means giving the worst jobs the highest priority. This will release you from dreading them all day long. As our friend Danny Cox says, "If you have a frog to swallow, the quicker you swallow it, the better. If you have more than one frog to swallow, start with the biggest one first!"

Reviewing the Things to Do List at the End of the Day

At the end of your work period you should review the entire list of "Things to Do" and move ahead those tasks that you didn't complete during the day. You might want to move all of those tasks to the next day, or portion them out over the next week. The important thing is that once you've entered each task into your time management software, you'll have a complete list of everything you need to do, all in one place.

At first glance this system may seem complicated. However, making good time management a habit is a real key to the Weekend Millionaire Mindset. Nothing is more important than how you use your time, because however rich you become, you'll never be able to buy any more of it. Queen Elizabeth I said on her deathbed, "I'll give everything I own for one more moment of time." At some time or another, that thought will occur to each of us. Football coach Vince Lombardi used to say he could win every game if only the clock never ran out. Weekend Millionaires know they could accomplish anything in life if they had an endless supply of time.

Time is the one and only nonnegotiable thing in our lives. You can never buy it or sell it, and other people can't give it to you. You can only organize time better.

Learn to organize your time better. Learn the art of getting the most out of every minute of every day. Remember, if you can take control of your time, you can take control of your life and channel your internal energy into building financial independence. It's a critical part of the Weekend Millionaire Mindset.

Key Points from This Chapter

- Time is the one thing we all have in common. We cannot make time, save time, or buy time.
- Good time management frees up your time for important things like creative thinking and strategic planning.
- Good time management takes the stress out of life and makes working more fun.
- Good time management enables you to plan more life for recreation and family life.
- Good time management gives you a reputation for reliability.
- Concentrate on one thing at a time.
- Use a daily planning system that you customize to complement the way you work.
- Prioritize your work, so that you're working on the most important things first.
- Give yourself deadlines by scheduling blocks of time.
- Read paper just once.
- Don't ask for time to think things over.
- Do the hardest job first so you don't have to think about it the rest of the day.
- Develop a daily planning system that works for you.
- Create a projects file that is cross-referenced to your daily planner.

37

Think Like an Investor, Not Like a Consumer

When we work with new investors, one of our big challenges is to get them to think like investors, not consumers. If they have not yet built any investment capital, it's usually because they've spent virtually all of their income on consumer items and very little on investment items. In the old days we would call that being broke. Nowadays, with the overabundance of consumer credit, being broke is just a marker on a long slippery slope. You can zoom by broke these days and still have plenty of money to spend.

Let's a take a look at an ordinary family. They've been married for 20 years and make around $50,000 a year. They've got 2.2 kids, a barking dog, and a picket fence. They're filling out a financial statement at a bank, perhaps because they need to borrow money for a college loan for their youngest son. They start out listing their assets, which might include a home, a car, a life insurance policy, furniture, and electronic items such as televisions, appliances, and computers. Wanting to put the best possible light on things, they would list the home at the price the one down the street is listed at, and would put a value on the furniture and appliances that is close to what they paid for them. This side of the financial statement looks pretty good. Perhaps they have $200,000 or more in assets.

Then comes the depressing side—the liabilities. They refinanced the home a couple of times, so there isn't much equity there, and they haven't even figured out what it would cost to sell the home if they had to. By the time they've fixed up the home for sale and paid the real estate broker, there may be no equity at all. They owe more on the car than it's worth, and they have credit card debt that totals $50,000. They come to the reluctant conclusion that they have no net worth.

How can that be? They're good people. They work hard. In the last 20 years they have earned over $1 million but have nothing to show for it. What went wrong? What went wrong was that they spent the last 20 years thinking and acting like consumers and not investors.

Investors think, "How I can I make money from the money that I spend?" Consumers think, "Can I afford the payments to pay for what I want?" (Unfortunately, many of them don't even give it that much thought!)

Investors think, "How can I make money from what I just learned?" Consumers think, "What's that going to cost me?" Here's an example: Both the investor and the consumer read in the local newspaper that the city council is discussing building a bridge from the island that will hook up to the freeway. The investor thinks, "How can I make money from this? What's going to happen to property values on each side of the bridge if this happens?" The consumer thinks, "There goes our taxes again. How much is this going to cost us?" or worse yet, "Who's getting money under the table on this one?"

Michael Crowe, an English friend of Roger's, once told him, "There's one big difference between this country and England, and it's what makes this country so successful. If a man is digging a ditch in England and he sees a man driving by in a Rolls Royce, he's likely to say, 'I wonder who he's stealing from?' If an American is digging a ditch and sees a man driving by in a Cadillac, he says, 'I'm going to get one of those myself one day.'"

Our first challenge is to get you to stop thinking like a consumer. This will involve three field trips.

Field Trip 101. Drive down to your local Wal-Mart or Target store and spend an hour looking carefully at all the merchandise piled up in there.

Think Like and Investor, Not Like a Consumer

Keep repeating to yourself, "My goodness, look at all the stuff in here that I don't need." If at the end of the hour you are able to walk out of the store without buying something and still thinking, "There's nothing in there that I need," you may move on to Field Trip 201.

Field Trip 201. If you're a man, spend an hour at a Home Depot or Lowe's home improvement store. If you're a woman, spend an hour at Nordstrom or a top department store. Imagine that you have been given a $500 gift certificate that expires today. If you can spend an hour in the store and still come out thinking, "There is nothing in there that I need to have," you may move on to Field Trip 301.

Field Trip 301. (Don't try this until you've graduated from the first two field trips. It could be disastrous!) Think of your dream car; perhaps a bright red Ferrari or a gleaming white top-of-the-line Lexus. Go take it for a long test drive. If you can walk away from the showroom thinking, "Wow, I would love to have that car, but not now. I'm an investor; I have a Weekend Millionaire Mindset. I only spend money on things that will show me a return. I will own that car one day, but not until I can pay for it from my investment earnings rather than from the sweat of my brow." Now, our friend, you are an investor!

From this moment on you are to think of yourself only as an investor. Every penny you think of spending, you say to yourself, "Will this show me a return on my investment?" If it won't, figure out a way to avoid spending that penny unless it will show you a return.

Another thing about the Weekend Millionaire Mindset: Consumers think, wonder what it costs. Investors don't worry about this. They are only concerned with the return on investment. A consumer might say, "I'm not going to pay $300,000 for that rental house. I remember when I could have bought it for only $150,000." An investor doesn't think like that. To an investor it doesn't matter what it costs. Again, what matters is: What will the return on investment be?

It doesn't matter to an investor if IBM stock is selling for $80 or $120. An investor's only thought is, "What is my return on investment going to be?" When you ordered this book, we hope that you weren't thinking, "This should be an interesting way to spend a couple of hours." We hope you were thinking, "How quickly will I get my $20 back from this investment and how many times over will I get it back?" Congratulations! Now you're thinking like an investor!

Key Points from This Chapter

- Don't spend so much on consumer items that your liabilities stay ahead of your assets.
- Think: "How much money can I make from the money I spend?"
- Don't think: "How can I make the payments to pay for what I want?"
- View each new event as an opportunity to think like an investor: "How can I make money from this?"
- Spend an hour at Wal-Mart looking at all the stuff you don't need.
- Spend an hour in Neiman Marcus or Home Depot looking at all the stuff you don't have to have.
- Take a dream car for a drive and come away thinking: "Not until my investments are able to pay for it."
- Never think, what does it cost?
- Always think, what will be my return on this investment?

PART VI

A Kick in the Pants That Will Improve Your Life

Throughout this book we have shared experiences that helped shape our lives and develop our Weekend Millionaire Mindsets. Several times we've urged you to keep a note pad nearby and make notes if any of our stories remind you of events from your past. If you're sitting there with no notes, you're already behind those who followed that recommendation. If you heeded our advice, now it's time to get out your notes and start the process of developing your own Weekend Millionaire Mindset.

The moral or the point of the everyday experiences the stories usually related were the important lessons we learned and the discoveries we made. Not all of these experiences were good, not all of them were bad, but in any case, we learned from each one—because we were looking for ways to achieve what we wanted, not excuses for failing to do so. When people gave us advice, we didn't summarily disregard it because others said it wouldn't work—we listened. When advice worked, we improved upon it; when it didn't, we looked for the reasons why and learned from those too.

As you begin constructing your Weekend Millionaire Mindset, we hope you'll recognize that all the things you need to achieve wealth, happiness, fame, or anything else you desire from life is all around you, except the desire to look for it. That comes from within. The Weekend Millionaire Mindset expands in direct proportion with your ability to create desire and eliminate excuses. In other words, it's up to you. What you do and how you act determines what you accomplish. We are amazed at the number of people who think they can buy books, audio programs, and other learning materials, put them on their shelves and expect great things to happen. It reminds us of the old Chinese proverb, "Man sit in chair with mouth open for very long time waiting for roast duck to fly in."

Building a Weekend Millionaire Mindset is like building a solid brick house: It's done by laying one brick at a time. Changing your thinking, building emotional security and financial independence, is done the same way: one step at a time. There aren't any shortcuts, so the sooner you get started, the quicker you will begin to see results. In this final part, we are not only going to show you how to create desire and eliminate excuses, but how to get started doing so immediately.

Now get your note pad, turn the page, and let's create some desire.

38

Creating Desire

Everyone knows that unless you're motivated to do something, chances are you aren't going to do it. People rarely do things for no reason, which is why motivation is so important. To motivate means to provide a reason or motive for doing something, but that can span a broad spectrum. We've had many people ask us, "What can you do to get me motivated?" Seldom do we hear them say, "How can I motivate myself?" And herein lies the difference between ordinary people and extraordinary people.

We refer to the two extremes of motivation as fear and desire. The closer you get to either extreme, the more intense the motivation becomes. Let's look at an example that illustrates this phenomenon.

Suppose a group of children are playing ball in the middle of a seldom-used highway. Over the course of several minutes, one mother comes out and tells her child to stop playing in the road and come in for dinner, another also scolds hers for playing in the road and says it's time to come in and do homework, and still another sees her children in the highway and starts running after them trying to get them out of the road. All the while, the children are procrastinating and making excuses as they continue playing their game. Dinner, homework, or even mad parents should all be good reasons for the kids to get out of the road, but none of the children are close enough to either extreme on the motivational spectrum to get them moving.

Suddenly a huge tractor-trailer rig comes barreling around the curve. The driver sees the children playing in the road and knows he can't stop. He slams on the brakes, reaches up and grabs the cord for the air horn. When the children hear the screeching tires and the ominous blast from the horn, they instantly dive for the ditch on the side of the road. They don't even look to see if it's full of rocks or mud or snakes or anything else. They'll deal with whatever is in the ditch later. At the moment, their fear of death is greater than anything else. They are motivated! They have just experienced fear motivation to the extreme. (Many parents use fear motivation to a lesser extreme with their threats to spank or ground their children.)

Now let's suppose that the children in the road are fully engrossed in their game when one of them spots another child petting a fawn in the backyard of a house next to where they're playing. He screams, "Look, everybody! There's a baby deer in Johnny's backyard and he's petting it. Let's go pet it too!"

The rest of the children instantly drop everything and start running for the backyard. They clear the roadway just as quickly as if a tractor-trailer truck were bearing down on them, but do so for a totally different reason. None of them have ever seen a little fawn before, especially one they could pet. They practically knock each other down trying to be the first to get to it. They're motivated! They have just experienced an extreme level of desire motivation.

Though the results in these two examples were the same, the motivation was entirely different. In both instances the children got out of the road as quickly as possible, but with the truck, because they feared for their lives, and with the fawn, because of inner desire. With the truck, the motivation came from the outside; from the fear of being physically harmed. The motivation to see and pet the fawn came from within. Neither little Johnny nor the fawn applied any outside force to get the children out of the road. Their inner desire was enough motivation to get them to react as quickly as if their life had been threatened. Very interesting, isn't it?

Creating Desire

Fear from the outside and desire from within form the extremes of motivation, but when these roles are reversed, it can be counterproductive. Either inner fear or desire induced from the outside can kill motivation. The inner fear of failure, ridicule, criticism, loss, harm, or even fear of success can restrain a person from developing the motivation needed to tackle and solve problems. That fear could keep them from enjoying great success. On the other hand, desire created from the outside; the old carrot-on-the-stick approach to get the donkey to pull the cart, can also be counterproductive unless the donkey gets to eat the carrot occasionally. Employers are often guilty of doing this when they dangle big bonuses in front of employees to encourage them to reach for unrealistic goals. It only takes a few times of busting your hump reaching for someone else's goals and coming up short for the promised rewards to lose their value.

In contrast, the desire created by setting your own goals can provide the motivation to overcome almost any obstacle that stands in the way of reaching those goals. Mike learned this at an early age when he wanted his first bicycle. The day his mother told him, "Honey, I'm sorry we can't afford to get you a bicycle, but if you really want one, I'll bet you can find a way to get it," was a turning point in his life. If you recall, his desire for the bicycle was greater than any of the obstacles he encountered to getting it. How do we know? It's simple: He did get the bicycle. Sure, he had to solve a lot of problems and overcome some difficulties, but his desire was strong enough to carry him through the tough times. In the same way, you can determine if your desires are strong enough. If you're consistently reaching your goals, they are. If you aren't consistently reaching them, they aren't.

So, how do you create this kind of intense desire? That's where your notes come into play. Did any of our stories remind you of times when you wanted something so much that you sacrificed to get it? If so, great! What we're trying to find out is if you ever sacrificed today in order to get something weeks or months later that you really wanted. If you have, we want you to think about how you felt while you were sacrificing, and contrast that with the way you felt when you finally got what you wanted. Wasn't the thrill of accomplishment worth the sacrifice?

Now think back about the times you wanted something and weren't willing to wait or to sacrifice for it. Times like when you bought a new car and went in debt so you could have it now. Within months the new smell disappeared; it probably picked up a few scratches and dings, but those payments kept coming. By the time it was paid off, you were probably sick of writing the checks, or else you traded up and rolled the remainder of the debt into a new loan and started all over again. But even if you paid off the loan, by the time the last payment was made, the car was probably close to being worn-out, and that's depressing. (Go back and review the story about the Chevrolet and the Cadillac in Chapter 4.)

The Weekend Millionaire Mindset materializes when you develop the ability to create desires so strong that they keep you on track when temptation arises. This is done by starting with small goals, experiencing some success, then gradually moving on to larger and larger goals. It also involves learning to rebound from setbacks and disappointments without giving up on your dreams.

If you haven't yet done so, stop now, sit down with a note pad and jot down a list of significant events from your past. If you have already made your list, great: Study this list and think about each incident. Whether the experiences were good or bad is not important. Write down what made them memorable and what you learned from them. If you can't do this, your first task will be to pay more attention to what's going on around you. You won't be able to create strong desires until you learn to recognize and deal with your surroundings.

In Chapter 22 we described an incident between Mike and another gentleman that occurred while they were bowling. Had Mike not learned to grasp what was taking place around him, he would have probably missed the lesson he learned from this encounter; a lesson that created a strong desire to control his emotions. Creating desire is not about coming up with a wish list. It's about learning to think two or three steps ahead; it's about anticipating the outcome of your actions and putting in place alternative actions if you get less than the desired results. Desire is strengthened by successes, and these come when you anticipate potential outcomes and prepare yourself to meet them.

Successes strengthen desires because they give you confidence that you'll ultimately be able to achieve your goals; therefore, as you strive to build a Weekend Millionaire Mindset. It's important that you start with small goals. Yes, you need big, long-term goals, but you have to break them down into small short-term goals that are easier to accomplish. This is important because successfully reaching each small goal gives you a feeling of accomplishment and allows you to measure your progress toward the bigger long-term goals. As you complete each small step, your desire level will grow, especially when you see yourself moving closer to the big goals.

Desire is such a subjective term that it's hard to define, but as we mentioned in the beginning of this book, when we refer to success, we are primarily talking about financial success. Of course, there are many different types of success and the word can mean different things to different people, but the principles we're discussing here apply to any type of success. Desire has to come first, followed by effort, before success can be realized. The kind of desire that creates motivation, which leads to effort, which leads to success, must come from within; otherwise, success is just a fleeting dream.

People react differently to fear and desire motivation, and therein lies one of the secrets to developing a Weekend Millionaire mindset. Fear motivation doesn't work, because people motivated by fear never do more than it takes to eliminate the fear. Nothing we can say or do, either in this book or in person, will create the inner desire you will need to become financially independent; only you can do that. The old saying, "If it's going to be, it's up to me," is so true.

Throughout the book, we've discussed accepting personal responsibility, developing a pattern of investing, repelling negative influences, and many other traits you need to become a Weekend Millionaire, but the most important of all is creating desire, and that has to come from within. Until your desire for financial independence—or any other goal—is strong enough to make you receptive to learning and employing every legal and ethical method of achieving it, you will find yourself making one excuse after another, which leads us to the next chapter, where we will discuss eliminating excuses.

Key Points from This Chapter

- The two extremes of motivation are fear and desire.
- The closer you get to either extreme, the more intense the motivation becomes.

A Kick in the Pants That Will Improve Your Life

- Fear comes from outside you. Desire comes from inside you.
- Fear from the inside can kill your motivation.
- You can't rely on desire artificially induced from the outside by others, because it is depressing and will kill your motivation when you reach for someone else's goals and come up short.
- Unless you're consistently reaching your goals, your desire is not strong enough.
- Crank up your desire by setting small goals that you consistently achieve.
- You must accept responsibility for creating and nurturing your inner desires.

39

Eliminating
Excuses

Just as desire comes from within, so do excuses, but the difference between them is huge. Desires form the building blocks of the Weekend Millionaire Mindset, but excuses are the termites that will devour it if you allow them to do so. The term "good excuse" may be life's biggest oxymoron. There is no such thing as a good excuse. As long as your goals are realistic, the only reason for not reaching them is you. That may sound harsh, but it's true. If your commitment is lacking, you will make up any excuse to justify failure.

Most people never set goals, and the few who do are often reluctant to share them. Sharing your goals exposes you to ridicule, especially if you lack the commitment to see them through to a successful completion. As a result, people often start making excuses as soon as obstacles begin to appear. We believe they do this because they confuse excuses with reasons. Their excuses are nothing but face-saving ways to avoid having to admit they lack the commitment and willingness to learn how to overcome the obstacles.

A Kick in the Pants That Will Improve Your Life

Excuses start simple enough and creep into all walks of life. You oversleep, so you call your employer and say, "My alarm clock didn't go off and I overslept so I'll be a few minutes late today." Then on the way to work you get caught in heavy traffic, you end up having to park at the far side of the parking lot because all the nearby spaces are already taken, then you have trouble getting into the building because you rushed out and left your security pass at home. You've just arrived and it's already been a rough day. As you pass the boss's office, you stick you head in the door and say, "I've finally made it; you wouldn't believe what I've been through this morning. It started when my clock didn't go off, and then I got caught in a traffic jam, and blah blah blah."

Do you think the boss cares? No! All the excuses do is help you rationalize in your own mind why you weren't at work when you were supposed to be. If you had 50 excuses, it doesn't change the fact that you were late to work.

Setting and reaching goals work the same way. Either you reach the goal or you don't. If you don't, all the excuses in the world won't change that. How many times have you heard people say, "I would have done _____ (you fill in the blank), but .... " Whatever follows the "but" is usually an excuse, especially if it is something they could have controlled.

The difference between an excuse and a reason is who controls the situation. Obstacles over which you have no control or ability to overcome are reasons, but these are few and far between.

Someone tells you, "I could have been a marathon runner, but I lost my leg in a car accident." Try telling that to Denny Chipollini of Skippack, Pennsylvania. He was in a car accident that severed both his legs. Doctors reattached them but eventually his left leg had to be amputated due to massive injury and infection. Ask him about this and he'll tell you that he refers to the accident as a "gift" because it changed his life for the better. Four years after the accident he ran a five-kilometer race on his artificial leg. By 2001 he had run in the Pittsburgh, New York City, and San Diego marathons. He founded a nonprofit organization that he called Generation Hope and used his "gift" to inspire people to overcome adversity with his "no excuses and no limits" attitude toward life. This proves that even an amputee can run marathons, because if his desire is strong enough he will give himself enough reasons.

Eliminating Excuses

Doesn't that put excuses into perspective? We want you to quit making excuses and start giving yourself enough reasons to want to be successful. Acknowledge the fact that excuses are inexcusable. If you don't reach your goals, all the excuses in the world won't change that. The only thing that will change it is eliminating the excuses and creating the desire to be successful. Understand that setbacks are merely part of the learning process.

The first step on your journey to a Weekend Millionaire Mindset and the financial independence that follows is to pledge that from this moment on you will never, ever, blame anyone else for what's going on in your life. You alone are responsible for setting your life's goals, and you alone are responsible for attaining them.

The most well-known example of setting and achieving a goal of which we are aware began on May 25, 1961, with President John F. Kennedy's Special Message to Congress on Urgent National Needs. In his speech, he said, "I believe that this nation should commit itself to achieving the goal, before this decade is out, of landing a man on the moon and returning him safely to Earth." The key word in this statement is "commit." This became a goal that galvanized the nation. It was specific: " … to land a man on the moon and return him safely to Earth." It had a time frame: " … before this decade is out." And he didn't add any qualifiers like: " … unless one of our rockets blows up, some of our astronauts are killed, or we encounter some other unforeseen events that cause problems." He simply said we will do it by the end of the decade.

All of the above mentioned obstacles and many more occurred, but commitment to the goal kept us focused. When the setbacks and disappointments arose, we learned from them and kept moving forward. Each one brought more intense study that resulted in better technology. Then right on schedule, July 20, 1969, the world heard the words: "Houston, Tranquility Base here, the Eagle has landed."

As exciting as the landing was, it was merely one more step toward successfully reaching the goal President Kennedy had set eight years before. Not until four days later, on July 24, 1969, when the command module splashed down in the Pacific Ocean and the crew was safely aboard the USS *Hornet*, was the goal declared accomplished. The mission objective for Apollo 11 was very simply stated: "Perform a manned lunar landing and return."

Think of the excuses that could have been given to abort the mission: President Kennedy was assassinated, the mission was extremely expensive, astronauts died while preparing for it, NASA chief James Webb was opposed to it, there were political disagreements over funding, and the list could go on and on. But none of these was even considered as an excuse to stop. With each small step, we drew closer to the goal and the commitment grew stronger. *Commitment is the key to eliminating excuses.*

Now go back to your notes and review your list of memorable life experiences. Think about the commitment level you had during the ones that were successful and compare this to the commitment level you had during the ones when you didn't succeed. First, think about the successful ones: Did the obstacles you encountered and overcame strengthen your resolve and make you more determined to succeed? Now compare this with the ones when you didn't succeed: Did you turn those obstacles into excuses? Be honest! We know how easy it was when you succeeded to take credit for the victories, but when you failed, did you accept personal responsibility for the failures or did you try to blame the outcome on others?

Before you can truly develop a Weekend Millionaire Mindset, you have to learn to eliminate excuses and accept full responsibility for your life. When you do so, it toughens you like an old piece of leather, so you can bend without breaking. You learn to treat your goals like games that aren't over until you win. You don't give up when you encounter obstacles; you learn to go over, under, around, or through them until you achieve your objectives. Failure ceases to be an option.

In the last chapter we described how desire must come from within. Well, so does eliminating excuses. These two characteristics separate people with Weekend Millionaire Mindsets from ordinary people. But the exciting part is that *ordinary people can achieve extraordinary success*, because anyone willing to make the commitment can develop a Weekend Millionaire Mindset. But first you have to get started, and that's what we're going to show you how to do in the last chapter.

Key Points from This Chapter

- Don't let a lack of commitment cause you to make excuses.

Eliminating Excuses

- There is no such thing as a good excuse.
- The difference between an excuse and a reason is: Who controls the situation?
- Even an amputee can run marathons if his desire is strong enough.
- Never, ever, blame anyone else for what's going on in your life.
- Commitment is the key to eliminating excuses.
- Eliminate excuses and accept full responsibility for your life.
- Ordinary people can achieve extraordinary success.

40

Getting Started

The final chapter of any good self-help book should be titled "Getting Started." We hope you've learned a great deal from spending your time with us, but unless you put what we've taught you to work, you've wasted it. Throughout these chapters, we included stories and anecdotes to tie the lessons we were sharing to the real-life events from which we learned them. We feel this approach makes for more enjoyable reading and can help you better relate these lessons to events from your life. The message we want you to get is that anyone can develop a Weekend Millionaire Mindset. Yes, even *ordinary people can achieve extraordinary success* when they create enough desire to be successful and fully commit themselves to doing so.

When we were starting out, nobody would have thought that we would become successful. Mike was raised in a dirt poor coal-mining town in West Virginia. Roger's father was a taxicab driver in London, England. If we can do it, we know you can too!

By now you should know the things you need to do. The only thing left is to get started, right? That's the impression given by many motivational gurus, but we disagree. We know there's much more to it than that. Sure, you have to get started, but don't we all start things that we never finish? It takes more than just starting and having good intentions to develop a Weekend Millionaire Mindset. It's not how you start that makes the difference, but how you finish. We want to close with another story that illustrates what can happen once you acquire this mindset.

As we've mentioned a number of times, Mike is a licensed multi-engine airplane pilot. What we haven't told you is that he quit flying in 1990 following a serious medical scare and did not fly again until 2002. When 12 years had passed with no recurrence of the problem, he decided it was time to get back in the air. He made an appointment with an FAA medical examiner to renew his medical certificate, and then visited a local flight school based at the Asheville airport to begin the process of getting checked out to fly again. He took his first flight on May 1, 2002, in a small single-engine Cessna 172. This was quite a switch from the much larger twin-engine prop jet he had been flying for several years prior to 1990.

It took less than two hours to be checked out in the 172 and signed off to take it up solo and start building some flying hours. During the month of May he rented the 172 five more times and practiced the instrument approaches and other procedures with which he had once been so familiar. He was surprised that his flying skills came back so quickly, and before the end of the month he was itching to buy an airplane. To his astonishment, when he inquired about getting insurance on another prop jet, no insurance company would even consider writing liability coverage, let alone insuring the plane against damage. They all wanted him to have 100 to 200 hours of multiengine time before they would consider it.

In his Weekend Millionaire Mindset way, Mike considered his options and then began to formulate a plan. He made several calls to insurance companies and finally found one that would write liability insurance for him to fly a Beechcraft Duke if he would get five hours of instruction prior to flying solo. He inquired about a Duke because he had owned one of these in the early 1980s and had logged about 1,000 hours of time in that make and model airplane. The Duke is a pressurized twin-engine plane with turbocharged piston engines, and just as he had in the 1980s, he decided it would be a good interim plane in which to build up enough hours to get back into a prop jet.

Although the Duke is an older airplane, Mike found one that had been completely refurbished, including having the latest avionics installed. He took a test flight in the plane and quickly discovered that navigation had changed dramatically in the 12 years since he'd been flying. The Loran and RNAV instruments he once used were now obsolete, and this plane was equipped with a new digital GPS navigation system, including a Multifunction Display that would actually display airways, airports, navigation stations, terrain, and even the instrument approach procedures on a video screen installed in the instrument panel. It even showed the airplane's location on the map as it tracked across the screen. Great equipment, but he didn't have a clue how to use it. Another obstacle!

Following the test flight, he agreed to buy the plane, and without delay put it into a maintenance facility for a complete inspection and to have his own registration number painted on the tail. While the plane was in the shop, he went to work on the obstacle. He took the manuals for the new navigation instruments home, and they became his reading materials for several days. Needless to say, they were far more technical and difficult reading than this book.

When the work was completed and the plane was ready to fly, Mike hired an instructor to give him the required five hours of refresher training the insurance company required. This was interesting, because the instrumentation was so new, the instructor hadn't seen it either and had to learn how to use it. So between them, they gradually figured it out, and by the end of the five hours Mike had been checked out on the plane's systems, received a biennial flight review and an instrument competency check, and was ready to fly.

As the months passed, Mike had made several flights in the Duke and was becoming more proficient with each one. He was anticipating the day he would be back in a prop jet. In the meantime, Roger paid him a visit to try to persuade him to coauthor a book on real estate investing. Mike was more interested in flying, and the fact that he'd purchased a plane led Roger to ask if Mike would take him for a ride. Mike jumped at the opportunity to fly, and they headed to the airport. When Roger saw the plane, he was impressed. He'd been expecting to go for a ride in a two-passenger Piper Cub, not a six-passenger airplane that could cruise at 25,000 feet and fly more than 270 miles per hour.

Mike invited Roger to join him in the cockpit, and as they were going through the start, taxi, and departure checklist, he shared his goal of flying the Duke for a couple of years and then moving back into a prop jet. As they taxied past a row of planes, he pointed out a Beechcraft King Air like the one he eventually wanted to buy. Mike shared his goal with his best friend without fear of ridicule or criticism. Nearly 20 years of friendship had taught Roger not to doubt him.

When they returned from the sightseeing flight, Roger went back to work on his goal: getting Mike to coauthor a real estate book with him. Just to humor his good friend, Mike joined him in preparing an outline for the book, and before he left, Roger got him to agree to join him in writing it if he found a publisher. Mike gave his commitment lightly and assumed that would be the end of it. But Roger didn't take it that way, and within a few weeks a contract from the McGraw-Hill Publishing Company landed on Mike's desk for their first book, *The Weekend Millionaire's Secrets to Investing in Real Estate*. It turned out to be a huge best-seller, and now here we are, completing the second book in the Weekend Millionaire series. Roger had accomplished his goal and more, but what about Mike and the prop jet?

First, you need to understand that they are very different people with very different goals in life. Roger is an accomplished boat captain and owns a lovely sailboat, but wouldn't think of getting behind the controls of an airplane. Mike, on the other hand, feels right at home in the air but could care less about sailing. (Once with Roger was enough to cure him.) Roger loves to travel and earns his living traveling around the world teaching negotiating skills to some of the world's largest corporations. Mike prefers to stay closer to home and devotes most of his time to overseeing his real estate holdings. Although he speaks occasionally at special events, speaking is not his primary source of income, as it is for Roger. But even though they're very different, both Mike and Roger have developed Weekend Millionaire Mindsets. Both are goal-oriented and committed to achieving what they go after. Both are also perfect examples of two ordinary people who have achieved extraordinary success. Neither come from affluent backgrounds nor hold university degrees ... unless Ph.D.'s from the University of Hard Knocks count.

When we told you in the beginning of this chapter that it takes more than just starting in order to achieve financial independence, we did so for a reason. We want you to understand that whatever your goals, until you can picture yourself accomplishing them, you aren't ready to start. You need to ratchet up the desire until you believe in yourself enough to see yourself crossing the finish line. No excuses!

That's the kind of desire Roger had, a little over two years ago, when he set a goal to get Mike to write a book with him. He could see them doing it, he believed in himself, he never doubted his ability or let Mike talk him out of his goal. That's also the kind of desire Mike had at the time, when he set a goal to once again own and fly a Beechcraft King Air.

As a result of Roger's desire and commitment, they've done their second book together and have more to follow. Writing books is hard work, and you need a strong desire to keep yourself motivated and committed, so they agreed that when this manuscript (which you are now reading in book form) was finished, they would reward themselves with something they really wanted. Well, guess what? On the very day that he typed the last words, Mike rewarded himself by making a deposit on a 10-passenger King Air. No excuses! Missions accomplished! Roger rewarded himself with a new necktie. As we mentioned earlier, they are very different people with very different goals, but for 20 years they've remained the best of friends.

Granted, their goals today may be different from what most ordinary people set in the beginning, but they provide perfect examples of what can happen to ordinary people who develop a Weekend Millionaire Mindset. Remember, starting is important, but not as important as how you finish. We challenge you to get started today and then, in the words of Sir Winston Churchill, "Never give in. Never, never, never, never ... never give in."

We thank you for staying with us through all these pages and hope you enjoyed learning about our journeys to financial independence. Now, we wish you our best as you start your journey. Just remember as you work on developing your Weekend Millionaire Mindset, you will hit some rough spots, there will be some tough times, and you may even feel like quitting, but before you do, stop and look up in the sky. If you happen to see a beautiful white prop jet with blue and gold striping flying over, wave. It may just be Mike flying in to give you *a kick in the pants that will improve your life*.

Happy investing!

Mike Summey and Roger Dawson

Mike@weekendmillionaire.com

Roger@weekendmillionaire.com

Key Points from This Chapter

- Even ordinary people can achieve extraordinary success when they have enough desire to be successful and fully commit themselves to doing so.
- If we can do it, you can too!
- It's not how you start that counts, it's how you finish.
- Be sure that you are pursuing goals that excite and motivate you.
- Once you start, never, never, never give up.